S.J. Zammit
Ing.P.Eur., P.Eng., M.S.E., M.I.Eng.Sc., A.I.E.D.

Motor vehicle engineering science for technicians

Longman

An imprint of **Pearson Education**

Harlow, England · London · New York · Reading, Massachusetts · San Francisco
Toronto · Don Mills, Ontario · Sydney · Tokyo · Singapore · Hong Kong · Seoul
Taipei · Cape Town · Madrid · Mexico City · Amsterdam · Munich · Paris · Milan

Pearson Education Limited
Edinburgh Gate
Harlow
Essex CM20 2JE
England

and Associated Companies throughout the world

Visit us on the World Wide Web at:
www.pearsoned.co.uk

First published 1987

Zammit, S.J.
   Motor vehicle engineering science for technicians
   Level 2. – (Longman technician series)
   1. Automobiles – Design and construction
   I. Title
   629.2   TL255
   ISBN 0-582-41302-8

20 19 18 17 16 15
08 07 06 05 04

Printed in Malaysia, PA

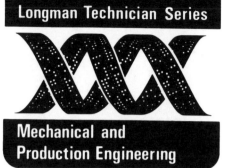

Longman Technician Series

Mechanical and Production Engineering

General Editors – Mechanical and Production Engineering

H.G. Davies
Vice Principal and Head of Department of Science, Carmarthen Technical and Agricultural College

G.A. Hicks

Contents

Preface
Acknowledgements

Chapter 1 Angular motion 1
1.1 Equations of linear motion with constant acceleration 1
1.2 Angular motion 4
1.3 The radian 4
1.4 Length of arc 5
1.5 Angular velocity 5
1.6 Angular acceleration 7
1.7 Equations of angular motion with constant
    angular acceleration 8
1.8 Relationship between linear and angular motion 8
Exercise 1.1 – Review questions 12
Exercise 1.2 – Problems 12

Chapter 2 Force, mass and acceleration 14
2.1 Newton's first law of motion 14
2.2 Mass and inertia 15
2.3 Momentum 15
2.4 Change of momentum – Newton's second law
    of motion 15
2.5 Weight 20
2.6 Newton's third law of motion 20
Exercise 2.1 – Review questions 23
Exercise 2.2 – Problems 24

Chapter 3 Work, energy and power 26
3.1 Work 26
3.2 Work done in lifting objects 27
3.3 Energy 29
3.4 Potential energy (PE) 29
3.5 Kinetic energy (KE) 30
3.6 Principle of conservation of energy 32

3.7   Power   35
Exercise 3.1 − Review questions   36
Exercise 3.2 − Problems   37

Chapter 4   Friction   40
4.1   Force of friction   40
4.2   Laws of friction for dry surfaces   40
4.3   The coefficient of friction   41
4.4   Advantages and disadvantages of friction   42
4.5   Friction in a journal bearing   45
4.6   Torque and power transmitted by a clutch   47
4.7   Disc brakes   50
4.8   Elementary theory of the shoe brake   53
Exercise 4.1 − Review questions   56
Exercise 4.2 − Problems   58

Chapter 5   Properties of lubricating oils   61
5.1   Purposes of lubrication   61
5.2   Forms of lubrication   62
5.3   Properties of lubricating oils   62
5.4   Oil viscosity tests   63
5.5   SAE viscosity rating   65
5.6   Viscosity index   66
5.7   Multi-grade oils   66
5.8   Lubricating oil additives   67
Exercise 5.1 − Review questions   69

Chapter 6   Stress and strain   71
6.1   Direct stress   71
6.2   Direct strain   74
6.3   Elasticity and Hooke's law   76
6.4   Spring stiffness   78
6.5   The tensile test   81
6.6   Stress−strain graphs for various materials   84
6.7   Working stress and factor of safety   87
6.8   Shear stress   88
6.9   Shear strain   90
6.10   Modulus of rigidity   91
Exercise 6.1 − Review questions   93
Exercise 6.2 − Problems   94

Chapter 7   Vehicle suspension springs   98
7.1   Function and types of suspension springs   98
7.2   Laminated or 'semi-elliptic' leaf springs   98
7.3   Coil springs   101

7.4 Torsion bars   101
7.5 Rate of springs   102
Exercise 7.1 – Review questions   104

Chapter 8   Forces acting at a point   106
8.1 Representation of a force   106
8.2 Terms used in problems involving a number of forces
    acting at a point   106
8.3 Parallelogram of forces   107
8.4 Triangle of forces   108
8.5 Bow's notation   109
8.6 Polygon of forces   115
8.7 Resolution of a force into two components   117
8.8 Body resting on a smooth inclined plane   119
Exercise 8.1 – Review questions   121
Exercise 8.2 – Problems   121

Chapter 9   Simply supported beams   127
9.1 Introduction   127
9.2 The moment of a force   127
9.3 Equilibrium under the action of parallel forces   128
9.4 Simply supported beams   131
9.5 Experimental determination of beam reactions   136
Exercise 9.1 – Review questions   137
Exercise 9.2 – Problems   138

Chapter 10   Simple machines   140
10.1 Introduction   140
10.2 Definitions of terms used in simple machine theory   140
10.3 Relationship between load and effort – The law
     of a machine   143
10.4 Limiting efficiency of a machine   144
10.5 Pulley systems   148
10.6 Weston differential pulley block   152
10.7 The screw jack   154
10.8 Levers   156
10.9 Gear systems   159
Exercise 10.1 – Review questions   163
Exercise 10.2 – Problems   164

Chapter 11   Vehicle transmission and steering   168
11.1 Introduction   168
11.2 Gearbox gear ratio   170
11.3 Rear-axle ratio   171
11.4 Overall gear ratio   173

11.5   Practical determination of the gearbox and rear-axle ratios of a vehicle without dismantling any of these components   173

11.6   Torque ratio   175

11.7   Steering box calculations   179

Exercise 11.1 – Review questions   181

Exercise 11.2 – Problems   182

Chapter 12   Temperature and quantity of heat   186

12.1   Temperature   186

12.2   Temperature scales   186

12.3   Heat energy   188

12.4   Unit of heat energy   188

12.5   Specific heat capacity   189

12.6   Heat energy transfer in mixtures   191

Exercise 12.1 – Review questions   195

Exercise 12.2 – Problems   196

Chapter 13   Change of state and latent heat   199

13.1   Change of state   199

13.2   Sensible heat and latent heat   199

13.3   Melting points of solids   200

13.4   Freezing points of liquids   200

13.5   Specific latent heat of fusion   202

13.6   To determine the melting point of a substance from a cooling curve   204

13.7   Boiling of liquids   206

13.8   Specific latent heat of vaporization   207

13.9   Effect of pressure on the boiling point of a liquid   209

Exercise 13.1 – Review questions   210

Exercise 13.2 – Problems   212

Chapter 14   Expansion of solids and liquids   214

14.1   Effect of temperature change on solids and liquids   214

14.2   Expansion and contraction of solids   214

14.3   Coefficient of linear expansion   215

14.4   The bimetallic strip   215

14.5   Coefficient of superficial expansion   220

14.6   Coefficient of cubical expansion   220

14.7   Expansion and contraction of liquids   221

Exercise 14.1 – Review questions   222

Exercise 14.2 – Problems   223

Chapter 15 The gas laws 226
15.1 Introduction 226
15.2 Pressure of a gas 226
15.3 Atmospheric pressure 227
15.4 Gauge pressure and absolute pressure 228
15.5 Pressure gauges 229
15.6 Vacuum gauges 231
15.7 Relationship between pressure and volume of a gas:
      Boyle's law 231
15.8 Relationship between volume and temperature of a gas:
      Charles' law 234
15.9 Combination of Boyle's and Charles' laws: The general
      gas equation 236
15.10 Standard temperature and pressure (STP) 238
15.11 Relationship between pressure and temperature of a gas
      at constant volume: Pressure law 239
15.12 Compression ratio 240
Exercise 15.1 – Review questions 245
Exercise 15.2 – Problems 245

Chapter 16 Fuels and combustion 249
16.1 Introduction 249
16.2 Elements, compounds and mixtures 249
16.3 The atom and relative atomic mass 250
16.4 The molecule and relative molecular mass 251
16.5 Combustion 251
16.6 Combustion equations 252
16.7 Complete combustion of carbon to carbon dioxide 253
16.8 Incomplete combustion of carbon to carbon monoxide 253
16.9 Combustion of carbon monoxide to carbon dioxide 254
16.10 Complete combustion of hydrogen to water vapour 254
16.11 Complete combustion of sulphur to sulphur dioxide 254
16.12 Theoretical mass of air required for combustion 255
16.13 Liquid fuels 256
16.14 Petroleum or crude oil 256
16.15 By-products from coal gas manufacture 258
16.16 Vegetable matter 258
16.17 Properties of liquid fuels 258
Exercise 16.1 – Review questions 260

Chapter 17 Engine cycles 263
17.1 The constant volume or Otto cycle 263
17.2 The constant pressure or Diesel cycle 265

17.3   The dual combustion cycle   266
Exercise 17.1 − Review questions   268

Chapter 18   Engine testing   270
18.1   Introduction   270
18.2   Brake power and engine torque   270
18.3   Brake power and torque curves   273
18.4   The indicator diagram   277
18.5   Mean effective pressure   277
18.6   Indicated power   277
18.7   Calculation of indicated power   278
18.8   Mechanical efficiency   279
18.9   Curves of i.p., b.p., f.p. and mechanical efficiency   280
18.10   Brake mean effective pressure   281
18.11   The Morse test   284
18.12   Fuel consumption   285
18.13   Thermal efficiency   286
18.14   Curves of fuel consumption and thermal efficiency   287
18.15   Other performance curves   287
Exercise 18.1 − Review questions   292
Exercise 18.2 − Problems   293

Answers to review questions   300
Answers to problems   301

Index   305

Preface

This book has been written to meet the requirements of the Business and Technician Education Council (BTEC) Level 2 Unit in Motor Vehicle Science (Syllabus U82/876) for motor vehicle technicians. The aim is to give a basic mechanical science background for motor vehicle technicians and to develop the student's understanding of statics, dynamics, energy, machines and engine power.

Each topic considered in the text is presented in a way that assumes in the student only the knowledge attained at BTEC Level 1 in Physical Science (Syllabus U80/682) and in Mathematics (Syllabus U80/863).

Chapter 6 on Stress and Strain has been extended slightly to include useful information and problems on shear stress and modulus of rigidity.

The book contains 137 illustrations and over 140 worked examples are included, the solutions being given in full and units have been presented in squared brackets to enable the student to become as familiar with units as with actual numerical calculation. There are also about 530 questions for exercises which include short answer and objective type questions, as well as conventional problems. Answers are provided at the end of the book.

Some of the conventional type questions have been taken from past examination papers set by the Examining Bodies listed under Acknowledgements. I am most grateful to these authorities for granting permission to use such questions. It should be pointed out, however, that responsibility for the modifications in some questions and for any errors which may arise, particularly in any given solution and in the included answers, must be borne by the author.

I would like to express my appreciation for the friendly cooperation and helpful advice given to me by the publishers.

Finally, I would like to add a word of thanks to the Series General Editors, Gwyn Davies and Gordon Hicks, for their valuable comments and suggestions.

S.J. Zammit,
Department of Mechanical Engineering,
Malta Government Technical Institute, Paola, Malta, June 1986

Acknowledgements

We are indebted to the following for permission to reproduce copyright material:

Autobooks for fig. 7.8 from fig. 8.9 p. 82 *Ford Transit V4 (1965–77 Autobook) OWM 756* 6th edition 1978, by K. Ball; Oxford University Press for fig. 7.6 from fig. 33 p. 35 *Laboratory Exercises for Motor Vehicle Students* Vol. 2, 1971 edition by W.P. Jonker and D.W. Harris.

and to the following Examining Bodies for permission to reproduce past examination questions:

City and Guilds of London Institute; East Midland Further Education Council (this authority has, from 1 January 1982, merged with the Regional Advisory Council for Further Education to form the unitary body EMFEC); North Western Regional Advisory Council for Further Education incorporating the Union of Lancashire and Cheshire Institutes (NWRAC/UCLI); and West Midlands Advisory Council for Further Education incorporating the Union of Educational Institutions (WMAC/UEI).

Chapter 1

Angular motion

1.1 Equations of linear motion with constant acceleration

Although the equations of linear motion may be familiar to the reader, they are derived here to provide useful revision.

Consider a body moving with a uniform or constant acceleration a so that its initial velocity u changes to a final velocity v in time t while travelling a distance s. The velocity–time graph representing the motion of the body will be a straight line as shown in Fig. 1.1.

The gradient (or slope) of the graph gives the acceleration of the body. Thus, from Fig. 1.1,

$$\text{Gradient} = \frac{\text{BD}}{\text{AD}}$$

i.e. $a = \dfrac{v - u}{t}$

from which $v = u + at$ [1.1]

The area under the graph gives the distance travelled. Since the graph is a trapezium, its area is given by:

$$\text{Area} = \frac{\text{OA} + \text{CB}}{2} \times \text{OC}$$

i.e. $s = \left(\dfrac{u + v}{2}\right) \times t$ [1.2]

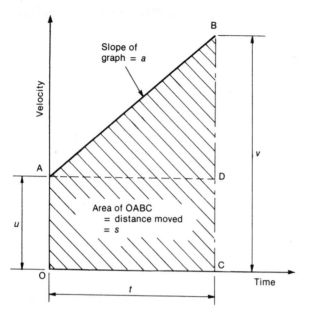

Figure 1.1 Velocity–time graph for a body moving with uniform acceleration

This would also be equal to the distance travelled by a body moving for time t with a velocity equal to the *average velocity* $\frac{1}{2}(u + v)$.

Now, substituting for v from equation [1.1] in equation [1.2], we get:

$$s = \left(\frac{u + u + at}{2}\right) \times t$$

so that $s = ut + \frac{1}{2}at^2$ [1.3]

By squaring both sides of equation [1.1], we get:

$$\begin{aligned}
v^2 &= (u + at)^2 \\
&= u^2 + 2uat + (at)^2 \\
&= u^2 + 2a(ut + \tfrac{1}{2}at^2)
\end{aligned}$$

but $ut + \frac{1}{2}at^2 = s$ from equation [1.3]

$\therefore$ $v^2 = u^2 + 2as$ [1.4]

Equations [1.1], [1.2], [1.3] and [1.4] are those used for solving problems involving linear motion with uniform or constant acceleration. It should be noted that in these equations a is positive when the body is accelerating and negative when it is retarding or decelerating. It is recommended that basic SI units are to be used, namely: metres (m) for distance s; seconds (s) for time t; metres per second (m/s) for velocities u and v; and metres per second squared (m/s²) for acceleration a.

Example 1.1

A vehicle is accelerated uniformly at 1.5 m/s^2 from a speed of 27 km/h. Calculate:

(a) the time required to attain a speed of 81 km/h
(b) the distance travelled in this time.

Solution

Initial velocity, u = 27 km/h = 7.5 m/s
Final velocity, v = 81 km/h = 22.5 m/s
Acceleration, a = 1.5 m/s^2
Time taken, t = ? (to be determined)
Distance travelled, s = ? (to be determined)

(a) $v = u + at$ from equation [1.1]

or $t = \dfrac{v - u}{a}$

$$= \frac{22.5 - 7.5}{1.5} \left[\frac{m/s}{m/s^2} \right] = 10 \, s$$

(b) $v^2 = u^2 + 2as$ from equation [1.4]

or $s = \dfrac{v^2 - u^2}{2a}$

$$= \frac{(22.5)^2 - (7.5)^2}{2 \times 1.5} \left[\frac{m^2/s^2}{m/s^2} \right] = 150 \, m$$

Answer: (a) Time to attain 81 km/h = 10 s
           (b) Corresponding distance travelled = 150 m

Example 1.2

If the vehicle of Example 1.1 is brought to rest with uniform retardation from the speed of 81 km/h in a further distance of 225 m, find (a) the retardation and (b) the time taken.

Solution

$u = 81$ km/h = 22.5 m/s $a = ?$ (to be determined)
$v = 0$ (the vehicle has stopped) $t = ?$ (to be determined)
$s = 225$ m

(a) Since $v^2 = u^2 + 2as$

     then $a = \dfrac{v^2 - u^2}{2s} = \dfrac{0 - (22.5)^2}{2 \times 225} \left[\dfrac{m^2/s^2}{m} \right]$

$$= -1.125 \, m/s^2$$

This is negative since the vehicle is being brought to rest; therefore the retardation is $1.125\,\text{m/s}^2$.

(b) Now $\quad s = \left(\dfrac{u + v}{2}\right) \times t \quad$ from equation [1.2]

i.e. $\qquad 225 = \left(\dfrac{22.5 + 0}{2}\right) \times t$

$\therefore \qquad\quad t = \dfrac{225 \times 2}{22.5} = 20\,\text{s}$

Answer: (a) Retardation $= 1.125\,\text{m/s}^2$; (b) Time taken $= 20\,\text{s}$

1.2 Angular motion

When a body rotates about an axis it is said to have *angular motion*. It is common practice to express the speed of rotating parts in revolutions per minute (rev/min), but in dealing with problems connected with angular motion it is more convenient to express the speed of rotation in terms of the angle turned through in unit time.

1.3 The radian

The *radian* (abbreviated 'rad') is the fundamental unit of angular displacement, and is defined as the angle subtended at the centre of a circle by an arc whose length is equal to the radius of the circle. An angle of one radian is illustrated in Fig. 1.2.

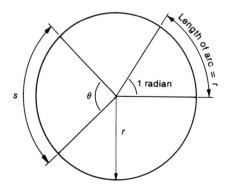

Figure 1.2

1.4 Length of arc

Referring again to Fig. 1.2, let *s* be the length of an arc subtending an angle θ rad at the centre of a circle of radius *r*. Then:

$$\text{Angle turned through} = \frac{\text{Length of arc}}{\text{Radius of circle}}$$

i.e. $$\theta = \frac{s}{r}$$

or $$s = r\theta \qquad [1.5]$$

The arc length for one complete revolution is the whole circumference of the circle, $2\pi r$. Substituting this for *s* in equation [1.5], we get:

$$2\pi r = r\theta$$
so that $\theta = 2\pi$

But the number of degrees subtended by the whole circle is 360. Hence there are 2π rad in 360° or in one complete revolution.

Example 1.3
A road wheel of diameter 560 mm turns through an angle of 150°. Calculate the distance moved by a point on the tyre tread of the wheel.

Solution
Since there are 2π rad in 360°, then:

$$150° = 150 \times \frac{2\pi}{360} = 2.618 \text{ rad}$$

Now $s = r\theta$ from equation [1.5]

where $r = 280$ mm and $\theta = 2.618$ rad

∴ $s = 280 \times 2.618 = 733$ mm

Answer: Circumferential distance moved by point = 733 mm

1.5 Angular velocity

Angular velocity is defined as the rate of change of angular displacement, i.e. angle turned through per unit time. Angular velocity is denoted by ω (the Greek letter 'omega'), and the unit used is the *radian per second* (rad/s).

Consider an arm OA rotating anticlockwise about pivot O at constant speed (see Fig. 1.3). If the arm takes *t* seconds to rotate through an angle θ rad, then:

Angular velocity $= \dfrac{\text{Angle turned through (rad)}}{\text{Time taken (s)}}$

i.e. $\qquad \omega = \dfrac{\theta}{t} \text{ rad/s}$ $\hspace{4cm}$ [1.6]

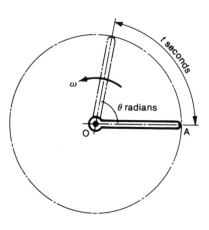

Figure 1.3

We shall often require to convert rev/min to rad/s. Suppose the arm OA in Fig. 1.3 to be rotating at a constant speed of N rev/min. Then, the number of rev/s is $N/60$. Now since the arm rotates through 2π rad in one complete revolution,

Angular velocity $= 2\pi \times \dfrac{N}{60} \text{ rad/s}$

i.e. $\qquad \omega = \dfrac{2\pi N}{60} \text{ rad/s}$ $\hspace{4cm}$ [1.7]

Example 1.4

A shaft has an angular velocity of 125 rad/s. Find the time it would take to make 350 complete revolutions.

Solution

$$\omega = \dfrac{\theta}{t} \quad \text{from equation [1.6]}$$

$$\therefore \quad t = \dfrac{\theta}{\omega}$$

where $\theta = 350 \times 2\pi = 2200$ rad (since there are 2π rad in one
and $\omega = 125$ rad/s $\hspace{5cm}$ revolution)

Hence $t = \dfrac{2200}{125} \left[\dfrac{\text{rad}}{\text{rad/s}} \right] = 17.6\,\text{s}$

Answer: Time taken for 350 rev = 17.6 s

Example 1.5
Calculate the angular velocity, in rad/s, of an engine flywheel when it is rotating at 2800 rev/min.

Solution

Angular velocity, $\omega = \dfrac{2\pi N}{60}$ rad/s [where N = 2800 rev/min]

$$= \dfrac{2\pi \times 2800}{60} = 293.3\,\text{rad/s}$$

Answer: Angular velocity of flywheel = 293.3 rad/s

1.6 Angular acceleration

Angular acceleration is defined as the rate of change of angular velocity, i.e. the change in angular velocity per unit time. Angular acceleration is denoted by α (the Greek letter 'alpha'), and the unit used is the *radian per second squared* (rad/s²).

If the angular velocity of a point moving in a circular path changes uniformly from ω_1 rad/s to ω_2 rad/s in time t seconds, the angular acceleration, α rad/s², of the point is given by:

$$\alpha = \dfrac{\omega_2 - \omega_1}{t} \qquad\qquad [1.8]$$

Example 1.6
The angular velocity of a disc changes from 10 rad/s to 40 rad/s in 12 s. What is the angular acceleration if it is assumed to be constant over the time interval concerned?

Solution

Angular acceleration $= \dfrac{\text{Change in angular velocity}}{\text{Time taken}}$

i.e. $\qquad\qquad \alpha = \dfrac{\omega_2 - \omega_1}{t}$

where $\omega_1 = 10$ rad/s; $\omega_2 = 40$ rad/s; $t = 12$ s

$\therefore \qquad \alpha = \dfrac{40 - 10}{12} \dfrac{\text{rad/s}}{\text{s}} = 2.5\,\text{rad/s}^2$

Answer: Angular acceleration of disc $= 2.5\,\text{rad/s}^2$

1.7   Equations of angular motion with constant angular acceleration

It is possible to establish equations of angular motion with constant angular acceleration which are directly comparable with the equations of motion [1.1], [1.2], [1.3] and [1.4] given in Section 1.1 for constant linear acceleration. These are given below in angular terms:

$$\omega_2 = \omega_1 + \alpha t \qquad\qquad\qquad\qquad\qquad\qquad [1.9]$$

$$\theta = \left(\frac{\omega_1 + \omega_2}{2}\right) \times t \qquad\qquad\qquad\qquad [1.10]$$

$$\theta = \omega_1 t + \tfrac{1}{2}\alpha t^2 \qquad\qquad\qquad\qquad\qquad [1.11]$$
$$\omega_2^2 = \omega_1^2 + 2\alpha\theta \qquad\qquad\qquad\qquad\qquad [1.12]$$

where θ = angle turned through (rad)
  t = time taken (s)
  ω_1 = initial angular velocity (rad/s)
  ω_2 = final angular velocity (rad/s)
  α = constant angular acceleration (rad/s^2)

1.8   Relationship between linear and angular motion

Consider a flywheel, radius r metres, to be rotating about centre O with uniform angular velocity ω rad/s, as shown in Fig. 1.4. The linear velocity v m/s of a point on the rim of the flywheel will always be directed along a tangent at right angles to the radius to the point. Let the initial position of the point be A and after time t seconds let it be at B. The radius OA will then have turned through an angle $\theta = \omega t$ rad. In this time, the point will have moved through the arc AB of length

$$s = r\theta \quad \text{from equation [1.5]}$$
i.e. $s = r\omega t$

The linear velocity of the point on the rim of the flywheel will be given by:

$$\text{Linear velocity} = \frac{\text{Distance moved}}{\text{Time taken}}$$

i.e. $v = \dfrac{s}{t} = \dfrac{r\omega t}{t}$

∴ $v = r\omega \qquad\qquad\qquad\qquad\qquad\qquad\qquad [1.13]$

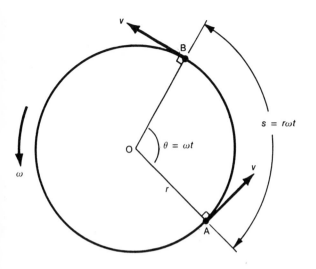

Figure 1.4

Putting this into words:

Linear velocity = Radius × Angular velocity

A similar relationship exists between linear and angular acceleration. If the flywheel is rotating about centre O with an angular acceleration α rad/s^2, the linear acceleration a m/s^2 of the point on its rim is given by:

$$a = r\alpha \qquad\qquad [1.14]$$

Putting this into words:

Linear acceleration = Radius × Angular acceleration

Example 1.7

A wheel rotating at 5 rad/s accelerates uniformly at 0.5 rad/s^2 for 30 s. Find:

(a) the angular velocity after the 30 s
(b) the angle turned through by the wheel during this time.

Solution

$\omega_1 = 5$ rad/s $\qquad\qquad \alpha = 0.5$ rad/s^2
$\omega_2 = ?$ (to be determined) $\qquad t = 30$ s
$\theta = ?$ (to be determined)

$$(a)\ \ \omega_2 = \omega_1 + \alpha t \quad \text{from equation } [1.9]$$
$$= 5 + (0.5 \times 30)$$
$$= 5 + 15 = 20 \text{ rad/s}$$

(b) $\theta = \omega_1 t + \frac{1}{2}at^2$ from equation [1.11]
$$= (5 \times 30) + (\tfrac{1}{2} \times 0.5 \times 30^2)$$
$$= 150 + 225 = 375 \, rad$$

Alternatively,

$$\theta = \left(\frac{\omega_1 + \omega_2}{2}\right) \times t \quad \text{from equation [1.10]}$$

$$= \left(\frac{5 + 20}{2}\right) \times 30 = 25 \times 15 = 375 \, rad$$

Answer: (a) Angular velocity after 30 s = 20 rad/s
(b) Angle turned through in this time = 375 rad

Example 1.8
A grinding wheel has a diameter of 200 mm. If it rotates at 2100 rev/min, what is the circumferential grinding speed in m/s?

Solution

Angular velocity, $\omega = \dfrac{2\pi N}{60}$ rad/s [where N = 2100 rev/min]

$$= \frac{2\pi \times 2100}{60} = 220 \, rad/s$$

The circumferential grinding speed is the same as the tangential speed of a point on the periphery of the wheel. Hence, from equation [1.13],

$$v = r\omega$$
$$= 0.1 \, [m] \times 220 \, [rad/s] = 22 \, m/s$$

Answer: Circumferential grinding speed = 22 m/s

Example 1.9
The road wheels of a motor vehicle increase their speed uniformly from 50 rev/min to 1100 rev/min in 40 s. Calculate the angular acceleration of the wheels in rad/s². If the diameter of the wheels is 0.7 m, what is the linear acceleration of a point on the tyre tread?

Solution

Initial angular velocity, $\omega_1 = 2\pi \times \dfrac{50}{60} = 5.24$ rad/s

Final angular velocity, $\omega_2 = 2\pi \times \dfrac{1100}{60} = 115.2$ rad/s

Angular acceleration, $\alpha = \dfrac{\omega_2 - \omega_1}{t}$ from equation [1.8]

$$= \frac{115.2 - 5.24}{40} \left[\frac{\text{rad/s}}{\text{s}}\right] = 2.75 \, \text{rad/s}^2$$

Linear acceleration, $a = r\alpha$ from equation [1.14]
$$= 0.35 \, [\text{m}] \times 2.75 \, [\text{rad/s}^2]$$
$$= 0.9625 \, \text{m/s}^2$$

Answer: Angular acceleration of wheels $= 2.75 \, \text{rad/s}^2$
Linear acceleration of point on tyre tread $= 0.9625 \, \text{m/s}^2$

Example 1.10
A wheel is rotating at 2000 rev/min and when a brake is applied the wheel is brought to rest with uniform retardation in 400 revolutions. Find the time taken to bring the wheel to rest and the angular retardation in rad/s².

Solution

Since angular velocity, $\omega = \dfrac{2\pi N}{60}$ rad/s [where N = rev/min] then:

$$\omega_1 = 2\pi \times \frac{2000}{60} = 209.4 \, \text{rad/s}$$

$\omega_2 = 0$ (since wheel is brought to rest in 400 rev)

Angle turned through $= 2\pi \times$ Number of revolutions
$$= 2\pi \times 400 = 2513 \, \text{rad}$$

Now, to find time t, we use equation [1.10],

i.e. $\qquad \theta = \left(\dfrac{\omega_1 + \omega_2}{2}\right) \times t$

so that $\quad 2513 = \left(\dfrac{209.4 + 0}{2}\right) \times t$

$\therefore \qquad t = \dfrac{2513 \times 2}{209.4} = 24 \, \text{s}$

To find the angular retardation, we use equation [1.12],

i.e. $\qquad \omega_2^2 = \omega_1^2 + 2\alpha\theta$
so that $\qquad 0 = (209.4)^2 + (2 \times 2513 \times \alpha)$
$$0 = 43\,848 + 5026\alpha$$

$\therefore \qquad \alpha = -\dfrac{43\,848}{5026} = -8.724 \, \text{rad/s}^2$

The negative sign in the above result indicates retardation.

Answer: Time taken to bring the vehicle to rest $= 24 \, \text{s}$
Angular retardation of wheels $= 8.724 \, \text{rad/s}^2$

Exercise 1.1 — Review questions

1 The unit of angular displacement is the ....
2 Define the radian.
3 In one revolution there are .... radians.
4 Define angular velocity.
5 The unit of angular velocity is the ....
6 Define angular acceleration.
7 The unit of angular acceleration is the ....
8 If a flywheel is rotating at a constant speed of N rev/min, its angular velocity ω rad/s is given by the expression:

$\omega = ...$ rad/s

9 Write down the relationship existing between the angular velocity ω rad/s of a rotating wheel and the linear velocity v m/s of a point on the wheel distant r metres from the axis of rotation.
10 Write down the relationship existing between the linear acceleration a m/s^2 and the angular acceleration α rad/s^2 of a body rotating in a circular path of radius r metres.
11 Two of the equations of linear motion with constant acceleration are:

(a) $s = ut + \frac{1}{2}at^2$
(b) $v^2 = u^2 + 2as$

Write down the corresponding equations relating to angular motion.

Exercise 1.2 — Problems

1 A motor vehicle travels round a bend of 30 m radius at 54 km/h. What is the angle turned through by the vehicle in one second (a) in radians and (b) in degrees?
2 If a road wheel makes 25 complete revolutions in 12 s, what is the rotational speed in rev/min and in rad/s? What is the angle turned through in radians, by a point on the tyre tread in 5 s?
3 A disc has a diameter of 700 mm and is rotating at 150 rev/min. Determine:

(a) the angular velocity of the disc, in rad/s
(b) the tangential (linear) velocity of a point on the rim of the disc, in m/s.

4 A disc is rotating with an angular velocity of 40 rad/s. Determine the angular acceleration required to increase the angular velocity uniformly to 120 rad/s in 32 s.
5 A wheel starts from rest and accelerates uniformly with an angular acceleration of 3 rad/s^2. What will be its angular velocity after 8 s and the angle turned through in that time?

6 A disc is rotating with a constant angular velocity of 55 rad/s. Calculate the number of revolutions made by a point on the disc in 8 s.

7 A wheel of diameter 1 m rotates with an angular velocity of 10 rad/s. Calculate the difference between the linear velocity of a point on its rim and that of a point 200 mm from the axis of rotation.

(EMEU)

8 The wheels of a motor vehicle are 1 m in diameter over the tyres. Assuming that no slip takes place between the wheels and the road surface, calculate the angular velocity of the wheels when the vehicle is travelling at a speed of 90 km/h.

(NWRAC/ULCI)

9 The road wheels of a vehicle are 600 mm in diameter. Calculate the linear speed of the vehicle, in km/h, if the wheels rotate at 560 rev/min.

10 A flywheel of diameter 360 mm increases its speed uniformly from 630 rev/min to 1050 rev/min in 11 s. Calculate:

(*a*) the angular acceleration of the wheel, in rad/s^2
(*b*) the number of revolutions made during the speed change
(*c*) the linear acceleration of a point on the rim of the wheel, in m/s^2.

11 A vehicle with wheels 750 mm in diameter moving at 27 km/h is brought to rest under a uniform retardation in a distance of 60 m. Find:

(*a*) the retardation of the vehicle, in m/s^2
(*b*) the initial angular velocity of the wheels, in rad/s
(*c*) the angular retardation of the wheels, in rad/s^2.

12 A drum makes 70 revolutions while accelerating uniformly to a final speed of 1050 rev/min in 5 s. Find:

(*a*) the initial speed of the drum, in rev/min
(*b*) the angular acceleration, in rad/s^2.

13 A wheel, initially at rest, is subjected to a uniform angular acceleration of 2.5 rad/s^2 for 80 s, and is then immediately retarded uniformly until it comes to rest 100 s later. Calculate:

(*a*) the maximum angular velocity attained, in rad/s
(*b*) the total number of revolutions made by the wheel
(*c*) the angular retardation, in rad/s^2.

Chapter 2

Force, mass and acceleration

2.1 Newton's first law of motion

The behaviour of bodies under the action of forces was observed by Sir Isaac Newton in the late seventeenth century, and his first law of motion may be stated as follows:

'A body continues in a state of rest, or of uniform motion in a straight line, unless acted upon by an external resultant force.'

This law will be readily understood by considering some facts. If, for instance, a motor vehicle is standing on a level road, it tends to remain at this standstill position unless an external force is applied to make it move. If the vehicle is already moving, only friction and air resistance have to be balanced to keep the vehicle moving with the same velocity. When the propelling force provided by the engine exceeds the forces opposing motion, the vehicle will accelerate steadily along the road. This is due to a resultant force acting in the direction of motion of the vehicle. On the other hand, if the engine is switched off, the only forces acting will be the retarding forces (air resistance and friction) causing the vehicle to slow down and stop.

It follows, therefore, that a body remains at rest or continues to move with uniform velocity only as long as there is no resultant force acting on it. Whenever a body accelerates in a given direction, there must be a resultant force acting in that direction. Conversely, whenever a resultant force acts on a body, the body will accelerate in the direction of this force.

2.2 Mass and inertia

The *mass* of a body may be defined as the quantity of matter which it contains. The SI unit of mass is the *kilogram* (kg). Small masses are often measured in *grams* (g) and large masses are usually measured in *megagrams* (Mg), where:

1 kg = 1000 g and 1 Mg = 1000 kg

The megagram is also called the *tonne* (t).

The tendency of a body to maintain a state of rest or of uniform motion is called its *inertia*, and this property is found to be dependent upon the mass of the body. Hence, the larger the mass of a body the greater is its inertia, i.e. the more difficult it would be to make it move when at rest, or to stop it when in motion. It can also be said that the larger the mass of a body, the smaller the acceleration produced by a given force, and the greater the time required for the velocity of the body to change by a given amount.

2.3 Momentum

Momentum can be defined as the quantity of motion possessed by a moving body. It is measured by the product of the mass m of the body and its velocity v. Thus:

Momentum = mv [2.1]

The unit of momentum is the *kilogram metre per second* (kg m/s).

Momentum has magnitude, and its direction and sense correspond to that of the velocity. Momentum is therefore a vector quantity.

Example 2.1
Determine the momentum of a motor vehicle of mass 2 Mg which is travelling with a uniform velocity of 72 km/h.

Solution
Momentum = mv from equation [2.1]

where m = 2 Mg = 2000 kg

$$v = 72 \text{ km/h} = \frac{72 \times 1000}{60 \times 60} = 20 \text{ m/s}$$

∴ Momentum = 2000 [kg] × 20 [m/s]
= 40 000 kg m/s

Answer: Momentum of vehicle = 40 000 kg m/s

2.4 Change of momentum – Newton's second law of motion

Whenever the momentum of a body changes, there must always be a force causing the change. The rate at which the momentum is changed will depend upon the size of this force. This is expressed in Newton's second law of motion which states that:

'The rate of change of momentum of a body is proportional to the externally applied force and takes place in the direction in which the force acts.'

Suppose a resultant force F acts on a body of mass m for a time t and causes its velocity to change from u to v. Then:

$$\text{Change of momentum} = mv - mu$$

$$\text{Rate of change of momentum} = \frac{mv - mu}{t}$$

According to Newton's second law,

$$F \propto \text{Rate of change of momentum}$$

i.e. $F \propto \dfrac{mv - mu}{t}$

If the mass, m, of the body remains unchanged, this may be written:

$$F \propto m \left(\frac{v - u}{t} \right)$$

But $\dfrac{v - u}{t}$ = Rate of change of velocity = Acceleration a

$\therefore \quad F \propto ma$

This relationship can be turned into an equation by putting in a constant. Hence:

$$F = \text{Constant} \times ma \qquad\qquad [2.2]$$

Now, the SI unit of force is the *newton* (N), and this is defined as the force which gives a mass of 1 kg an acceleration of 1 m/s². Substituting $F = 1\,\text{N}$, $m = 1\,\text{kg}$ and $a = 1\,\text{m/s}^2$ in equation [2.2], we get:

$$1\,\text{N} = \text{Constant} \times 1\,\text{kg} \times 1\,\text{m/s}^2$$

Thus, the constant has a numerical value of unity and Newton's second law of motion may be written in the form:

$$\text{Force} = \text{Mass} \times \text{Acceleration}$$

i.e. $F = ma \qquad\qquad [2.3]$

It should be pointed out that the unit of force can be expressed in terms of the units of mass, length and time, e.g.

$$1\,\text{N} = 1\,\text{kg} \times \text{m/s}^2 = 1\,\frac{\text{kg m}}{\text{s}^2}$$

Example 2.2

Calculate the force required to produce an acceleration of $3 \, \text{m/s}^2$ on a motor vehicle having a mass of $1100 \, \text{kg}$. If the initial velocity of the vehicle is $12 \, \text{m/s}$, what will be the final velocity if this force is applied for $5 \, \text{s}$?

(EMEU)

Solution

Applying equation [2.3]:

Accelerating force, $F = ma$
$$= 1100 \, [\text{kg}] \times 3 \, [\text{m/s}^2]$$
$$= 3300 \, \text{N} = 3.3 \, \text{kN}$$

Now,

$$v = u + at \quad \text{from equation [2.1]}$$

where $u = 12 \, \text{m/s}; \, a = 3 \, \text{m/s}^2; \, t = 5 \, \text{s}$

Then $v = 12 + (3 \times 5) = 27 \, \text{m/s}$

Answer: Force producing acceleration of the vehicle $= 3.3 \, \text{kN}$
  Final velocity attained in $5 \, \text{s} = 27 \, \text{m/s}$

Example 2.3

A valve and tappet assembly fitted to an overhead camshaft engine has a mass of $200 \, \text{g}$. At a given engine speed, the force to open the valve is $250 \, \text{N}$. Calculate the acceleration of the valve under these conditions.

(EMEU)

Solution

$$\text{Force} = \text{Mass} \times \text{Acceleration}$$

i.e. $F = ma$

$\therefore$ Acceleration, $a = \dfrac{F}{m}$ where $F = 250 \, \text{N}$
$m = 200 \, \text{g} = 0.2 \, \text{kg}$

Hence $a = \dfrac{250}{0.2} \left[\dfrac{\text{N}}{\text{kg}} = \dfrac{\text{kg m/s}^2}{\text{kg}} \right] = 1250 \, \text{m/s}^2$

Answer: Acceleration of valve $= 1250 \, \text{m/s}^2$

Example 2.4

Calculate the force required to accelerate a vehicle uniformly from $30 \, \text{km/h}$ to $75 \, \text{km/h}$ in $20 \, \text{s}$. The mass of the vehicle is $2 \, \text{Mg}$.

Solution

Time taken $= t = 20 \, \text{s}$

Initial velocity $= u = 30\,\text{km/h} = \dfrac{30 \times 1000}{60 \times 60} = 8.33\,\text{m/s}$

Final velocity $= v = 75\,\text{km/h} = \dfrac{75 \times 1000}{60 \times 60} = 20.83\,\text{m/s}$

Now,

Acceleration, $a = \dfrac{v - u}{t}$ from equation [1.1]

$\qquad = \dfrac{20.83 - 8.33}{20} = 0.625\,\text{m/s}^2$

Applying equation [2.3]:

Accelerating force, $F = ma$
$\qquad\qquad = 2000\,[\text{kg}] \times 0.625\,[\text{m/s}^2]$
$\qquad\qquad = 1250\,\text{N}$

Answer: Force required to accelerate vehicle $= 1250\,\text{N}$

Example 2.5

A motor vehicle of mass 1250 kg is braked from a speed of 108 km/h and comes to rest with uniform retardation after travelling a distance of 150 m. Determine:

(*a*) the magnitude of the braking force
(*b*) the time taken by the vehicle to come to rest.

Solution

(*a*) $u = 108\,\text{km/h} = \dfrac{108 \times 1000}{60 \times 60} = 30\,\text{m/s}$

$\quad v = 0$ (the vehicle is brought to rest by the brakes)
$\quad s = 150\,\text{m}$

Now, $v^2 = u^2 + 2as$ from equation [1.4]

so that $a = \dfrac{v^2 - u^2}{2s}$

$\qquad = \dfrac{0 - 30^2}{2 \times 150}\left[\dfrac{\text{m}^2/\text{s}^2}{\text{m}}\right] = -3\,\text{m/s}^2$

This is negative; therefore the retardation is 3 m/s². Applying equation [2.3]:

Braking force $=$ Mass of vehicle $\times$ Retardation
$\qquad\qquad = 1250\,[\text{kg}] \times 3\,[\text{m/s}^2]$
$\qquad\qquad = 3750\,\text{N} = 3.75\,\text{kN}$

(b) To find time taken by vehicle to come to rest:

$$s = \left(\frac{u + v}{2}\right) \times t \quad \text{from equation [1.2]}$$

i.e. $150 = \left(\frac{30 + 0}{2}\right) \times t$

$$\therefore \quad t = \frac{150 \times 2}{30} = 10\,\text{s}$$

Answer: (a) Braking force = 3.75 kN
(b) Time taken by vehicle to come to rest = 10 s

Example 2.6

A force of 650 N is applied to a body of mass 200 kg for a period of 12 s. If the only other force acting on the body is a constant frictional force of 400 N in opposition to its motion, find:

(a) the acceleration of the body
(b) the distance moved by the body in this time.

Solution (see Fig. 2.1)

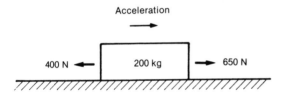

Figure 2.1 Example 2.6

(a) Accelerating force, F = Resultant force in the direction of motion
= Applied force − Frictional force
= 650 N − 400 N = 250 N

But $\qquad\qquad F = ma$ from equation [2.3]

$$\therefore \qquad \text{Acceleration, } a = \frac{F}{m}$$

$$= \frac{250}{200} \left[\frac{\text{kg m/s}^2}{\text{kg}}\right] = 1.25\,\text{m/s}^2$$

(b) To find distance moved by the body.

Applying equation [1.3]:

$$s = ut + \tfrac{1}{2}at^2$$

where $u = 0$; $t = 12\,\text{s}$; $a = 1.25\,\text{m/s}^2$

Then, by substitution,

$$s = 0 + (\tfrac{1}{2} \times 1.25 \times 12^2) = 90 \text{ m}$$

Answer: (*a*) Acceleration of body $= 1.25 \text{ m/s}^2$
(*b*) Distance moved in 12 s $= 90 \text{ m}$

2.5 Weight

The force with which a body is attracted towards the earth, known as the force due to gravity, is called the *weight* of the body. This is determined by the product of the mass of the body and the acceleration due to gravity.

If W is the weight of a body, m is its mass and g is the acceleration due to gravity, then:

$$W = mg \qquad\qquad\qquad [2.4]$$

It must here be remarked that the magnitude of g varies with the distance from the centre of the earth. Since the earth is not a perfect sphere, its radius being less at the poles than it is at the equator, the weight of a body then varies slightly at different places on the earth's surface. However, an average value of g equal to 9.81 m/s^2 has been adopted which is sufficiently accurate for most engineering purposes. (At sea-level near London area, g is almost exactly 9.81 m/s^2.)

Example 2.7
Determine the gravitational force acting on a body of mass 160 kg.

Solution
Gravitational force, $W = mg$ from equation [2.4]
where $m = 160 \text{ kg}$ and $g = 9.81 \text{ m/s}^2$
Hence $W = 160 \text{ [kg]} \times 9.81 \text{ [m/s}^2\text{]} = 1570 \text{ N}$

Answer: Gravitational force acting on body (i.e. weight of body) $=$ 1570 N

Note: For the purpose of simplifying calculations, g is frequently taken as 10 m/s^2. Hence, by using this value in the above example, the gravitational force acting on the body becomes 1600 N. It will be observed that the error involved is less than 2 per cent.

2.6 Newton's third law of motion

Newton's third law of motion tells us that forces always act in pairs of equal and opposite forces. It states that:

'To every action there is an equal and opposite reaction.'

This is sometimes stated as: 'If a body A exerts a force on another body B, then B will exert on A a force of equal magnitude but in the opposite direction.'

This law applies to both bodies at rest and bodies in motion, and can best be explained by considering the following cases.

(*a*) A body resting on a table exerts a force (action) equal to its weight downwards on the table. The fact that the body is stationary indicates that the force system is in equilibrium, i.e. in balance, and that the table exerts an equal and upward force (reaction) on the body.

(*b*) If a body is attached to a string and allowed to hang vertically, the weight of the body exerts a downward pull (acting force) on the string. By Newton's third law, there is a reacting force in the string supporting the body, acting vertically upwards.

(*c*) If a vehicle is towing a trailer and pulls on the tow-rope with a given force (action), it should be appreciated that the tow-rope tends to pull the vehicle backwards with an equal force (reaction).

Example 2.8

A load of 200 kg is suspended stationary on the end of a wire rope. Determine the tension in the rope.

Solution (see Fig. 2.2)

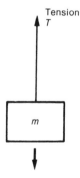

Figure 2.2   Example 2.8

From equation [2.4],

Downward force exerted by load on the rope
= Weight of the load
= mg
= 200 [kg] × 9.81 [m/s²] = 1962 N

From Newton's third law, the rope is exerting an equal and opposite force on the load. This force is known as the *tension* in the rope. In Fig. 2.2, it is denoted by T. Hence:

Tension in the rope, T = Weight of the load
$$= 1962\,\text{N}$$

Answer: Tension in the rope = 1962 N

Note: The tension in the rope would also have been equal to 1962 N had the load been raised or lowered by the rope with uniform velocity.

Example 2.9

What would be the tension in the rope if the load in the previous example is raised by the rope with a constant acceleration of $1.5\,\text{m/s}^2$?

Solution (see Fig. 2.3)

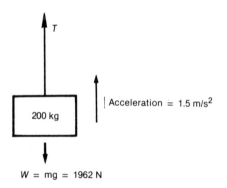

W = mg = 1962 N

Figure 2.3   Example 2.9

Force to accelerate the load, $F = ma$ from equation [2.3]

where m = 200 kg and $a = 1.5\,\text{m/s}^2$

Hence $F = 200\,[\text{kg}] \times 1.5\,[\text{m/s}^2] = 300\,\text{N}$

For accelerated motion upwards, the tension T in the rope is greater than the weight W, so that

Accelerating force, F = Resultant force (upwards)
$$= \text{Tension } T - \text{Weight } W$$
i.e. $300\,\text{N} = T - 1962\,\text{N}$
∴ $T = 1962 + 300 = 2262\,\text{N}$

It will therefore be noticed that the tension in the rope (for this particular case) is made up of two parts:

1. The tension required to balance the weight of the load.

2. The tension required to accelerate the load.

Answer: Tension in the rope $= 2262\,\text{N}$

Note: For accelerated motion downwards, W will be greater than T, in which case, $F = W - T$.

Exercise 2.1 – Review questions

1 State Newton's first law of motion.
2 The resistance that a body has to motion or change of motion is called ....
3 The amount of .... that a body possesses can be measured in terms of its mass.
4 The mass of a body is the .... contained in the body.
5 A resultant force applied to a body produces ....
6 Define the term 'momentum'.
7 A body of mass 5 kg, moving at 12 m/s, has a momentum of
   ....
8 State Newton's second law of motion.
9 Force = ... × ....
10 Define the newton.
11 $1\,\text{N} = 2\,\text{kg} \times$ ....
12 The gravitational force acting on a body is called ....
13 A mass of 50 kg is suspended on the end of a rope. The tension in the rope is ....
14 State Newton's third law of motion.
15 The acceleration imparted to a mass of 250 kg by a force of 2 kN is

   (a) $0.125\,\text{m/s}^2$ (b) $0.5\,\text{m/s}^2$ (c) $8\,\text{m/s}^2$ (d) $500\,\text{m/s}^2$

16 The tractive force required to accelerate a vehicle of mass 2 tonne at a rate of $0.75\,\text{m/s}^2$ is

   (a) $750\,\text{N}$ (b) $1500\,\text{N}$ (c) $2000\,\text{N}$ (d) $75\,\text{kN}$

17 A vehicle of mass 800 kg is being propelled along a level road by a force of 1.3 kN. If the acceleration produced is $1.2\,\text{m/s}^2$, the total resistance to motion is

   (a) $340\,\text{N}$ (b) $960\,\text{N}$ (c) $1040\,\text{N}$ (d) $1540\,\text{N}$

A vehicle having a mass of 950 kg accelerates uniformly from 15 m/s to 25 m/s in 5 s. Use this data to answer Problems 18 to 21, selecting the nearest correct solution from those given below.

(a) $50\,\text{m}$ (b) $9500\,\text{kg m/s}$ (c) $1900\,\text{N}$ (d) $8\,\text{m/s}^2$
(e) $100\,\text{m}$ (f) $9500\,\text{N}$ (g) $2\,\text{m/s}^2$ (h) $1900\,\text{kg m/s}$

18 Determine the acceleration of the vehicle.

19 Determine the distance travelled during the 5 s.
20 Determine the force producing the acceleration.
21 Determine the change in momentum of the vehicle.

A vehicle of mass 1800 kg is brought to rest from 72 km/h in 200 m. Use this data to answer Problems 22 to 24, selecting the nearest correct solution from those given below.

(a) $-1\,\text{m/s}^2$ (b) 1.8 kN   (c) 36 s   (d) 20 s   (e) 1 m/s^2 (f) 9 kN

22 Determine the retardation of the vehicle.
23 Determine the braking force required.
24 Determine the time taken by the vehicle to stop in this distance.

Exercise 2.2 – Problems

1 The inlet valve of a modern small car engine has a mass of 50 g and its maximum acceleration during the opening period is 8000 m/s^2. Calculate the force necessary to produce this acceleration.
(CGLI) (Modified)

2 A piston assembly has a mass of 0.5 kg and at a given instant the force on the gudgeon pin is 500 N. Determine the acceleration of the piston.
(EMEU)

3 A vehicle has a force of 1.5 kN acting on it due to the engine, and the acceleration produced is 1.2 m/s^2. Calculate the mass of the vehicle.

4 A vehicle having a mass of 1 tonne and travelling at 54 km/h is brought to rest in a distance of 30 m with uniform retardation. Determine the value of the retarding force and the time taken by the vehicle to come to rest.

5 A commercial vehicle having a total mass of 8 tonne is accelerated uniformly from rest at the rate of 0.75 m/s^2. Determine:

(a) the force producing the acceleration
(b) the velocity at the end of 16 s
(c) the distance covered during this time.

6 The speed of a vehicle of mass 1 tonne is reduced from 81 km/h to 27 km/h by the action of a mean retarding force of 3 kN. Find the distance covered during this reduction of speed.

7 A resultant force of 60 N acts on a body of mass 2.4 kg for 0.3 s. Determine the change in velocity.

8 At a given instant, a vehicle of mass 1000 kg has a speed of 18 km/h when it is subjected to a uniform acceleration of 2 m/s^2 until its speed is 72 km/h. Determine:

(a) the time taken to increase the speed

(*b*) the distance travelled during the acceleration
(*c*) the accelerating force.

(WMAC/UEI)

9   A body of mass 20 kg is acted upon by two forces, one of 50 N and the other of 120 N in the opposite direction. In which direction will the body accelerate and what will be the value of the acceleration?

10 A box of mass 250 kg is pulled along a horizontal plane against a frictional resistance of 200 N. Calculate the force, exerted parallel to the plane, which will be required to produce an acceleration of 3 m/s^2.

(EMEU)

11 A lorry of mass 10 Mg reaches a speed of 63 km/h in 20 s, starting from rest with uniform acceleration. It travels 2 km at this speed and is then brought to rest in a distance of 125 m. Determine:

(*a*) the momentum at 63 km/h
(*b*) the accelerating and braking forces required.

12 The speed of a vehicle of mass 960 kg is increased from 18 km/h to 54 km/h. Determine the change in momentum.

13 What propulsive force is required to produce the change in momentum of the vehicle in Problem 12 above if the change takes place in 12 s?

14 A racing car has a force of 10 kN acting on it due to the engine, and the frictional and air resistance total 2 kN. If the acceleration is 2 m/s^2, calculate the mass of the car.

15 A vehicle having a mass of 750 kg is being propelled along a level road by a force of 1.2 kN against a total resistance to motion of 300 N. Calculate:

(*a*) the acceleration of the vehicle
(*b*) how far the vehicle will travel from rest in the first 15 s
(*c*) the velocity of the vehicle at the end of this time.

16 A lift cage has a mass of 800 kg. Determine the tension in the lifting cable when the cage is

(*a*) ascending with uniform velocity
(*b*) accelerating upwards at 1.5 m/s^2
(*c*) accelerating downwards at 1.5 m/s^2.

Take $g = 10 \text{ m/s}^2$.

17 A caravan of mass 1000 kg is towed by means of a rope attached to a vehicle which is accelerating steadily at 1.25 m/s^2 along a level road. If the frictional resistances amount to 500 N, what is the tension in the tow-rope?

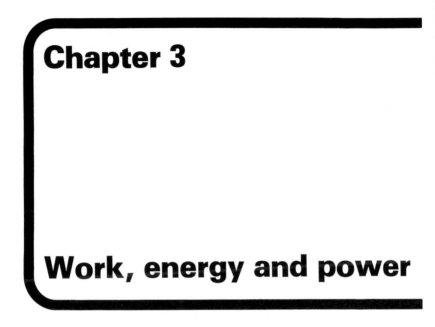

Chapter 3

Work, energy and power

3.1 Work

Work is said to be done when a force is applied to a body and causes it to move in the direction of the force. If the applied force is constant, the amount of work done is measured by the product of that force and the distance moved by the body.

Let a constant force F act on a body through a distance s. Then:

Work done = Force × Distance moved in the direction of the force
i.e. Work done = Fs [3.1]

The unit of work is the *joule* (J), and this is defined as the amount of work done when a force of one newton acts through a distance of one metre in the direction of its application. Hence, one joule is equal to one newton metre of work. In symbols, 1 J = 1 N m.

Example 3.1
A vehicle is towed along a straight level road by a force of 120 N. Calculate the work done in towing the vehicle through a distance of 70 m.

Solution
Work done = Force × Distance moved in direction of force
= 120 [N] × 70 [m]
= 8400 J = 8.4 kJ

Answer: Work done in towing the vehicle = 8.4 kJ

Example 3.2

An engine has a stroke of 80 mm. If the average force acting on the piston crown during the power stroke is 3.5 kN, calculate the work done during this stroke.

Solution

The stroke is the distance moved by the piston from top dead centre position to bottom dead centre position.

Work done = Average force on piston × Distance moved
= 3500 [N] × 0.08 [m]
= 280 J

Answer: Work done during the power stroke = 280 J

3.2 Work done in lifting objects

When an object is lifted at a steady speed, the direct force applied to raise the object is simply the upward force to overcome the downward gravitational pull on the object, which is the weight of the object (see Section 2.5).

From equation [2.4], the gravitational force acting on an object of mass m kg is mg newtons, where g is the acceleration due to gravity having the value of 9.81 m/s². When the object is lifted through a certain height, the work done is given by the product of the force to overcome the downward gravitational pull and the vertical distance moved by the object.

Example 3.3

Find the amount of work done by a hydraulic hoist in lifting a vehicle of mass 1500 kg to a height of 2 m.

Solution

Force to overcome when lifting the vehicle
= mg from equation [2.4]
= 1500 [kg] × 9.81 [m/s²]
= 14 715 N
Work done = Force × Vertical distance moved
= 14 715 [N] × 2 [m]
= 29 430 J = 29.43 kJ

Answer: Work done in lifting vehicle = 29.43 kJ

Example 3.4

A motor car of mass 800 kg is being propelled up a hill of gradient 1 in 15 at a steady speed of 63 km/h. Find the work done against gravity per minute. Neglect frictional resistance.

Solution

It must here be pointed out that the gradient used for roads is the ratio of height change for a corresponding distance along the slope. Hence, a gradient of 1 in 15 means that the hill or slope rises vertically 1 m for every 15 m measured along the road (see Fig. 3.1).

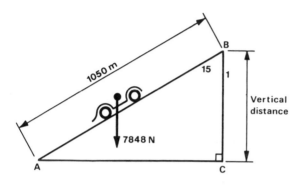

Figure 3.1   Example 3.4

Now, 63 km/h $= \dfrac{63 \times 1000}{60} = 1050$ m/min

The distance travelled (measured along the road) by the car in one minute is then 1050 m.

Mass of car is 800 kg; therefore gravitational force acting on a mass of 800 kg

$= 800 \times 9.81 = 7848$ N

Since the work done against the gravitational force of 7848 N is required, the distance moved in one minute must be measured along the line of action of this force. This is the vertical distance BC (Fig. 3.1). Thus:

Vertical distance BC $= \dfrac{\text{Distance AB}}{\text{Gradient}}$

$= \dfrac{1050 \text{ m}}{15} = 70 \text{ m}$

Work done against gravity per minute

$=$ Force $\times$ Vertical distance moved
$= 7848 \text{ [N]} \times 70 \text{ [m]}$
$= 549\ 360 \text{ J} = 549.36 \text{ kJ}$

Answer: Work done against gravity/min = 549.36 kJ

3.3 Energy

Energy is defined as the capacity for doing work, and is measured in the same unit, i.e. the joule (J). It exists in many forms such as mechanical energy, electrical energy, heat energy, chemical energy and so on. In this chapter, we are concerned with mechanical energy which is of two distinct types, namely, potential energy and kinetic energy.

3.4 Potential energy (PE)

The *potential energy* of a body is the energy it possesses due to its position in a gravitational field, i.e. due to its height above the ground (or any convenient reference level).

If a body of mass m kg is lifted through a vertical distance of h metres above the ground (see Fig. 3.2), work is done because the body is being lifted against the gravitational force which acts on the body.

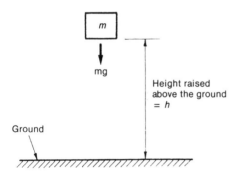

Figure 3.2

Work done = Force × Vertical distance
$$= mg \times h$$
$$= mgh \text{ joules}$$

This amount of work done will be stored in the body as potential energy by virtue of its position relative to the ground. In other words, the body will be capable of doing mgh joules of work if allowed to fall back to the ground. Thus, energy is transferred to a body when it is lifted.

Potential energy (PE) = mgh joules   [3.2]

3.5 Kinetic energy (KE)

The kinetic energy of a body is the energy it possesses due to its velocity. This energy can be made available to do work against a resistance if the moving body is brought to rest.

Let a constant unresisted force F newtons act on a body of mass m kg, initially at rest, and displace it in a straight line through a distance s metres. Then the work done is Fs joules.

If a m/s^2 is the acceleration produced, then from equation [2.3],

Accelerating force, $F = ma$
so that   Work done $= (ma) \times s$ $\qquad$ [3.3]

If the velocity reached in a distance s metres is v m/s, then from equation [1.4] for linear motion with constant acceleration,

$$s = \frac{v^2 - u^2}{2a} = \frac{v^2}{2a} \quad (\text{since } u = 0)$$

Substituting for s in equation [3.3], we have:

Work done $= ma \times \dfrac{v^2}{2a} = \tfrac{1}{2}mv^2$

(*Units:* kg $\times \dfrac{\text{m}^2}{\text{s}^2} = \dfrac{\text{kg m}}{\text{s}^2} \times \text{m} = \text{N m} = \text{J}$)

Now, the expression $\tfrac{1}{2}mv^2$ is the kinetic energy possessed by the body when moving with the velocity v m/s. Hence, the work done by the force to set the body in motion will be stored in the body in the form of kinetic energy, so that

Kinetic energy (KE) $= \tfrac{1}{2}mv^2$ joules $\qquad$ [3.4]

Work is the process by which energy is transferred to a body, and the energy thus gained by the body could be in the form of either potential energy or kinetic energy.

Example 3.5
A body of mass 5 kg is supported 12 m above the ground. Determine the potential energy possessed by the body due to its position with respect to the ground.

Solution
PE possessed by body $= mgh$ from equation [3.2]

where $m = 5$ kg; $g = 9.81$ m/s^2 ; $h = 12$ m

$\therefore \qquad\qquad$ PE $= 5 \times 9.81 \times 12 = 588.6$ J

Answer: PE possessed by body $= 588.6$ J

Example 3.6

A motor vehicle of mass 2 tonne is travelling at 50.4 km/h. Determine the kinetic energy of the vehicle at this speed.

Solution

KE of vehicle $= \frac{1}{2}mv^2$ from equation [3.4]

where $m = 2$ tonne $= 2000$ kg

$$v = 50.4 \text{ km/h} = \frac{50.4 \times 1000}{60 \times 60} = 14 \text{ m/s}$$

$$\therefore \quad \text{KE} = \frac{1}{2} \times 2000 \times 14^2 = 196\,000 \text{ J} = 196 \text{ kJ}$$

Answer: Kinetic energy of vehicle $= 196$ kJ

Example 3.7

A vehicle of mass 1600 kg increases its speed uniformly from 36 km/h to 72 km/h by the action of a resultant force of 2.4 kN. Determine the increase in the kinetic energy of the vehicle during the acceleration period. Show that this increase in kinetic energy is equal to the work done by the accelerating force.

Solution

Increase in KE $= \frac{1}{2}m(v^2 - u^2)$

where $m = 1600$ kg; $u = 36$ km/h $= 10$ m/s; $v = 72$ km/h $= 20$ m/s

$\therefore$ Increase in KE $= \frac{1}{2} \times 1600\,(20^2 - 10^2)$
$$= 240\,000 \text{ J} = 240 \text{ kJ}$$

We shall now proceed to show that this increase in KE is equal to the work done by the accelerating force.

Acceleration, $a = \dfrac{F}{m}$ from equation [2.3]

where $m = 1600$ kg and $F = 2.4$ kN $= 2400$ N

$$\therefore \quad a = \frac{2400}{1600}\left[\frac{\text{kg m/s}^2}{\text{kg}}\right] = 1.5 \text{ m/s}^2$$

Distance covered, $s = \dfrac{v^2 - u^2}{2a}$ from equation [1.4]

$$= \frac{20^2 - 10^2}{2 \times 1.5}\left[\frac{\text{m}^2/\text{s}^2}{\text{m/s}^2}\right] = 100 \text{ m}$$

Work done $= F \times s$
$$= 2400\,[\text{N}] \times 100\,[\text{m}] = 240\,000 \text{ J}$$
$$= \text{Increase in KE}$$

Answer: Increase in kinetic energy $= 240$ kJ

3.6 Principle of conservation of energy

The *principle of conservation of energy* states that energy can neither be created nor destroyed. Energy can be readily converted from one form to another, but it is found that a loss of energy in any one form is always accompanied by an equivalent increase in another form. In all such conversions, therefore, the total amount of energy remains constant.

There are many cases in which the potential energy of a body is converted into kinetic energy (and vice versa). When a motor vehicle freewheels down an incline, it gives up some of its potential energy but at the same time, it gains an equal amount of kinetic energy. Hence, the total energy possessed by the vehicle at any instant on the incline remains constant. In practice, friction is always present and work has to be done in overcoming the frictional resistances (this amount of work done is dissipated as heat). In such cases:

Final energy = Initial energy − Work done against friction

Let us consider again the body of mass m kg raised to the height h metres above the ground (Fig. 3.2). We have seen that the potential energy possessed by the body due to its position with respect to the ground is mgh joules. If the body is allowed to fall freely from that height until it is just about to strike the ground, all its available potential energy will be given up. Assuming no external work is done on or by the body during its time of fall then, by the principle of conservation of energy, the body will gain kinetic energy equal in amount to the initial potential energy.

Suppose the body reaches a speed of v m/s just before contact with the ground. Then, since energy is conserved, we may write:

KE on reaching the ground = Initial PE
i.e. $\qquad\qquad\qquad \tfrac{1}{2}mv^2 = mgh$
so that $\qquad\qquad\qquad\quad v = \sqrt{(2gh)}$ $\qquad\qquad$ [3.5]

Example 3.8

An engine has a mass of 150 kg and is suspended from a crane by a sling 4 m above ground level.

(a) Determine the potential energy of the engine due to its position above the ground.
(b) Due to a fault in the sling, the engine falls freely to the ground from that height. Calculate the velocity and the kinetic energy of the engine at the point of impact with the ground.
(c) Determine the kinetic energy and the potential energy of the engine after falling 3 m.

Neglect air resistance.

Solution

(a) PE of engine = mgh
$$= 150 \times 9.81 \times 4 \ [\text{kg} \times \text{m/s}^2 \times \text{m}]$$
$$= 5886 \, \text{J}$$

(b) Neglecting air resistance, the velocity of the engine as it strikes the ground is given by equation [3.5], that is:

$$v = \sqrt{(2gh)}$$
$$= \sqrt{(2 \times 9.81 \times 4)} \ [\text{m/s}^2 \times \text{m}]$$
$$= 8.859 \, \text{m/s}$$

KE of engine at point of impact with the ground

$$= \tfrac{1}{2}mv^2$$
$$= \tfrac{1}{2} \times 150 \times 8.859^2 \ [\text{kg} \times \text{m}^2/\text{s}^2]$$
$$= 5886 \, \text{J}$$
$$= \text{Initial PE (since air resistance is neglected)}$$

(c) KE gained by engine after falling a distance $x = 3 \, \text{m}$

$$= \text{PE given up}$$
$$= mgx$$
$$= 150 \times 9.81 \times 3 \ [\text{kg} \times \text{m/s}^2 \times \text{m}]$$
$$= 4414.5 \, \text{J}$$

PE still possessed by engine

$$= 5886 \, \text{J} - 4414.5 \, \text{J} = 1471.5 \, \text{J}$$

Check: PE still possessed by engine

$$= mg \, (h - x)$$
$$= 150 \times 9.81 \, (4 - 3) = 1471.5 \, \text{J}$$

Answer: (a) PE of engine = 5886 J
(b) Velocity at impact with the ground = 8.859 m/s
KE at impact with the ground = 5886 J
(c) KE after falling 3 m = 4414.5 J
PE still possessed by engine = 1471.5 J

Example 3.9

A motor vehicle of mass 800 kg stands on an incline whose gradient is 1 in 10. The handbrake is released and the vehicle runs down the incline. If the frictional resistance to motion is 40 N, find the speed of the vehicle after running 200 m down the incline.

Solution

From Fig. 3.3, we have:

$$h = 200 \sin \theta = 200 \times \tfrac{1}{10} = 20 \, \text{m}$$

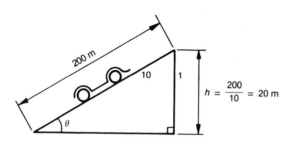

$$h = \frac{200}{10} = 20 \text{ m}$$

Figure 3.3 Example 3.9

PE at top of incline $= mgh$
$$= 800 \times 9.81 \times 20 \text{ [kg} \times \text{m/s}^2 \times \text{m]}$$
$$= 156\,960 \text{ J}$$
Work done against friction $= Fs$
$$= 40 \text{ [N]} \times 200 \text{ [m]}$$
$$= 8000 \text{ J}$$

By the principle of conservation of energy,

KE gained at bottom of incline

$= $ PE given up $-$ Work done against friction
$= 156\,960 \text{ J} - 8000 \text{ J} = 148\,960 \text{ J}$

But $\quad$ KE $= \frac{1}{2}mv^2$
i.e. $\quad 148\,960 = \frac{1}{2} \times 800 \times v^2$

$\therefore \qquad v = \sqrt{\left(\frac{148\,960 \times 2}{800}\right)} = 19.3 \text{ m/s}$

Answer: Speed after running 200 m $= 19.3 \text{ m/s}$ (69.5 km/h)

Example 3.10

A motor vehicle of mass 1200 kg is travelling along a level road at 54 km/h. The brakes are then applied and the speed of the vehicle is reduced to 18 km/h over a distance of 50 m. If the frictional resistance to motion is constant at 160 N, calculate the effective braking force of the brakes.

Solution

Work done by retarding forces $=$ Loss of KE of vehicle
i.e. $\qquad (F_B + F_F) \times s = \frac{1}{2}m\,(u^2 - v^2)$

where $F_B = $ the required braking force, in N
$\quad F_F = $ the frictional force $= 160 \text{ N}$
$\quad m = $ the mass of the vehicle $= 1200 \text{ kg}$
$\quad s = $ the distance moved during braking $= 50 \text{ m}$
$\quad u = $ the initial velocity $= 54 \text{ km/h} = 15 \text{ m/s}$
$\quad v = $ the final velocity $= 18 \text{ km/h} = 5 \text{ m/s}$

Now, substituting these values in the above equation, we get:

$$(F_B + 160) \times 50 = \tfrac{1}{2} \times 1200 \times (15^2 - 5^2)$$
$$= 120\,000$$

$$F_B + 160 = \frac{120\,000}{50} = 2400$$

$$\therefore \qquad F_B = 2400 - 160 = 2240\,\text{N}$$

Answer: Braking force = 2240 N

3.7 Power

Power is defined as the rate of transfer of energy. If the energy transfer is in the form of mechanical work, then:

$$\text{Power} = \frac{\text{Work done}}{\text{Time taken}} \tag{3.6}$$

$$= \frac{\text{Force} \times \text{Distance moved}}{\text{Time taken}} \tag{3.7}$$

But $\dfrac{\text{Distance moved}}{\text{Time taken}}$ is the velocity v of the body. Hence:

$$\text{Power} = \text{Force} \times \text{Velocity} = Fv \tag{3.8}$$

The unit of power is the *watt* (W), which is the rate of doing one joule of work every second. Thus:

$$1\,\text{W} = 1\,\text{J/s} = 1\,\text{N m/s}$$

Example 3.11
If an engine drives a car against a total resistance of 1.2 kN over a distance of 250 m in 30 s, what power is being developed by the crankshaft?

Solution
If the vehicle is to overcome a resistance of 1.2 kN, the engine must provide a force of 1.2 kN at the crankshaft.

Power developed at the crankshaft

$$= \frac{\text{Force} \times \text{Distance moved}}{\text{Time taken}}$$

$$= \frac{1200 \times 250}{30} \left[\frac{\text{N m}}{\text{s}}\right] = 10\,000\,\text{W} = 10\,\text{kW}$$

Answer: Power developed at the crankshaft = 10 kW

Example 3.12

A vehicle hauls a trailer at 72 km/h when exerting a steady pull of 800 N at the tow-rope. Calculate the power required.

Solution

Power required = Force × Velocity

$\qquad\qquad$ = $F \times v$ from equation [3.8]

where F = 800 N and v = 72 km/h = 20 m/s

$\therefore$ Power required = 800 [N] × 20 [m/s]

$\qquad\qquad\qquad$ = 16 000 W = 16 kW

Answer: Power required = 16 kW

Example 3.13

The velocity of a body of mass 16 kg is increased from 5 m/s to 20 m/s in 12 s. Calculate the power required to produce the change in kinetic energy of the body.

Solution

Change in KE of body = $\frac{1}{2}m (v^2 - u^2)$

where m = 16 kg; u = 5 m/s; v = 20 m/s

$\therefore\qquad$ Change in KE = $\frac{1}{2} \times 16 \times (20^2 - 5^2)$ = 3000 J

$\qquad$ Power required = $\dfrac{\text{Change in KE}}{\text{Time taken}}$

$\qquad\qquad\qquad\qquad$ = $\dfrac{3000}{12} \left[\dfrac{\text{J}}{\text{s}}\right]$ = 250 W

Answer: Power required = 250 W

Exercise 3.1 − Review questions

1 Define the term 'work' and name its unit of measurement.
2 Energy is the capacity for ....
3 List four forms in which energy can exist, illustrating your answer by reference to the energy forms at work in the motor vehicle.
4 Distinguish between 'potential energy' and 'kinetic energy'.
5 Write down the formula for calculating:

   (*a*) potential energy,   (*b*) kinetic energy.

6 Give one motor vehicle example of each of the following:

   (*a*) potential energy,   (*b*) kinetic energy.

$\qquad\qquad\qquad\qquad\qquad\qquad\qquad\qquad\qquad\qquad$ (NWRAC/ULCI)

7 State the principle of conservation of energy.
8 Define the term 'power' and name its unit.
9 Complete the following:

(*a*) Work done = Force × ....
(*b*) Work done = Weight × ....
(*c*) Power = Force × ....

10 The power produced when a force F acts through a distance s for

a time t is given by $\dfrac{.........}{.........}$.

Exercise 3.2 — Problems

1 Calculate the work done when a casting is moved 15 m along a workshop floor by a force of 3.5 kN.
2 A force of 250 N is applied to a body. If the work done is 6 kJ, determine the distance through which the body is moved in the direction of the force.
3 The work done in raising the front end of a vehicle was 360 J. If the vehicle was raised to a height of 120 mm, determine the magnitude of the force exerted by the lifting jack.
4 A force of 120 N acts on a body moving it through a distance of 5 m in the direction of the force in 8 s. Determine (*a*) the energy transferred to the body and (*b*) the power used.
5 In moving a distance of 20 m, a force does 7.5 kJ of work. Calculate:

(*a*) the magnitude of the force
(*b*) the time taken if the power output is 625 W.

6 A piston moved at a uniform velocity of 7 m/s against a resistance of 250 N. Find the power developed.
7 A motor car required a power of 10 kW to maintain a steady speed of 36 km/h on a level road. Calculate the magnitude of the propelling force required to sustain this speed.
8 A vehicle of mass 4 tonne is raised by a hydraulic hoist through a distance of 2.25 m in 36 s. Calculate the power required to perform this task.
9 The work done in raising eight motor vehicle components on the back of a lorry 1.25 m above the ground is 4905 J. Calculate the mass of each component.
10 An electric motor driving a lifting machine has a power rating of 2.8 kW. Find the time taken by the machine to raise a motor vehicle rear axle of mass 240 kg to a height of 3.5 m. (Take $g = 10\,\text{m/s}^2$.)
11 The total resistance to motion of a vehicle travelling along a level

road at 42 km/h is 1.5 kN. Calculate:

(a) the work done per minute against the resistance
(b) the power required to keep the speed steady.

12 A loaded vehicle of total mass 4 tonne climbed a gradient of 1 in 50, the gradient being 1.5 km long. Calculate:

(a) the work done in reaching the top of the gradient
(b) the power used for climbing if the speed of the vehicle was 27 km/h.

(Take $g = 10 \, \text{m/s}^2$.)

13 Determine the power of a pump used to raise 75 litres of water to a height of 16 m in 24 s. What is the potential energy of the water in the final position?
(1 litre of water has a mass of 1 kg.)

14 The energy expended in lifting an engine of mass 150 kg is 6 kJ. Calculate the height through which it has been lifted.
(Take $g = 10 \, \text{m/s}^2$.)

15 A metal box and its contents have a mass of 25 kg. The box is pulled 8 m along a workshop floor by applying a force of 60 N, and is then lifted 3 m on to a bench. Determine:

(a) the total work done
(b) the amount of energy that is transformed into potential energy.

(Take $g = 10 \, \text{m/s}^2$.)

16 A motor vehicle of mass 1650 kg is travelling on the level at a speed of 72 km/h. Determine its kinetic energy.
    If the engine is switched off, how far will the vehicle travel before coming to rest? The resistance to motion may be assumed constant at 2.2 kN.

17 The inlet valve of a modern small car engine has a mass of 50 g and reaches a maximum acceleration of 8000 m/s² during the opening period in 0.001 s from rest. Calculate the kinetic energy of the valve at the end of the acceleration.

(CGLI) (Modified)

18 (a) The speed of a vehicle of mass 1500 kg is reduced from 54 km/h to 18 km/h by the action of an average retarding force of 3 kN. Calculate the change in kinetic energy.
   (b) Show that this change in kinetic energy is equal to the work done by the retarding force.

(NWRAC/ULCI) (Modified)

19 A vehicle of mass 800 kg has an initial velocity of 108 km/h when a retarding force of 4 kN is applied for a distance of 50 m. Determine the final velocity of the vehicle.

20 A body of mass 20 kg is supported 50 m above the ground. If the body is allowed to fall freely from this height, calculate the poten-

tial energy and the kinetic energy of the body at the following positions: (*a*) 50 m above the ground, (*b*) 20 m above the ground, and (*c*) just above the ground.
(Take $g = 10 \text{ m/s}^2$.)

21 In a drop-forging operation, the top die and its holder, which have a combined mass of 50 kg, fall freely on to the bottom die. Calculate:

(*a*) the kinetic energy of the top die just before striking the bottom die if its velocity at that instant is 7.8 m/s

(*b*) the height through which the top die has fallen.

22 A body of mass 10 kg falls freely from rest through a vertical distance of 6 m when its velocity is decreased to 6 m/s by imparting energy to a machine. Calculate the amount of energy given to the machine.

(NWRAC/ULCI)

23 A vehicle has a mass of 600 kg and stands at the top of a hill having a gradient of 1 in 8. When the brakes are released there is a frictional resistance of 300 N. Find the vehicle speed after it has rolled 160 m.
(Take $g = 10 \text{ m/s}^2$.)

(NWRAC/ULCI)

Chapter 4

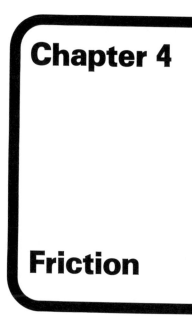

Friction

4.1 Force of friction

Whenever one surface moves (or attempts to move) over another, a resisting force, acting tangentially to the surfaces, is set up so as to oppose the motion. This resisting force is called the *force of friction*.

It is found that the force of friction is usually slightly greater before one surface starts to move over the other than after this movement has started. In other words, it requires a slightly greater force to overcome the friction of rest, known as *static friction*, than it does to overcome the friction of motion, known as *sliding* or *dynamic friction* (see Section 4.3).

4.2 Laws of friction for dry surfaces

The following laws have largely resulted from experimental observations. They form the basis from which friction problems are tackled.

1. The sliding frictional force opposing motion, once motion has started, is directly proportional to the normal force between the surfaces.
2. The sliding frictional force is dependent upon the nature of the surfaces in contact.
   (Relative motion is more difficult with rough surfaces than with smooth surfaces.)

3. The sliding frictional force is dependent upon the physical properties of the materials involved.
   (For the same force pressing the sliding surfaces together, steel slides more easily over nylon than it does over rubber.)
4. The sliding frictional force is independent of the area of the surfaces in contact.
   (Provided the surfaces are of the same material and condition, and have the same force pressing them together, the resistance to sliding will be the same for a small area of contact as for a large area.)
5. For low speeds of relative motion of the surfaces, the frictional force is independent of the speed of sliding.

4.3 The coefficient of friction

Static friction

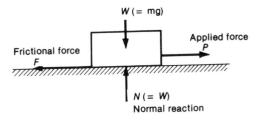

Figure 4.1

Figure 4.1 shows a body of mass m resting on a flat horizontal surface. The weight W of the body (equal to mg) acts vertically downwards. For equilibrium, there will be an equal and opposite reacting force N, acting vertically upwards. Suppose now a horizontal force P is applied to the body, tending it to move to the right. A frictional force F (equal to P) will be created between the surfaces to act in opposition to P, i.e. to the left. As P is increased in magnitude, F also increases and will reach an upper limiting value when the body is just about to move. This limiting or maximum value of F is called the force of static friction between the surfaces under these conditions.

Sliding or dynamic friction

Once the body has started to move, it will be found that the magnitude of the applied force P can be reduced slightly to keep the body moving at a steady speed along the surface. This is because sliding or dynamic friction (i.e. the friction of motion) is less than static friction (i.e. the friction of rest). This particular value of P is then equal to the force of sliding friction.

By the first law of friction given in Section 4.2, the sliding frictional force is directly proportional to the reaction force normal to the surfaces in contact. Thus:

$$F \propto N$$

or $\quad \dfrac{F}{N} =$ Constant

The constant is called the *coefficient of friction* between the two surfaces concerned, and is denoted by μ (the Greek letter 'mew').

$\therefore \quad$ Coefficient of friction, $\mu = \dfrac{F}{N}$ $\qquad\qquad$ [4.1]

Since the forces F and N are expressed in the same units, μ is just a number and has no units of its own.

Table 4.1 gives some average values for the coefficient of friction between dry surfaces.

Table 4.1 Average values of coefficient of friction

Materials	μ
Metal on metal	0.2
Clutch lining material on cast iron	0.35
Brake lining material on cast iron	0.4
Rubber tyre on road surface	0.6

4.4 Advantages and disadvantages of friction

Friction can be used to great advantage in a motor vehicle when applied to such units as tyres, clutches and brakes, in which instances the surfaces must be dry and free from oil or grease. In bearings and other moving parts, however, friction is a disadvantage and systems of lubrication must be used to reduce friction to a minimum.

Example 4.1

A metal block lined with Ferodo and having a mass of 4.8 kg requires a horizontal pull of 17 N to move it at a steady speed along a horizontal steel surface. Calculate the coefficient of friction for Ferodo on steel.

Solution

Referring to Fig. 4.2,

Total weight of block, $W = mg$
$$= 4.8 \text{ [kg]} \times 9.81 \text{ [m/s}^2\text{]} = 47.1 \text{ N}$$

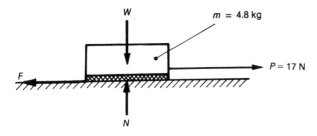

Figure 4.2 Example 4.1

∴   Normal reaction N between Ferodo and steel surface $= 47.1\,N$

Since the block is moving at a steady speed, then:

Frictional force, $F =$ Applied force, P
$\qquad\qquad\qquad = 17\,N$

Coefficient of friction, $\mu = \dfrac{F}{N}$ from equation [4.1]

$$= \frac{17}{47.1}\left[\frac{N}{N}\right] = 0.36$$

Answer: Coefficient for friction for Ferodo on steel $= 0.36$

Example 4.2

A vehicle has a mass of 1325 kg and the coefficient of friction between the tyres and ground is 0.4. What is the maximum retarding force which can be used to stop it without causing it to skid? If the actual retarding force at the ground is 0.75 of the maximum, and is constant, determine the work done in bringing the vehicle to rest in a distance of 20 m.

(EMEU) (Modified)

Solution

Weight of vehicle, $W = mg$
$\qquad\qquad\qquad = 1325\ [\text{kg}]\ \times\ 9.81\ [\text{m/s}^2]$
$\qquad\qquad\qquad = 13\,000\,N$

From equation [4.1],

Maximum retarding force, $F = \mu N = \mu W$
$\qquad\qquad\qquad\qquad\qquad = 0.4 \times 13\,000\,N$
$\qquad\qquad\qquad\qquad\qquad = 5200\,N = 5.2\,kN$
Actual retarding force at ground $= 0.75 \times 5200\,N$
$\qquad\qquad\qquad\qquad\qquad\qquad = 3900\,N$

44

Work done in bringing the vehicle to rest
= Actual retarding force × Distance moved
= 3900 [N] × 20 [m]
= 78 000 J = 78 kJ

Answer: Maximum retarding force = 5.2 kN
                Work done to bring vehicle to rest = 78 kJ

Example 4.3

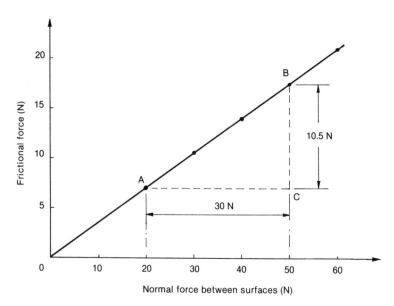

Figure 4.3   Example 4.3

In an experiment to determine the coefficient of friction between clutch lining and steel, a block faced with material was drawn at uniform speed across a horizontal steel surface. The following results were obtained:

Normal force between surfaces (N)	20	30	40	50	60
Horizontal force required to cause motion (N)	7	10.5	14	17.5	21

Plot these values on a graph and hence determine the coefficient of friction.

Solution

For uniform speed across the steel surface, the frictional force just balances the applied force that causes the motion of the block. Thus, plotting values of the frictional force against corresponding values of the reaction force normal to the surfaces in contact gives the graph shown in Fig. 4.3. It will be observed that the graph is a straight line passing through the origin, illustrating that the frictional force is directly proportional to the normal force between the surfaces. The gradient of the graph represents the coefficient of friction between the rubbing surfaces. Hence, from the graph,

$$\text{Coefficient of friction, } \mu = \frac{BC}{AC} = \frac{17.5 - 7}{50 - 20} \left[\frac{N}{N}\right]$$

$$= \frac{10.5}{30} = 0.35$$

Answer: Coefficient of friction for clutch lining material on steel = 0.35

4.5 Friction in a journal bearing

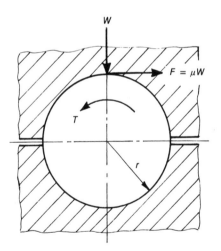

Figure 4.4 Friction in a journal bearing

Let W be the load (in newtons) on the bearing. The tangential frictional force F acts to oppose the rotation of the shaft (see Fig. 4.4), so if $\mu =$ coefficient of friction between shaft and bearing, then from equation [4.1],

Frictional force, $F = \mu W$

Now let r be the radius of the shaft in metres, then:

Frictional torque resisting rotation of shaft (see Section 18.2),

$\quad T_F$ = Frictional force × Radius of shaft

i.e. $\quad T_F = \mu Wr$ N m $\hfill$ [4.2]

At steady speed conditions, the frictional torque T_F is balanced by the equal and opposing driving torque T.

$\quad$ Work done in overcoming friction in one revolution of the shaft

$\quad$ = Frictional force × Circumference

$\quad$ = $\mu W \times 2\pi r$

or $\quad$ = $\mu Wr \times 2\pi$ J

If the shaft is running at a speed of N rev/min, then:

$\quad$ Work done against friction per minute

$\quad$ = $\mu Wr \times 2\pi N$ J $\hfill$ [4.3]

From Section 1.5, the expression $2\pi N$ gives the angle turned through by the shaft in rad/min. Hence, equation [4.3] may be written thus:

$\quad$ Work done against friction per minute

$\quad$ = Frictional torque × Angle turned through in rad/min

Now since 1 W = 1 J/s, then:

$\quad$ Power absorbed by friction

$\quad$ = Work done against friction in J/s

$\quad$ = $\mu Wr \times \dfrac{2\pi N}{60}$ W $\hfill$ [4.4]

Again, from Section 1.5, the expression $2\pi N/60$ gives the angular velocity ω of the shaft in rad/s. Hence, equation [4.4] may be written thus:

Power absorbed by friction = $T_F \times \omega$ W $\hfill$ [4.5]

Example 4.4

The main journal bearings of an engine crankshaft carry a total load of 10 kN when the engine speed is 3500 rev/min. If the coefficient of friction between each bearing and shaft is 0.015 and the diameter of the shaft is 60 mm, calculate:

(a) the frictional torque on the shaft
(b) the power absorbed by friction
(c) the heat energy generated in the bearings per minute.

Solution

Load on bearings, W	$= 10 \times 10^3$ N
Shaft speed, N	$= 3500$ rev/min
Shaft radius, r	$= 0.03$ m
Coefficient of friction, μ	$= 0.015$

(a) Frictional torque, T_F
$\qquad = \mu W r$
$\qquad = 0.015 \times 10 \times 10^3 \times 0.03$
$\qquad = 4.5$ N m

(b) Power absorbed by friction $= T_F \times \dfrac{2\pi N}{60}$ W

$$= 4.5 \times \frac{2\pi \times 3500}{60} \text{ W}$$

$$= 1650 \text{ W} = 1.65 \text{ kW}$$

(c) Heat energy generated in bearings per minute due to friction

$\qquad = 1650 \times 60 \qquad$ [since 1 W $= 1$ J/s]
$\qquad = 99\,000$ J $= 99$ kJ

Answer: (a) Frictional torque on shaft $= 4.5$ N m
$\qquad\quad (b)$ Power asborbed by friction $= 1.65$ kW
$\qquad\quad (c)$ Heat energy generated in bearings/min $= 99$ kJ

4.6 Torque and power transmitted by a clutch

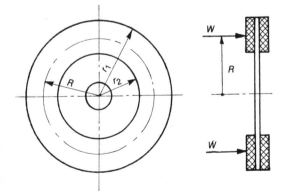

Figure 4.5 Forces acting on a single-plate clutch

With reference to Fig. 4.5, let

$W =$ total spring force (N)

r_1 = external radius of friction disc (m)
r_2 = internal radius of friction disc (m)
n = number of pairs of friction surfaces in contact
μ = coefficient of friction between disc and driving surfaces.

Now,

Mean or effective radius, $R = \frac{1}{2}(r_1 + r_2)$

Tangential force acting at distance R from centre of rotation,

$F = \mu W$

$\therefore$ Frictional torque transmitted,

$T_F = F \times R$
$\quad = \frac{1}{2}\mu W (r_1 + r_2)$

Since there are n pairs of friction surfaces in contact (for a single-plate clutch, $n = 2$), then the torque transmitted by a clutch is given by:

$$T_F = \frac{1}{2}\mu W n (r_1 + r_2) \, \text{N m} \qquad [4.6]$$

If N is the rotational speed of the clutch in rev/min, then, from equations [4.2] and [4.4]:

$$\text{Power transmitted} = T_F \times \frac{2\pi N}{60} \, \text{W}$$

Example 4.5

A single-plate clutch of 0.15 m effective diameter is lined with material of coefficient of friction 0.35. If the total spring force is 2.5 kN, calculate:

(a) the torque transmitted
(b) the power transmitted at 3000 rev/min.

Solution

Total spring force, W = 2.5 kN = 2500 N
Effective radius, R = 0.075 m
Pairs of contact surfaces, n = 2
Coefficient of friction, μ = 0.35
Rotational speed, N = 3000 rev/min

(a) Torque transmitted, $T_F = \mu W R n$
$\qquad = 0.35 \times 2500 \times 0.075 \times 2 \, \text{N m}$
$\qquad = 131.25 \, \text{N m}$

(b) Power transmitted $= T_F \times \dfrac{2\pi N}{60} \, \text{W}$

$\qquad = 131.25 \times \dfrac{2\pi \times 3000}{60} \, \text{W}$

$$= 41\,250\,\text{W} = 41.25\,\text{kW}$$

Answer: (a) Torque transmitted by clutch $= 131.25\,\text{N m}$
(b) Power transmitted by clutch $= 41.25\,\text{kW}$

Example 4.6

A six-cylinder engine running under full load conditions develops maximum torque at 1500 rev/min when the power is 22 kW. Calculate:

(a) The torque transmitted by the clutch.
(b) The force exerted by each of the eight springs if the clutch is a single-plate type. The friction surfaces are 0.25 m outside diameter and 0.18 m inside diameter, and the coefficient of friction is 0.32.

Solution

Outside radius of friction ring, $r_1 = 0.125\,\text{m}$
Inside radius of friction ring, $r_2 = 0.09\,\text{m}$
Coefficient of friction, $\mu = 0.32$
Pairs of friction surfaces, $n = 2$
Engine speed, $N = 1500\,\text{rev/min}$

(a) By equation [18.4],

$$\text{Power developed} = \text{Engine torque } (T) \times \frac{2\pi N}{60}\,\text{W}$$

i.e. $22 \times 10^3 = T \times \dfrac{2\pi \times 1500}{60}$

∴ $T = \dfrac{22 \times 10^3 \times 60}{2\pi \times 1500} = 140\,\text{N m}$

Maximum torque transmitted by clutch,

$T_F\,\text{max} = \text{Engine torque}$
$= 140\,\text{N m}$

Note: To allow for wear of the friction lining material and the lowering of the coefficient of friction between the contact surfaces due to the presence of oil or a high temperature, motor vehicle clutches are usually designed to have a torque capacity about $1\frac{1}{2}$ times the maximum torque of the engine.

Thus, in practice, the maximum capacity of the clutch would be equal to

Engine torque transmitted $\times 1.5 = 140 \times 1.5 = 210\,\text{N m}$

(b) Let W be the total spring force in newtons. Then, from equation [4.6],

$T_F\,\text{max} = \frac{1}{2}\mu Wn(r_1 + r_2)\,\text{N m}$
i.e. $140 = \frac{1}{2} \times 0.32 \times W \times 2 \times (0.125 + 0.09)$
or $140 = 0.32 \times 0.215 \times W$

so that $\quad W = \dfrac{140}{0.32 \times 0.215} = 2034 \, \text{N}$

Now,

Force exerted by each spring $= \dfrac{\text{Total spring force}}{\text{Number of springs}}$

$\qquad\qquad = \dfrac{2034}{8} = 254.25 \, \text{N}$

Answer: (*a*) Max. torque transmitted by clutch $= 140 \, \text{N m}$
             (*b*) Force exerted by each spring $= 254.25 \, \text{N}$

Example 4.7

The friction disc of a single-plate clutch has a face area of $0.025 \, \text{m}^2$ and a mean radius of $0.12 \, \text{m}$. If the spring force per m^2 of area is not to exceed $120 \, \text{kN}$, and the coefficient of friction between the lining material and the driving surfaces is 0.3, calculate the maximum power that could be transmitted by the clutch at $2000 \, \text{rev/min}$.

(CGLI) (Modified)

Solution

Total spring force,

$W =$ Spring pressure $\times$ Friction disc face area
$\quad = 120 \times 10^3 \, [\text{N/m}^2] \times 0.025 \, [\text{m}^2]$
$\quad = 3000 \, \text{N}$

Maximum torque transmitted by clutch,

$T_F \text{ max} = \mu W R n$
$\qquad\quad = 0.3 \times 3000 \times 0.12 \times 2 = 216 \, \text{N m}$

Maximum power transmitted by clutch,

$\qquad = T_F \text{ max} \times \dfrac{2\pi N}{60 \times 10^3} \, \text{kN}$

$\qquad = 216 \times \dfrac{2\pi \times 2000}{60 \times 10^3} = 45.25 \, \text{kW}$

Answer: Maximum power transmitted by clutch $= 45.25 \, \text{kW}$

4.7 Disc brakes

With reference to Fig. 4.6, let

$W =$ total force acting on friction pads (N)
$p =$ hydraulic pressure in brake line (Pa)

A = cross-sectional area of brake cylinder (m²)
R = effective radius of pads (m)
μ = coefficient of friction between pads and disc
n = number of pads pressing on disc (for a single pair of opposing friction pads, $n = 2$)

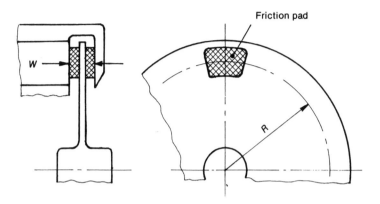

Figure 4.6 Thrust (force) on a simple disc brake pad

Now,

Force acting on each pad
   = Hydraulic pressure × Cross-sectional area of brake cylinder
   = pA

Total force W acting on pads
   = Force on each pad × Number of pads
   = pAn

Frictional force, $F = \mu W = \mu pAn$

Frictional torque T_F acting on the brake disc shaft
   = Frictional force × Effective radius
   = $F \times R$
i.e. $T_F = \mu pAnR$ N m   [4.7]

Example 4.8

Two disc brake pads operate at a mean radius of 0.14 m. The force applied to each pad is 4450 N and the coefficient of friction between each pad and disc is 0.35. When the disc rotates at 500 rev/min, calculate:

(*a*) the frictional torque acting on the disc
(*b*) the work done per minute by this torque
(*c*) the heat energy generated per second.

                                                (CGLI) (Modified)

52

Solution

(a) Frictional force on disc

$\qquad$ = Force applied to pads × Coefficient of friction
$\qquad$ = 4450 × 2 × 0.35
$\qquad$ = 3115 N

Frictional torque acting on disc

$\qquad$ = Frictional force × Effective radius of pads
$\qquad$ = 3115 [N] × 0.14 [m]
$\qquad$ = 436 N m

(b) From Section 4.6,

Work done per minute at the disc

$\qquad$ = Frictional torque × Angle turned through in rad/min
$\qquad$ = 436 × 2π × 500 = 1 370 000 J
$\qquad\qquad\qquad\qquad\qquad$ = 1370 kJ

(c) Heat energy generated/second $= \dfrac{\text{Work done/min}}{60}$

$$= \frac{1370}{60} = 22.83 \text{ kJ}$$

Answer: (a) Frictional torque acting on disc = 436 N m
$\qquad\qquad$ (b) Work done/min at the disc = 1370 kJ
$\qquad\qquad$ (c) Heat energy generated at the disc/second = 22.83 kJ

Example 4.9

A disc brake rotating at 500 rev/min has three opposing pairs of friction pads pressing on it at an effective radius of 0.15 m. Each pad is 50 mm diameter and the coefficient of friction between the pads and the disc is 0.3. If the pressure on each pad during braking is 490 kPa, determine:

(a) the frictional torque acting on the brake disc shaft
(b) the power developed.

$\qquad\qquad\qquad\qquad\qquad\qquad\qquad\qquad\qquad$ (CGLI) (Modified)

Solution

Contact area of each pad, $A = \dfrac{\pi}{4} \times 0.05^2 = 0.001\,964 \text{ m}^2$

Hydraulic pressure, p	= 490 kPa = 490 000 N/m²
Effective radius of pads, R	= 0.15 m
Coefficient of friction, μ	= 0.3
Number of pads, n	= 3 × 2 = 6
Disc brake speed, N	= 500 rev/min

(a) From equation [4.7],

Frictional torque acting on the brake disc shaft,

$$T_F = \mu p A n R$$
$$= 0.3 \times 490\,000 \ [\text{N/m}^2] \times 0.001\,964 \ [\text{m}^2] \times 6 \times 0.15 \ [\text{m}]$$
$$= 260 \ \text{N m}$$

(b) Power developed $= T_F \times \dfrac{2\pi N}{60 \times 10^3} \ \text{kW}$

$$= 260 \times \dfrac{2\pi \times 500}{60 \times 10^3} = 13.6 \ \text{kW}$$

Answer: (a) Frictional torque = 260 N m
(b) Power developed = 13.6 kW

4.8 Elementary theory of the shoe brake

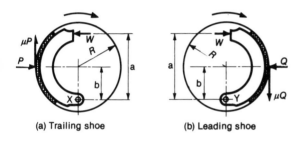

(a) Trailing shoe   (b) Leading shoe

Figure 4.7 Internal expanding brakes

When the brake is applied the forces acting on a trailing and a leading shoe are as illustrated in Fig. 4.7(a) and (b), respectively.

The drum is shown rotating in a clockwise direction. Hence, the shoe at (b) is called a *leading shoe* because the frictional drag on it tends to increase the radial thrust between it and the drum, whereas the shoe at (a), called a *trailing shoe,* has its radial thrust reduced.

Consider the trailing shoe shown at (a). The actuating force W will introduce a normal force P between the shoe and the brake drum. When the drum is rotating in the direction shown, the normal force P will produce a frictional force μP as indicated. The shoe is in equilibrium under the action of the forces shown. Thus:

Taking moments about the pivot X,

$$Wa = Pb + \mu PR$$
$$= P(b + \mu R)$$

so that
$$P = \dfrac{Wa}{b + \mu R} \qquad\qquad [4.8]$$

The braking torque, T_T, acting on the drum is due entirely to the frictional force μP. Thus:

$$T_T = \mu PR \qquad [4.9]$$

Substituting for P from equation [4.8], gives:

Braking torque, $T_T = \mu R \left(\dfrac{Wa}{b + \mu R} \right) \qquad [4.10]$

Now let us consider the leading shoe shown at (b). Since the shoe is in equilibrium under the action of the forces shown, then by taking moments about the shoe pivot Y, we get:

$$Wa = Qb - \mu QR$$
$$= Q(b - \mu R)$$

so that $\qquad Q = \dfrac{Wa}{b - \mu R} \qquad [4.11]$

As in the case of the trailing shoe, the braking torque, T_L, acting on the drum is due entirely to the frictional force μQ. Thus:

$$T_L = \mu QR \qquad [4.12]$$

Substituting for Q from equation [4.11], gives:

Braking torque, $T_L = \mu R \left(\dfrac{Wa}{b - \mu R} \right) \qquad [4.13]$

From equations [4.10] and [4.13], it can be observed that the torque developed by the brake when the shoe is a leading one is greater than that developed when the shoe is a trailing one, the other factors being equal. For this reason, two leading shoe type brakes are usually employed in the front wheels.

Example 4.10

A motor car brake drum has an internal diameter of 0.2 m. The distance between the shoe pivots and the points of application of the forces actuating the shoes is 0.16 m. Assuming that the shoes are centrally positioned in the drum and the coefficient of friction between the linings and drum is 0.4, determine the value of the braking torque exerted by an actuating force of 600 N on (a) the leading shoe, and (b) the trailing shoe.

Find also the total braking torque developed by the two shoes.

Solution

Actuating force, W $= 600$ N
Internal radius, R $= 0.1$ m
Coefficient of friction, $\mu = 0.4$

Since shoes are assumed to be centrally positioned in the drum, then, with reference to Fig. 4.7,

$a = 0.16 \, \text{m};$ $b = 0.08 \, \text{m}$

(a) For a leading shoe,

Braking torque, $T_L = \mu R \left(\dfrac{Wa}{b - \mu R} \right)$

$$= 0.4 \times 0.1 \left[\frac{600 \times 0.16}{0.08 - (0.4 \times 0.1)} \right]$$

$$= \frac{0.4 \times 0.1 \times 96}{0.04} = 96 \, \text{N m}$$

(b) For a trailing shoe,

Braking torque, $T_T = \mu R \left(\dfrac{Wa}{b + \mu R} \right)$

$$= 0.4 \times 0.1 \left[\frac{600 \times 0.16}{0.08 + (0.4 \times 0.1)} \right]$$

$$= \frac{0.4 \times 0.1 \times 96}{0.12} = 32 \, \text{N m}$$

Total braking torque developed by the two shoes

$= 96 + 36 = 128 \, \text{N m}$

Answer: (a) Leading shoe: 96 N m; (b) Trailing shoe: 32 N m
Total braking torque developed $= 128 \, \text{N m}$

Example 4.11

If the force between the brake shoe and drum on a motor vehicle is 1.25 kN and the coefficient of friction between them is 0.4, how many kilojoules of work are done against friction in 60 revolutions of the drum? The diameter of the drum is 0.28 m.

Solution

For two shoes,

Normal force between brake linings and drum
$= 2 \times 1.25 \times 10^3 = 2500 \, \text{N}$

Frictional force $= \mu \times$ Normal force
$= 0.4 \times 2500 = 1000 \, \text{N}$

Braking torque $=$ Frictional force $\times$ Drum radius
$= 1000 \, [\text{N}] \times 0.14 \, [\text{m}] = 140 \, \text{N m}$

Work done against friction
$=$ Braking torque $\times$ Angle turned in radians
$=$ Braking torque $\times 2\pi \times$ Number of revolutions
$= 140 \times 2\pi \times 60 \, [\text{N m} = \text{J}]$
$= 52\,800 \, \text{J} = 52.8 \, \text{kJ}$

Answer: Work done against friction in 60 rev of drum $= 52.8 \, \text{kJ}$

Exercise 4.1 — Review questions

1 Explain what is meant by 'friction'.
2 Distinguish between 'static friction' and 'dynamic friction'.
3 State any three laws which govern the effect of friction between dry surfaces.

(NWRAC/ULCI)

4 What is meant by the 'coefficient of friction' between two plane surfaces?

(CGLI)

5 Describe, with the aid of sketches, an experiment which can be performed to determine the coefficient of sliding friction between two flat surfaces. Explain how the effect of varying the load between the surfaces may be demonstrated, and state the conclusions which may be drawn from this experiment.

(WMAC/UEI)

6 Describe, with the aid of sketches, an experiment to show that friction is independent of the area of contact.

(NWRAC/ULCI)

7 Three examples where friction has a useful application in a motor vehicle are:

(1) ....
(2) ....
(3) ....

8 Three examples where friction is undesirable in a motor vehicle are:

(1) ....
(2) ....
(3) ....

9 It is found that a vehicle having a mass of 900 kg can be moved slowly and steadily along a horizontal surface by a pull of 5.74 kN with the wheels locked. The coefficient of friction between tyres and road is

(a) 0.157   (b) 0.65   (c) 0.883   (d) 1.54

10 An engine resting on a metal sled is drawn along a workshop floor with uniform speed. The total downward force exerted by the engine and sled on the floor is 1400 N. If the coefficient of friction between sled and floor is 0.25, the horizontal force necessary to move the engine is

(a) 250 N   (b) 350 N   (c) 1400 N   (d) 5600 N

11 A crankshaft bearing has a diameter of 50 mm and the shaft carries a load of 10 kN. If the coefficient of friction between the shaft and the bearing is 0.02, the frictional torque on the shaft is

(*a*) 5 N m (*b*) 10 N m (*c*) 0.2 kN m (*d*) 0.25 kN m

12 If the power lost due to friction in a journal bearing is 1.5 kW, the heat generated in the journal per minute is

(*a*) 1.5 J (*b*) 90 J (*c*) 1.5 kJ (*d*) 90 kJ

13 A single-plate clutch has a mean radius of 0.1 m. The total spring force is 2.5 kN and the coefficient of friction is 0.3. The maximum torque which the clutch can transmit is

(*a*) 75 N m (*b*) 150 N m (*c*) 750 N m (*d*) 1500 N m

14 For the clutch referred to in Question 13 above, the power that can be transmitted at a speed of 35 rev/s is

(*a*) 275 W (*b*) 550 W (*c*) 16.5 kW (*d*) 33 kW

Figure 4.8 shows the arrangement of a brake shoe, pivoted at A and subjected to an actuating force $W = 450$ N. F is the normal force between the shoe and the brake drum. The internal diameter of the drum is 0.2 m and μ for the lining material is 0.4. Use this data to determine the correct answer to Questions 15 to 18.

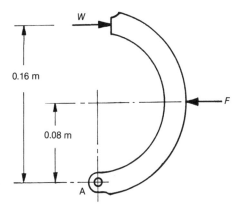

Figure 4.8

15 The magnitude of F when the shoe is a leading one is

(*a*) 180 N (*b*) 450 N (*c*) 900 N (*d*) 1800 N

16 The torque developed by the brake when the shoe is a leading one is

(*a*) 7.2 N m (*b*) 18 N m (*c*) 72 N m (*d*) 90 N m

17 The magnitude of F when the shoe is a trailing one is

(*a*) 180 N (*b*) 600 N (*c*) 900 N (*d*) 1800 N

18 The torque developed by the brake when the shoe is a trailing one is

(a) 18 N m   (b) 24 N m   (c) 60 N m   (d) 72 N m

Exercise 4.2 – Problems

1 A casting has a mass of 30 kg and requires a horizontal force of 70 N to drag it at constant speed along a level surface. Determine:

(a) the normal reaction between the casting and the surface
(b) the coefficient of friction.

2 A vehicle has a mass of 1400 kg. The coefficient of friction between road and tyres is 0.6. What is the greatest force that can be used to stop the vehicle on a level road without causing it to skid?

(EMEU) (Modified)

3 Determine the maximum load that may be moved across a horizontal surface by an effort of 175 N when the coefficient of friction between the materials in contact is 0.5.

(WMAC/UEI)

4 A tool box of total mass 75 kg is pulled along a horizontal workshop floor for a distance of 15 m by a horizontal force. If the coefficient of friction between the box and the floor is 0.32, calculate (a) the magnitude of the applied force, and (b) the work done.
(Take $g = 10 \, \text{m/s}^2$.)

5 A 50 mm diameter journal rotating in a bearing at a speed of 2100 rev/min is subjected to a normal load of 20 kN. If the coefficient of friction is 0.02, calculate:

(a) the frictional torque on the shaft
(b) the power absorbed by friction at the bearing.

6 A crankshaft has 50 mm diameter journals and is rotating in a bearing at 2800 rev/min. If the power absorbed by friction is 770 W when the load on the bearing is 3.5 kN, determine the coefficient of friction.

7 A compression-ignition engine has main bearing journals 80 mm in diameter. Under certain running conditions the downward load on the bearings is 15 kN. The coefficient of friction between the bearings and journals is 0.012. When the engine is running at a speed of 2000 rev/min, calculate:

(a) the power absorbed by friction
(b) the heat energy generated per minute due to friction.

8 A single-plate clutch transmits a torque of 240 N m. The total spring force acting on the pressure plate is 3360 N and the coefficient of friction of the lining material is 0.3. Calculate the outside diameter of the lining if it had a width of 26 mm.

9   A multi-plate clutch has eight annular friction surfaces of 250 mm external and 200 mm internal diameter. The coefficient of friction is 0.3. If the axial spring force on the pressure plate is 600 N, calculate the power that can be transmitted at a speed of 2100 rev/min.

(CGLI) (Modified)

10   The friction disc of a single-plate clutch has a face area of 0.025 m² and a mean radius of 0.12 m. If the spring pressure is 140 kN/m² of face area and the coefficient of friction is 0.35, determine the power which can be transmitted at 2500 rev/min.

(CGLI) (Modified)

11   A certain vehicle engine develops 26.4 kW at its maximum torque speed of 2100 rev/min. The torque is transmitted by a single-plate clutch having two friction faces of 0.24 m outside diameter and 0.16 m inside diameter. If the coefficient of friction is 0.3, calculate the minimum force which the clutch springs must exert, when the clutch is engaged, to prevent clutch slip.

12   (a) A motor vehicle is fitted with a single dry-plate clutch with external and internal lining diameters of 0.25 m and 0.15 m, respectively. Assuming a coefficient of friction of 0.35, calculate the total spring force necessary to transmit 50 kW at 2000 rev/min.
(b) If the clutch is engaged by eight springs, each of free length 0.060 m and stiffness of 30 kN/m, calculate the length to which the springs must be compressed to transmit the torque.

(CGLI)

13   A twin-plate clutch has a friction face mean diameter of 250 mm. The maximum torque capacity is $1\frac{1}{2}$ times maximum engine torque. Maximum torque occurs at 1200 rev/min at which speed the power output is 75 kW. Assuming a coefficient of friction of 0.4, determine the clamping force on the clutch plates.

(EMEU)

14   A disc brake rotating at 1000 rev/min has two pairs of friction pads pressing on it at an effective radius of 0.15 m. Each pad is 50 mm in diameter and the coefficient of friction between the pads and the disc is 0.3. If the pressure on each pad during braking is 400 kPa, determine:

(a) the frictional torque acting on the brake disc shaft
(b) the power developed.

(WMAC/UEI)

15   A disc brake rotating at 6 rev/s has a force of 240 N acting on each pad at a radius of 0.15 m. The coefficient of friction between the disc and the two pads is 0.4. Calculate:

(a) the torque acting on the disc

(*b*) the work done per minute at the disc

(*c*) the heat generated per minute by the work.

State the units of **each** answer.

(CGLI)

16 The disc of a disc brake assembly has a pair of opposing friction pads pressing on it at an effective radius of 0.125 m. The contact area of each pad is 0.002 m² and the coefficient of friction between pads and disc is 0.3. If the hydraulic pressure in the brake line during braking is 700 kPa and the disc speed reduces uniformly from 10 rev/s to 6 rev/s, determine:

(*a*) the braking torque per brake

(*b*) the power absorbed by the brakes of a vehicle fitted with four such brake assemblies

(*c*) the total heat generated per minute at the brakes.

17 Make a sketch of the simple mechanically-expanded brake and indicate the forces acting on the leading shoe when the brake is applied.

If the distance between the shoe fulcrum and the point of the actuating force, equal to 500 N, is 0.16 m, determine the value of the braking torque on the drum.

Assume that the shoe is centrally positioned in the drum, and that the coefficient of friction between the lining and drum is 0.4. Diameter of drum is 0.2 m.

(CGLI) (Modified)

18 A force of 750 N is applied to the brake shoes operating in a drum of 0.3 m diameter. If the coefficient of friction between the drum and lining is 0.4, find:

(*a*) the braking force at the drum

(*b*) the work lost in friction when the wheels rotate 420 times before coming to rest.

(NWRAC/ULCI) (Modified)

19 A vehicle brake drum has an internal diameter of 0.36 m and two brake shoes are pressing against it with a force on each of 600 N. The brake drum rotates at 350 rev/min and the coefficient of friction is 0.4. Calculate:

(*a*) the frictional torque on the drum

(*b*) the power absorbed in friction at the drum

(*c*) the heat generated at the drum per minute.

(CGLI) (Modified)

Chapter 5

Properties of lubricating oils

5.1 Purposes of lubrication

Although the surface of a piece of metal may appear to be perfectly
smooth, it will be found that, when seen under a microscope, the surface
is made up of ridges and craters. Therefore, when two such surfaces
are placed over each other, they will, in fact, be supported on the tips
of the ridges which tend to bite into each other and become interlocked,
as shown in Fig. 5.1. Before movement can take place, the interlocked
ridges have to be torn off, this tearing action producing a high frictional
resistance accompanied by heat which is generated at the surfaces. The
continual interlocking and tearing away of the ridges produces the wear
that occurs between two dry moving surfaces.

If the surfaces can be separated slightly by the application of a
suitable lubricant, generally oil, as in Fig. 5.2, the friction between
them is greatly reduced. Hence, the prime purposes of lubrication are:

(1) to reduce friction between moving surfaces by separating them with
    a lubricant
(2) to reduce the wear on the surfaces
(3) to carry away any heat which is generated at the surfaces, thus
    eliminating the risk of seizure.

Lubrication also protects the metal surfaces against rust and
corrosion.

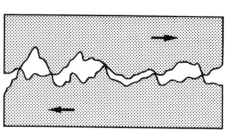

Figure 5.1 Unlubricated (dry) surfaces

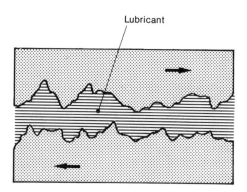

Figure 5.2 Surfaces separated by a lubricant

5.2 Forms of lubrication

Lubrication follows two main forms. The first of these is known as *boundary* or 'thin-film' lubrication, in which the moving surfaces are virtually in contact, being separated only by a film of lubricant which is insufficient to prevent occasional contact of the surfaces. Boundary lubrication conditions occur between the piston rings and cylinder walls immediately upon starting from cold or when running slow.

The second form of lubrication is that known as *fluid* or 'thick-film' lubrication, in which the moving surfaces are completely separated by a layer of lubricant. The only resistance to the moving surfaces sliding over one another is due to the very small internal friction of the lubricant. It is apparent, therefore, that thick-film lubrication is the ideal. Main and big-end bearings have thick-film lubrication.

5.3 Properties of lubricating oils

The two most important properties of lubricating oils are *oiliness* and *viscosity*.

Oiliness

This is difficult to define but can be described as the adhering property of a lubricant to a metal surface. Under severe conditions of loading and high rubbing speeds, seizure between a journal and its bearing would be less likely to occur with the lubricant of greater oiliness.

Vegetable oils, such as castor, possess a high degree of oiliness but they are expensive, short-lived and have a strong tendency to form gums, resulting in the sticking of piston rings in their grooves and the valves in their guides. Mineral oils, however, are cheaper and are less prone to gumming. They are used for all normal motoring and are obtained by the distillation and refining of crude petroleum.

Viscosity

The viscosity of a lubricating oil is a measure of its resistance to flow. High viscosity denotes a thick oil, and low viscosity denotes a thin oil. The viscosity of an oil decreases with a rise in temperature; in other words, an oil becomes thinner and flows more freely when heated.

The viscosity of oils is determined by means of a *viscometer*. This measures the time taken for a given volume of oil to flow through a calibrated orifice under controlled temperature conditions. In Great Britain, the *Redwood* viscometer is used, in which the time taken for 50 millilitres of oil at a given temperature to flow through an orifice of 1 mm^2 in area. The viscosity of the oil is then stated in Redwood seconds. In the USA, viscosity is measured by the *Saybolt* viscometer and is stated in Saybolt Universal seconds.

5.4 Oil viscosity tests

To determine the viscosity of a lubricating oil at varying temperatures using the Redwood viscometer. This apparatus (Fig. 5.3) consists of a vertical cylinder containing the lubricant which is allowed to flow through a calibrated orifice situated in the centre of the cylinder base. The orifice is closed by a ball valve when it is not actually being used. The oil cylinder is surrounded by a water jacket, which can maintain the lubricant under test at any required temperature by means of a bunsen burner flame applied to the heating tube. Facilities for measuring the temperatures of the lubricant and the surrounding water in the jacket are provided. The thermometer for the water in the jacket is mounted in a paddle-type stirrer which can be rotated by hand, using the handle shown.

Procedure

The water jacket is filled with water. With the orifice ball valve in position, oil is poured into the cylinder to the level of the pointer. A 50 ml measuring flask is placed centrally under the orifice. The water is

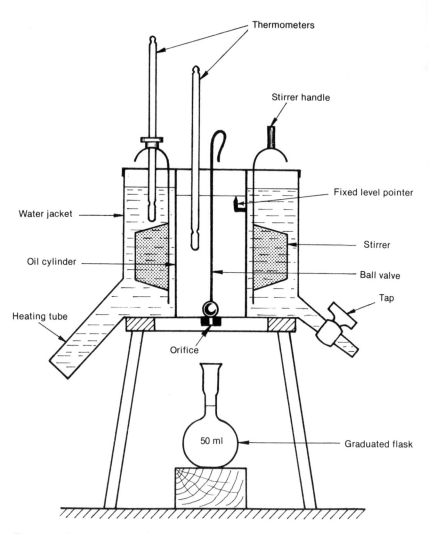

Figure 5.3 Determination of the viscosity of a lubricant by the Redwood viscometer

stirred gently until the two thermometers read the same temperature (room temperature, say, 15 °C). The temperature value is recorded. The ball valve is then raised and a stop-watch is used to obtain the time (in seconds) for 50 ml of oil to flow into the measuring flask.

The test is repeated with oil temperatures increasing by 10 °C each time up to, say, 95 °C. All data are tabulated and a graph is plotted of Redwood seconds against temperature, as shown in Fig. 5.4. Similar tests can be carried out to compare the viscosities of different grades of motor oils at varying temperatures.

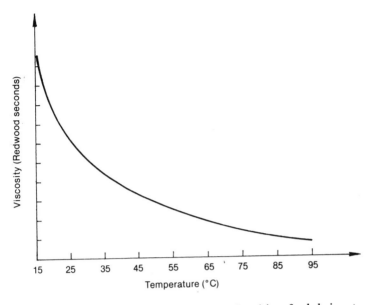

Figure 5.4 Viscosity–temperature relationship of a lubricant

5.5 SAE viscosity rating

The Society of Automotive Engineers (SAE) in America has devised a classification in which crankcase and transmission oils which come within a specified range of viscosities at a particular temperature are given an SAE number. A low SAE number denotes an oil of low viscosity, and vice versa. In other words, an oil with SAE rating of 5 would have a very low viscosity and would be suitable for use in cold climates or during winter weather. On the other hand, an oil with SAE rating of 50 would have a high viscosity at low temperatures and, therefore, would be more suitable for summer use.

The winter and summer SAE grades are given below. Note that the winter grade oils are followed by the letter W.

SAE winter grades (measured at −18 °C):
   5W (lowest viscosity); 10W; 20W (highest viscosity)

SAE summer grades (measured at 99 °C):
   20 (lowest viscosity); 30; 40; 50 (highest viscosity)

The above grades are for crankcase oils only. For transmission lubrication, however, the SAE grades commonly used are 80, 90, 140 and 250.

Table 5.1 gives the viscosity range at −18 °C, 20 °C and 95 °C for the various crankcase oils mentioned above.

Table 5.1 SAE crankcase oil classification

SAE number	Viscosity range (Redwood seconds)					
	− 18 °C		20 °C		95 °C	
	Min	Max	Min	Max	Min	Max
5W	—	3520	—	—	—	—
10W	5250	10 560	—	—	—	—
20W	10 560	42 000	—	—	—	—
20	—	—	750	850	43	55
30	—	—	1300	1400	55	67
40	—	—	1750	1850	67	8?
50	—	—	2350	2450	83	112

5.6 Viscosity index

The rate of change of viscosity with temperature is measured by the *viscosity index*. An oil whose viscosity varies widely with temperature is given a low or zero viscosity index. An oil whose viscosity varies very little with temperature is given a high viscosity index, usually from 100 to 115.

It is essential for modern top-quality motor oils to have a high viscosity index so that rapid distribution of the oil can be obtained when starting from cold, while the viscosity is well maintained at running temperatures to prevent breakdown of the oil film.

5.7 Multi-grade oils

Motor oils are nowadays produced to meet the requirements of more than one grade. These have very high viscosity indices and are known as *multi-grade* oils. Multi-grade oils have suitably low viscosity at low temperatures to provide the required conditions for starting in cold weather, while the viscosity is reasonably maintained at higher temperatures to prevent excessive and high oil consumption. A multi-grade oil of SAE 10W/30, for instance, possesses a viscosity within the SAE 30 range at 99 °C and will only thicken when the temperature drops to − 18 °C to within the viscosity range specified for SAE 10W oil. The effect of temperature on SAE 10W/30 multi-grade oil is shown in Fig. 5.5. Other examples of multi-grade oils in common use are 5W/20, 20W/40 and 20W/50.

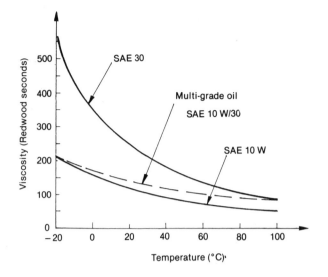

Figure 5.5 Effect of temperature on a multi-grade oil

5.8 Lubricating oil additives

Lubricating base oils produced from crude petroleum by normal refining processes are unable to withstand the severe operating conditions of modern vehicle engines, and are also liable to form unwanted effects in the engine. However, by the addition of certain chemical compounds known as *oil additives*, the performance of present-day engine lubricating oils is greatly improved.

Some of the more common additives are listed below.

1. Viscosity index improvers
2. Oxidation inhibitors
3. Detergents
4. Dispersants
5. Anti-foam preventers
6. Corrosion and rust inhibitors
7. Anti-wear additives
8. Extreme pressure additives

Viscosity index improvers

Modern motor oils are blended with chemicals so that their viscosity index is raised to 120 and over. Viscosity index improvers, as these chemicals are called, are polymeric in nature and have the property of reducing the change in the viscosity of the oil caused by change in temperature.

Oxidation inhibitors

When heated and agitated in the presence of metals, ordinary lubricating oils tend to oxidize, forming insoluble carbon compounds, corrosive acids and a varnish-like or gummy substance. This substance causes piston rings to stick in their grooves, giving rise to a loss of power and an increase in fuel consumption.

Another product of oxidation and contamination is a black, pasty substance known as sludge. This may be deposited on moving parts of the engine, in the crankcase, or may be held in suspension in the oil. It may sometimes choke or even block up vital passageways, causing bearings to be starved.

To prevent or delay the formation of sludge and harmful deposits, anti-oxidant additives, such as aromatic phenols, amines and zinc compounds, are added to the base oil.

Detergents

Modern engine oils contain special detergent additives to deal with deposits associated with both high-temperature and low-temperature operating conditions. These additives are usually oil soluble metallic soaps, typical examples being barium sulphonate, calcium sulphonate and barium phosphonate.

Detergent additives are added to the ordinary engine oil to prevent the formation of carbon deposits in the piston ring grooves, and lacquer or varnish-like deposits on the piston skirts, connecting-rod surfaces and on the exposed parts of the crankshaft.

Dispersants

Although most detergent oils have the necessary detergency for washing away deterioration products, they may not have the ability to maintain these in suspension. Thus, dispersant additives are used to break up large particles of sludge and facilitate their removal either by filtration or during the oil change.

Anti-foam preventers

Under certain operating conditions, an oil may foam or froth so that adequate supply of the oil to the bearing surfaces and other moving parts cannot be maintained. Foaming tendencies can be reduced by using anti-foam agents, such as the silicon esters.

Corrosion and rust inhibitors

When a vehicle is frequently used for short journeys in cold weather, or when it is used in heavy traffic with prolonged periods of idling, corrosion of the cylinder walls can occur, due to acid products of combustion left in the cylinders after the engine has been switched off. Apart from this, moisture in the cylinders and the crank chamber can cause rusting of the piston rings, connecting rods, crankshaft and the main and big-end bearings. Special inhibitors, e.g. petroleum sulphate derivatives, phosphate derivatives and amines, are employed to protect surfaces liable to rust or corrosion.

Anti-wear additives

To avoid metal-to-metal contact under boundary lubrication conditions, anti-wear compounds are added to the oil. These are substances that react chemically with the working surfaces so that a molecular film is built up quickly.

Extreme pressure additives

These additives are mainly organic compounds containing sulphur, phosphorus and chlorine. They have properties that increase the film strength and are used in gearbox and rear axle lubricating oils.

Oils used for hypoid gear lubrication are known as *hypoid* oils. These are special extreme pressure lubricants containing more active agents than those used for spiral bevel gears and in gearboxes, so that they can be able to withstand the heavy loading and sliding action imposed by hypoid gearing on the oil film.

Exercise 5.1 — Review questions

1 Three purposes for which lubrication is required are:

(1) ....

(2) ....

(3) ....

2 Distinguish between 'boundary' lubrication and 'fluid-film' lubrication.

3 Two important properties of a lubricating oil are:

(1) ....

(2) ....

4 Complete the following statements.

(*a*) Boundary lubrication conditions occur between ....

(*b*) In fluid lubrication the only resistance to motion is due to ....

(*c*) Oiliness can be described as ....

(*d*) The viscosity of a lubricating oil is a measure of ....

(*e*) In Great Britain viscosity is stated in ....

(*f*) In the USA viscosity is stated in ....

(*g*) SAE stands for ....

(*h*) The letter W in SAE 10W grade oil means ....

5 Explain what is meant by the following terms used in connection with lubricating oils:

(*a*) Viscosity
(*b*) SAE number
(*c*) Viscosity index
(*d*) Multi-grade
(*e*) Extreme pressure.

(WMAC/UEI)

6 State briefly the characteristics of an engine lubricating oil which has

(*a*) a low viscosity index
(*b*) a high viscosity index.

(NWRAC/ULCI)

7 State briefly the meaning of the following SAE specifications relative to crankcase lubricating oils:

(*a*) 10W   (*b*) 30   (*c*) 10W/30

(EMEU)

8 Explain how each of the following types of additives, when blended with the basic mineral oil, improve the properties and performance of an engine lubricating oil:

(*a*) Anti-oxidants   (*b*) Detergents   (*c*) Dispersants
(*d*) Rust inhibitors   (*e*) Anti-wear compounds
(*f*) Anti-foam agents.

9 Describe an experiment to determine the viscosity of a lubricating oil. Sketch and describe the apparatus used.

10 Draw a graph to show how the viscosity of an engine oil varies over the temperature range 15 °C to 95 °C.

11 Which of the following statements is false?

(*a*) Modern lubricating oils are obtained by the distillation and refining of crude petroleum.
(*b*) Vegetable oils possess a higher degree of oiliness than mineral oils.
(*c*) An oil becomes thinner and flows more freely when cooled.
(*d*) One of the basic properties required of all lubricating oils is a small rate of change of viscosity with temperature.

12 Which of the following statements is false?

(*a*) A low SAE number denotes an oil of low viscosity, and vice versa.
(*b*) Multi-grade oils have to be changed frequently to cater for the different needs of winter and summer.
(*c*) Detergents are used in lubricating oils in order to prevent carbon deposition and gum formation.
(*d*) Additives of the chlorine-sulphur-phosphorus type are used to produce lubricating oils capable of supporting heavy loads.

Chapter 6

Stress and strain

6.1 Direct stress

When a material is subjected to an external force (load) which tends to
cause deformation, internal forces are called into play to resist the
loading. While these resisting forces are in operation the material is
said to be in a state of *stress*.

Materials which are subjected to an external pull, called a *tensile
force*, are said to be in *tension* and the material will be in a state of
tensile stress. This is represented in Fig. 6.1(a).

Materials which are subjected to an external thrust, called a *compressive force*, are said to be in compression and the material will be in
a state of *compressive stress*. This is represented in Fig. 6.1(b).

Tensile and compressive stresses are referred to as *direct* or *normal
stresses* because, in both cases, the cross-sectional area being stressed is
at right angles to the line of action of the applied force.

The *intensity of stress*, often just called the stress, is a measure of
the load carried by unit cross-sectional area of the material.

The stress is defined as the force or load per unit cross-sectional
area.

Let σ = direct stress (i.e. tensile or compressive stress)
  F = applied force
  A = cross-sectional area of the material

then $\sigma = \dfrac{F}{A}$ [6.1]

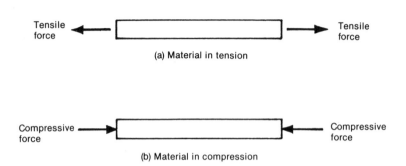

(a) Material in tension

(b) Material in compression

Figure 6.1 Direct stress

From this equation, it is possible to obtain the unit of stress as

$$\frac{\text{Unit of force}}{\text{Unit of area}} = \frac{\text{N}}{\text{m}^2} = \text{N/m}^2$$

It is sometimes more convenient to express the stress in larger units, such as kN/m^2, MN/m^2 and GN/m^2.

Now since $1\,\text{MN} = 10^6\,\text{N}$ and $1\,\text{m}^2 = 10^6\,\text{mm}^2$

then $1\,\text{MN/m}^2 = \dfrac{10^6\,\text{N}}{10^6\,\text{mm}^2} = 1\,\text{N/mm}^2$

Also $1\,\text{GN/m}^2 = 10^3\,\text{MN/m}^2 = 10^3\,\text{N/mm}^2 = 1\,\text{kN/mm}^2$

The unit of stress (and of pressure) is referred to as the *pascal* (symbol Pa). Hence, $1\,\text{Pa} = 1\,\text{N/m}^2$ and, say, $15\,\text{kPa} = 15\,\text{kN/m}^2 = 15\,000\,\text{N/m}^2$.

Example 6.1
A steel brake rod is subjected to a tensile force of 2.5 kN. If the diameter of the rod is 8 mm, calculate the stress induced in the rod.

Solution
Tensile force applied to rod, $F = 2.5\,\text{kN} = 2500\,\text{N}$
Cross-sectional area of rod, $A = \frac{1}{4}\pi \times 8^2 = 50.27\,\text{mm}^2$

Tensile stress, $\sigma = \dfrac{F}{A}$ from equation [6.1]

$$= \frac{2500}{50.27}\left[\frac{\text{N}}{\text{mm}^2}\right] = 49.7\,\text{N/mm}^2 \text{ or } 49.7\,\text{MPa}$$

Answer: Tensile stress produced in rod $= 49.7\,\text{MPa}$

Example 6.2
A hydraulic jack has a ram area of $2000\,\text{mm}^2$ and a lifting capacity of

30 kN. Calculate the compressive stress produced in the ram when the jack is used to 70 per cent of its maximum capacity.

(NWRAC/ULCI) (Modified)

Solution

Load raised by jack when used to 70 per cent of its maximum capacity

$$= \frac{30 \times 70}{100} = 21 \text{ kN} = 21\,000 \text{ N}$$

Compressive stress produced in ram

$$= \frac{\text{Compressive load}}{\text{Cross-sectional area}}$$

i.e. $\sigma = \dfrac{F}{A}$ from equation [6.1]

$$= \frac{21\,000}{2000} \left[\frac{N}{mm^2}\right] = 10.5 \text{ N/mm}^2 \text{ or } 10.5 \text{ MPa}$$

Answer: Compressive stress produced in ram = 10.5 MPa

Example 6.3

A cylinder head stud has a diameter of 14 mm at the bottom of the thread. If the maximum tensile stress allowed in the material is 30 MPa, calculate the safe load the stud can carry.

(CGLI) (Modified)

Solution

Cross-sectional area of stud at the bottom of the thread (i.e. at its root or core diameter),

$$A = \tfrac{1}{4}\pi \times 14^2 = 154 \text{ mm}^2$$

Allowable tensile stress, $\sigma = 30$ MPa $= 30$ N/mm^2

From equation [6.1],

Safe load $(F) =$ Tensile stress $(\sigma) \times$ Cross-sectional area (A)

$$= 30 \text{ [N/mm}^2] \times 154 \text{ [mm}^2] = 4620 \text{ N}$$

Answer: Safe load that stud can carry = 4620 N

Example 6.4

A cast-iron column of hollow cross-section has an outside diameter of 150 mm and is used to support a load of 70 kN. If the average compressive stress produced in the metal is 7140 kPa, calculate the inside diameter of the column.

Solution

Compressive load, $F = 70\,\text{kN} = 70\,000\,\text{N}$
Compressive stress, $\sigma = 7140\,\text{kPa} = 7.14\,\text{N/mm}^2$

From equation [6.1],

Cross-sectional area of column,

$$A = \frac{\text{Compressive load } (F)}{\text{Compressive stress } (\sigma)}$$

$$= \frac{70\,000}{7.14} \left[N \times \frac{\text{mm}^2}{N} \right] = 9804\,\text{mm}^2$$

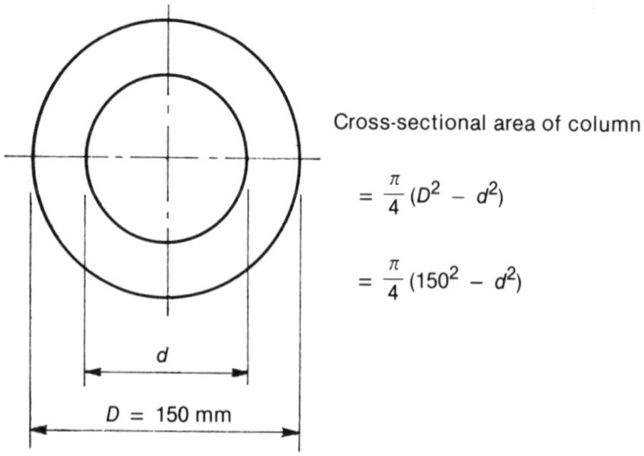

Cross-sectional area of column

$$= \frac{\pi}{4}(D^2 - d^2)$$

$$= \frac{\pi}{4}(150^2 - d^2)$$

d

$D = 150\,\text{mm}$

Figure 6.2   Example 6.4

Let d be the inside diameter of the column, in mm (see Fig. 6.2). Then:
$\frac{1}{4}\pi(150^2 - d^2) = 9804$

$$d^2 = 150^2 - \left(\frac{9804 \times 4}{\pi} \right) = 10\,020$$

so that $d = \sqrt{(10\,020)} = 100.1\,\text{mm}$

Answer: Inside diameter of column $= 100.1\,\text{mm}$

6.2   Direct strain

When a material is put in a state of stress, deformation takes place; in other words, the material undergoes a change of shape and size. This deformation, caused by the stress, is called *strain*.

A tensile stress will result in a *tensile strain*, producing an extension or increase in length. This is illustrated in Fig. 6.3(a).

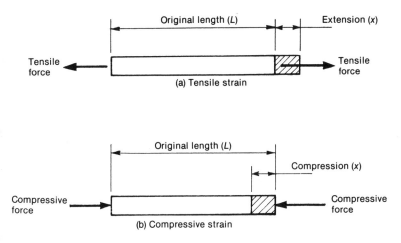

Figure 6.3 Direct strain

A compressive stress will result in a *compressive strain*, producing a compression or decrease in length. This is illustrated in Fig. 6.3(b).

The strain produced in a material is determined by dividing the change in length by the original length.

Hence, if ε = direct strain (i.e. tensile or compressive strain)

$\qquad L$ = original length

$\qquad x$ = change in length (in the direction of the applied force)

then $\qquad \varepsilon = \dfrac{x}{L}$ $\qquad\qquad\qquad\qquad$ [6.2]

Note that the units of x and L must be the same. Strain is therefore a ratio; in other words, it has no units.

Example 6.5

A steel brake rod is 1.25 m long and when subjected to a pull, the extension produced is 0.5 mm. Calculate the strain in the rod.

Solution

From equation [6.2],

$$\text{Tensile strain } (\varepsilon) = \frac{\text{Extension } (x)}{\text{Original length } (L)}$$

$$= \frac{0.5}{1.25 \times 1000} \left[\frac{\text{mm}}{\text{mm}} \right] = 0.0004$$

Answer: Strain produced in brake rod = 0.0004

6.3 Elasticity and Hooke's law

The materials used in the construction of a motor vehicle must, of necessity, be elastic, i.e. possess the property of *elasticity*. This is the property which allows a piece of material to return to its original shape and size when the load is removed.

A material remains elastic provided the load does not exceed a value called the *elastic limit*. If the load exceeds the elastic limit value, the material will not regain its original dimensions when the load is removed. The elastic limit, however, is very difficult to determine and for some materials it practically coincides with a point called the *limit of proportionality* (see Fig. 6.4).

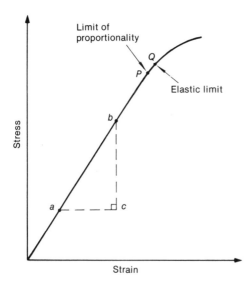

Figure 6.4

There is an important relationship between stress in a material and the strain it produces. This is known as *Hooke's law* which states that:

'Within the limit of proportionality, the strain produced in a material is directly proportional to the stress producing it.'

This may be expressed as follows:

Stress ∝ Strain

or $\dfrac{\text{Stress}}{\text{Strain}} = \text{Constant}$

If values of stress are plotted against corresponding values of strain, a graph similar to Fig. 6.4 will be produced. It is seen that it is a straight line (i.e. stress ∝ strain) up to point P, the limit of proportionality.

This constant of proportionality is called *Young's modulus of elasticity*, and is denoted symbolically by E. It is usually just called 'Young's modulus' or the 'modulus of elasticity'.

Young's modulus of elasticity may be regarded as a measure of the resistance which a material offers to tensile and compressive forces, i.e. the larger the value of E, the smaller is the extension (or compression) produced by a given load.

If $\quad \sigma$ = direct stress

$\quad\quad \varepsilon$ = direct strain

$\quad\quad E$ = Young's modulus of elasticity

then $\quad E = \dfrac{\sigma}{\varepsilon}$ [6.3]

Note that since strain is a ratio, the units of E are the same as those for stress. Typical values of E for some materials are given in Table 6.1.

Table 6.1 Typical values of E for various materials

Material	Young's modulus E (GPa)
Aluminium alloy	70
Brass	85
Phosphor-bronze	95
Copper	100
Cast iron	110
Steel	200−210
Tungsten	410

To determine the value of Young's modulus of elasticity either from a stress−strain graph or with the aid of a load−extension graph:

The slope of the graph in Fig. 6.4 gives the value of Young's modulus for the material. Thus, if two points, a and b, are chosen on the straight line, and vertical and horizontal lines (shown dotted) are drawn respectively through b and a to intersect at c, then:

Young's modulus, $E = \dfrac{bc}{ac}$

Now, since $\sigma = F/A$ and $\varepsilon = x/L$, then equation [6.3] becomes:

$$E = \frac{F/A}{x/L} = \frac{FL}{Ax}$$ [6.4]

For a material which obeys Hooke's law, the extension produced is directly proportional to the load which produces it. Hence, if a load–extension graph is plotted for the material, this will produce a graph similar to that shown in Fig. 6.4. The slope of the graph will then give a mean value of F/x.

Hence, from equation [6.4],

$$E = \frac{L}{A} \times \frac{F}{x}$$

or $\quad E = \frac{L}{A} \times$ slope of load–extension graph

6.4 Spring stiffness

Hooke's law also applies to springs where the deflection produced is directly proportional to the applied force.

The *stiffness* of a spring may be defined as the force required to cause unit deflection. Thus,

$$\text{Spring stiffness} = \frac{\text{Applied force}}{\text{Deflection}} \qquad [6.5]$$

Example 6.6

A helical spring carrying a load of 500 N is compressed by 20 mm. What would be the load required to compress the spring by 8 mm?

Solution

$$\text{Spring stiffness} = \frac{\text{Applied load}}{\text{Deflection}}$$

$$= \frac{500}{20} \left[\frac{\text{N}}{\text{mm}} \right] = 25 \, \text{N/mm}$$

$\therefore$ Load required to compress the spring by 8 mm

$$= \text{Spring stiffness} \times \text{Deflection}$$
$$= 25 \, [\text{N/mm}] \times 8 \, [\text{mm}] = 200 \, \text{N}$$

Answer: Load required $= 200 \, \text{N}$

Example 6.7

A handbrake has a leverage of $8 : 1$. The handbrake cable has an initial length of 2 m and a cross-sectional area of 20 mm². Determine:

(*a*) the stress in the cable when the driver applies a force of 100 N to the handbrake

(b) the strain in the cable when it is extended by 0.4 mm

(c) the modulus of elasticity for the material of the cable.

Solution

(a) Tensile force applied on handbrake cable

$$= \text{Driver's effort} \times \text{Leverage}$$

$$= 100 \times 8 = 800 \, \text{N}$$

Tensile stress produced in cable

$$= \frac{\text{Tensile force}}{\text{Cross-sectional area}}$$

i.e. $\sigma = \dfrac{F}{A}$

$$= \frac{800}{20} \left[\frac{\text{N}}{\text{mm}^2} \right] = 40 \, \text{N/mm}^2$$

$$= 40 \, \text{MN/m}^2 \text{ or } 40 \, \text{MPa}$$

(b) Tensile strain $= \dfrac{\text{Extension}}{\text{Original length}}$

i.e. $\varepsilon = \dfrac{x}{L}$

$$= \frac{0.4}{2 \times 10^3} \left[\frac{\text{mm}}{\text{mm}} \right] = 0.0002$$

(c) Modulus of elasticity $= \dfrac{\text{Stress}}{\text{Strain}}$

i.e. $E = \dfrac{\sigma}{\varepsilon}$

$$= \frac{40 \, \text{MPa}}{0.0002}$$

$$= 200 \times 10^3 \, \text{MPa} = 200 \, \text{GPa}$$

Answer: (a) Stress = 40 MPa; (b) Strain = 0.0002;
(c) Modulus of elasticity = 200 GPa

Example 6.8

A steel rod, 20 mm diameter, carries a pull of 60 kN. Calculate the extension produced, in mm, on a length of 1 m. (Take $E = 210 \, \text{GPa}$.)

Solution

Cross-sectional area of rod, A = $\frac{1}{4}\pi \times 20^2$ = 314.2 mm²
Tensile force applied to rod, F = 60×10^3 N
Original length of rod, L = 1000 mm
Young's modulus of elasticity, E = 210×10^3 MPa or
210×10^3 N/mm²
Extension produced in rod, x = ?

Now, since $E = \dfrac{FL}{Ax}$ from equation [6.4]

then $\quad x = \dfrac{FL}{AE}$

$\quad\quad = \dfrac{60 \times 10^3 \times 1000}{314.2 \times 210 \times 10^3} \left[\dfrac{\text{N} \times \text{mm} \times \text{mm}^2}{\text{mm}^2 \times \text{N}} \right]$

$\quad\quad = 0.91$ mm

Answer: Extension produced in rod = 0.91 mm

Example 6.9

A steel brake rod is 1.2 m long and is subjected to a maximum load of 4.5 kN. If the extension of the rod is not to exceed 0.384 mm, determine a suitable diameter for the rod.
(Young's modulus, $E = 200$ GPa.)

Solution

Tensile strain $(\varepsilon) = \dfrac{\text{Extension } (x)}{\text{Original length } (L)}$

$\quad\quad = \dfrac{0.384 \text{ mm}}{1.2 \times 10^3 \text{ mm}} = 0.000\,32$

From equation [6.3],

Maximum stress induced in the rod,

σ = Modulus of elasticity $(E) \times$ Strain (ε)
= $200 \times 0.000\,32 = 0.064$ GPa
= 64 MPa or 64 N/mm²

From equation [6.1],

Cross-sectional area $(A) = \dfrac{\text{Applied load } (F)}{\text{Stress } (\sigma)}$

$\quad\quad = \dfrac{4500}{64} \left[\dfrac{\text{N}}{\text{N/mm}^2} \right] = 70.31$ mm²

Let d be the diameter of the rod, in mm.

Then $\qquad \frac{1}{4}\pi d^2 = 70.31\,\text{mm}^2$

so that $\qquad d = \sqrt{\left(\dfrac{70.31 \times 4}{\pi}\right)} = 9.46\,\text{mm}$

Answer: Suitable diameter for rod = 9.5 mm

6.5 The tensile test

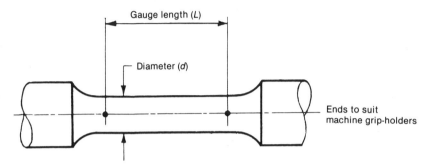

Figure 6.5 A tensile test piece

A tensile test on a material is carried out on a tensile testing machine. The test piece, or specimen (Fig. 6.5), is generally machined to comply with British Standard Specifications (refer to BS 18). The diameter of the ends and the overall length of the test piece are made to suit the testing machine. The reduced centre portion is joined to the enlarged ends by a smooth radius, so that the stress is not concentrated at the change of section. The extremities of the gauge length (note that the working length of the test piece is called the 'gauge length') are marked on the centre portion along the axis with centre punch dots so that, when the test piece is pulled to destruction, the broken parts are placed together and the final distance between the dots is measured. The value of the test piece diameter d is chosen such that the resulting calculations are made easier. For example, a diameter of 11.28 mm will give a cross-sectional area of 100 mm².

If recordings of load and extension are taken during a tensile test to destruction, i.e. up to fracture, a graph of load against extension (or stress against strain) can be plotted for the material. A typical load–extension graph for low carbon steels (e.g. mild steel) is shown in Fig. 6.6.

Limit of proportionality
From point O to point A the graph is linear, indicating that during this stage the material obeys Hooke's law, i.e. the extension is directly

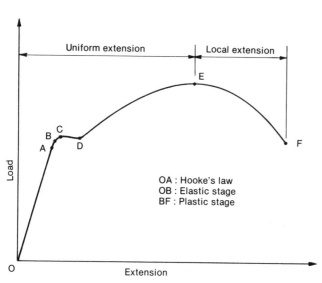

Figure 6.6 Typical load–extension graph for low carbon steels

proportional to the load (or the strain is directly proportional to the stress). Hence, point A denotes the *limit of proportionality*. The slope of line OA is used when determining Young's modulus of elasticity (see Section 6.3), that is, $E = (L/A) \times$ Slope of load–extension graph.

Elastic limit

At some load just beyond point A, a point B is reached called the *elastic limit*. The stress in the material at this point is the greatest stress that can be induced without producing permanent extension. Hence, up to point B the test piece returns to its original unstretched length when the load is removed. In practice, the points A and B are so close together that is is virtually impossible to distinguish between them.

Permanent set

Beyond B, the material is said to be *plastic*; if the test piece is loaded beyond this point and then unloaded, a permanent extension remains, called the *permanent set*.

Yield stress

As the load is further increased, a point is reached when the material begins to 'yield'; the test piece undergoes a sudden increase in length without any corresponding increase in load. This is represented by the portion CD on the graph. The point C at which this occurs is known as the *yield point*, the corresponding stress being termed the *yield stress*. This phenomenon of yielding is not found in all ductile materials (see

'Ductility' below), but is a marked feature of the softer irons and low carbon steels.

Tensile strength

At D the material recovers some of its resistance and additional load is required to produce further extension. Eventually, a point such as E will be reached which will be the maximum load reached during the test. The stress at this point is known as the *tensile strength* of the material. For all practical purposes, the tensile strength is the maximum stress that the original cross-sectional area can withstand. This is because up to point E the extension has taken place along the whole length of the test piece.

$$\text{Tensile strength} = \frac{\text{Maximum load}}{\text{Original cross-sectional area}} \qquad [6.6]$$

Necking

After point E, the extension is localized at a 'neck' or 'waist' which starts to form at the central portion of the test piece (see Fig. 6.7). The cross-sectional area at the neck decreases rapidly and the load required to continue extending the test piece also decreases until fracture occurs at point F.

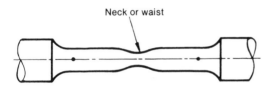

Neck or waist

Figure 6.7 Necking

Ductility

A material is said to be *ductile* if it can be drawn out and undergo a considerable permanent stretch before breaking. Ductility is important in certain manufacturing processes where material is to be bent or formed to shape. Copper is a good example of a ductile material and mild steel is the most ductile of the carbon steels. Ductility is measured in two ways: by the percentage elongation of the gauge length after fracture, and by the percentage reduction in area referred to the minimum section at the point of fracture.

$$\% \text{ Elongation} = \frac{\text{Final length} - \text{Original length}}{\text{Original length}} \times 100 \qquad [6.7]$$

$$\% \text{ Reduction in area} = \frac{\text{Original area} - \text{Final area}}{\text{Original area}} \times 100 \qquad [6.8]$$

6.6 Stress—strain graphs for various materials

Not all materials have a clearly defined yield point, as is shown in Fig. 6.8. Soft metals, such as copper and aluminium, are very ductile and a tensile test of these materials would give a stress—strain curve of the form shown for annealed copper. It can be seen that aluminium alloy is stronger than annealed copper but is less ductile, whereas hard-drawn brass is both strong and ductile.

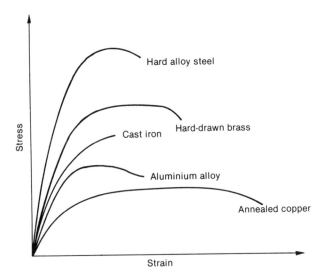

Figure 6.8 Stress—strain graphs for various materials

Also shown in Fig. 6.8 is the stress—strain curve for cast iron, which has little plasticity or ductility and does not neck down before fracture. A metal such as this is said to be *brittle*, and is particularly liable to break under shock loads (suddenly applied loads). Brittle materials fracture suddenly straight across the test piece (see Fig. 6.9) and the cup-and-cone fracture of ductile materials (see Fig. 6.10) does not occur. The first mentioned type of fracture is also characteristic of hard alloy steels, although these are very strong and carry a much higher breaking load than cast iron.

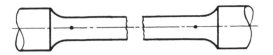

Figure 6.9 Test piece of brittle material after fracture

Figure 6.10   Test piece of ductile material after fracture

Example 6.10
The following results were obtained during a tensile test on a mild steel test piece of 11.28 mm diameter and 50 mm gauge length.

Load (kN)	4	8	12	16	20	24	28
Extension (mm)	0.01	0.02	0.03	0.04	0.05	0.06	0.08

Draw the load–extension graph, and from this graph, determine:

(*a*) the stress at the elastic limit
(*b*) the modulus of elasticity for mild steel.

Solution
The load–extension graph is drawn using the data given, and is shown in Fig. 6.11.

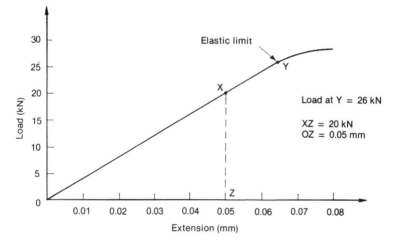

Figure 6.11   Example 6.10

(*a*) The elastic limit occurs at point Y on the graph. This has a load value of about 26 kN. Since the diameter of the specimen is 11.28 mm, this gives a cross-sectional area of 100 mm^2. Thus:

$$\text{Stress at elastic limit} = \frac{\text{Load at Y}}{\text{Cross-sectional area}}$$

$$= \frac{26 \times 10^3}{100} \left[\frac{N}{mm^2} \right] = 260 \, N/mm^2$$

$$= 260 \, MN/m^2 \text{ or } 260 \, MPa$$

(b) The slope of the straight line portion of the graph is:

$$\frac{XZ}{OZ} = \frac{20 \times 10^3}{0.05} \left[\frac{N}{mm} \right] = 400\,000 \, N/mm$$

Modulus of elasticity, $E = (\text{Slope of graph}) \times \dfrac{L}{A}$

$$= \frac{400\,000 \times 50}{100} \left[\frac{N}{mm} \times \frac{mm}{mm^2} \right]$$

$$= 200 \times 10^3 \, N/mm^2 \text{ or } 200 \, GPa$$

Answer: (a) Stress at elastic limit = 260 MPa
(b) Modulus of elasticity for steel = 200 GPa

Example 6.11

The following results were obtained during a tensile test to destruction on a specimen of low carbon steel of diameter 19.54 mm and gauge length 100 mm.

Load at yield point   = 86 kN
Maximum load on specimen   = 153 kN
Gauge length after fracture   = 136 mm
Diameter of specimen at fracture = 14.88 mm

From these results determine:

(a) the yield stress
(b) the tensile strength
(c) the percentage elongation
(d) the percentage reduction in area.

Solution

(a) Original cross-sectional area $= \dfrac{\pi \times (19.54)^2}{4} = 300 \, mm^2$

$$\text{Yield stress} = \frac{\text{Load at yield point}}{\text{Original cross-sectional area}}$$

$$= \frac{86 \times 10^3}{300} \left[\frac{N}{mm^2} \right] = 286.7 \, N/mm^2$$

$$= 286.7 \, MN/m^2 \text{ or } 286.7 \, MPa$$

(b) Tensile strength $= \dfrac{\text{Maximum load}}{\text{Original cross-sectional area}}$

$\qquad = \dfrac{153 \times 10^3}{300} \left[\dfrac{\text{N}}{\text{mm}^2} \right] = 510\,\text{N/mm}^2$

$\qquad = 510\,\text{MN/m}^2 \text{ or } 510\,\text{MPa}$

(c) % Elongation $= \dfrac{\text{Final length} - \text{Original length}}{\text{Original length}} \times 100$

$\qquad = \dfrac{136 - 100}{100} \left[\dfrac{\text{mm}}{\text{mm}} \right] \times 100 = 36\%$

(d) Cross-sectional area of specimen at fracture

$\quad = \dfrac{\pi \times (14.88)^2}{4} = 174\,\text{mm}^2$

$\quad$ % Reduction in area $= \dfrac{\text{Original area} - \text{Final area}}{\text{Original area}} \times 100$

$\qquad = \dfrac{300 - 174}{300} \left[\dfrac{\text{mm}^2}{\text{mm}^2} \right] \times 100 = 42\%$

Answer: (a) Yield stress = 287 MPa
$\qquad$ (b) Tensile strength = 510 MPa
$\qquad$ (c) Percentage elongation = 36%
$\qquad$ (d) Percentage reduction in area = 42%

6.7 Working stress and factor of safety

The tensile strength of a material is of vital importance in the design of the various components of a motor vehicle. A motor vehicle component such as an axle, or a spring, or any other part of the engine and transmission, must not be stressed beyond the *allowable safe working stress* and this must be below the elastic limit of the material. The designer will then ensure that the component remains elastic, i.e. that it retains its original dimensions when the stress is removed. To obtain the working stress it is usual to divide the tensile strength of the material by a suitable number called the *factor of safety*. Thus:

$$\text{Working stress} = \frac{\text{Tensile strength}}{\text{Factor of safety}} \qquad [6.9]$$

or $\quad$ $$\text{Factor of safety} = \frac{\text{Tensile strength}}{\text{Working stress}} \qquad [6.10]$$

The choice of a suitable factor of safety depends very much upon the physical properties of the material employed and upon the nature

88

of the loading. For a component subjected to a steady load of constant value, a low factor of safety is normally used. But for applications where the load might be repeatedly or suddenly applied, or where the load might be reversing, i.e. producing alternately tensile and compressive stresses in the material, high values of the factor of safety would be used.

When deciding what factor of safety to use, factors such as corrosion, expected life of the component, possibility of mishandling, etc., are also taken into consideration.

Example 6.12

A steel tie-rod has a cross-sectional area of 500 mm² and is subjected to a tensile load of 30 kN. If the tensile strength of the steel used is 450 MPa, calculate the factor of safety at which the rod is worked.

Solution

$$\text{Working stress} = \frac{\text{Working load}}{\text{Cross-sectional area}}$$

$$= \frac{30 \times 10^3}{500} \left[\frac{N}{mm^2} \right] = 60\,\text{N/mm}^2 \text{ or } 60\,\text{MPa}$$

$$\text{Factor of safety} = \frac{\text{Tensile strength}}{\text{Working stress}}$$

$$= \frac{450}{60} \left[\frac{MPa}{MPa} \right] = 7.5$$

Answer: Factor of safety = 7.5

6.8 Shear stress

Another type of stress to which a material may be subjected is called *shear stress*. Shear stress acts tangentially, i.e. parallel to the surface or section of the material. A material subjected to shear stress tends to fracture at any section by the two portions of the material sliding past one another.

Consider a single-riveted lap joint, Fig. 6.12(a), being subjected to load. The two equal and opposite forces, F, applied to the plates as shown, tend to shear the rivet across section AB (shown dotted). In other words, the upper half of the rivet tends to slide to the left relative to the lower half. Figure 6.12(b) gives a pictorial view of the rivet failing in shear across AB. Since the rivet is sheared across one plane only, it is said to be in *single shear*.

Now consider a clevis joint, Fig. 6.13(a), being subjected to load. When the tensile force or load F is applied to the rods, the joint may

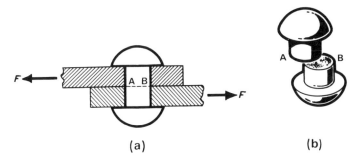

Figure 6.12 Lap joint (rivet subjected to single shear)

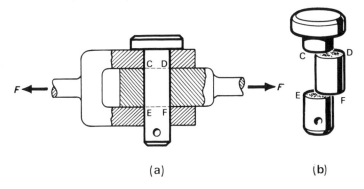

Figure 6.13 Clevis joint (pin subjected to double shear)

fail by the pin shearing at two sections CD and EF (shown dotted). The right-hand rod then carries away the centre portion of the pin with it. Figure 6.13(b) gives a pictorial view of the pin failing in shear across CD and EF. This is a case of *double shear*. The area resisting shear is therefore equal to **twice** the area of the cross-section of the pin.

The shear stress (symbol τ) is determined by dividing the shearing force (F) by the area of the section (A) resisting shear. Hence:

$$\tau = \frac{F}{A} \qquad\qquad [6.11]$$

(τ is the Greek letter 'tau'.)

The unit of shear stress is the same as that for direct stress, i.e. N/m^2 or Pa.

Example 6.13

The maximum pressure on an engine piston of 80 mm diameter is 3500 kPa. The hollow gudgeon pin is 24 mm outside diameter and 12 mm inside diameter. Calculate:

90

(*a*) the maximum force on the piston and gudgeon pin
(*b*) the shear stress in the material of the gudgeon pin.

(CGLI)

Solution

A pressure of 3500 kPa = 3.5 MPa or 3.5 N/mm².

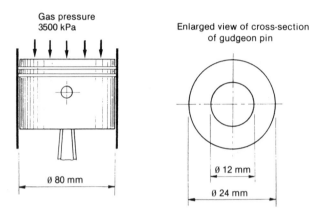

Gas pressure
3500 kPa

Enlarged view of cross-section
of gudgeon pin

Ø 12 mm

Ø 24 mm

Ø 80 mm

Figure 6.14   Example 6.13

(*a*) Maximum force on piston and gudgeon pin (see Fig. 6.14)

   = Cylinder pressure × Area of piston
   = 3.5 [N/mm²] × ($\frac{1}{4}\pi$ × 80²) [mm²]
   = 17 600 N or 17.6 kN

(*b*) Cross-sectional area of pin = $\frac{1}{4}\pi$ × (24² − 12²) = 339.3 mm²

Since this is a case of double shear, then total area of pin under shear = 2 × 339.3 = 678.6 mm².

Shear stress in the material of the gudgeon pin

$$= \frac{\text{Force on pin}}{\text{Total area under shear}}$$

$$= \frac{17\,600}{678.6} \left[\frac{\text{N}}{\text{mm}^2}\right] = 25.94\,\text{N/mm}^2 \text{ or } 25.94\,\text{MPa}$$

Answer: (*a*) Max. force on piston and gudgeon pin = 17.6 kN
   (*b*) Shear stress in gudgeon pin = 25.94 MPa.

6.9   Shear strain

Since shear stress tends to make one surface of the material slide over an adjacent surface, the resulting strain is determined as follows.

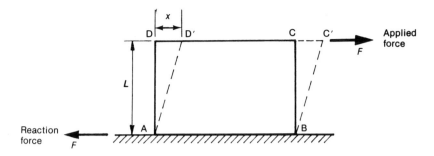

Figure 6.15 Shearing of a block of material

Consider a rectangular block of material ABCD firmly fixed at its base AB, as shown in Fig. 6.15. Under the action of the forces F the block will be deformed to the new position ABC′D′. If we denote DD′ by x and AD by L, the *shear strain* produced in the material is given by:

$$\text{Shear strain, } \phi = \frac{x}{L} \qquad [6.12]$$

6.10 Modulus of rigidity

Hooke's law applies equally well to shear stress as to direct stress. Thus, for a given material loaded in shear we have the following relationship:

$$\frac{\text{Shear stress}}{\text{Shear strain}} = \text{Constant}$$

This constant is called the *modulus of rigidity* or *shear modulus*, and is denoted symbolically by G. Hence:

$$\text{Modulus of rigidity, } G = \frac{\text{Shear stress}}{\text{Shear strain}} = \frac{\tau}{\phi} \qquad [6.13]$$

For mild steel the value of G is about 80 GPa. For aluminium, brass, copper and cast iron, the value of G lies between 25 and 50 GPa.

The modulus of rigidity is a measure of the resistance of a material to changing its shape and is of importance when dealing with stiffness of shafts and other components subjected to *torsion*.

A material which is subjected to *torsional stress* (torsion) tends to deform by twisting, and hence the nature of the stress at any point in the material is one of shear.

Some motor vehicle components subjected to torsion when under normal operation are crankshafts, propeller shafts, final drive axle half-shafts, starter motor armature shafts, coil springs and torsion bars.

Example 6.14

In an experiment to determine the modulus of rigidity of a sample of rubber, a rectangular block of the material, measuring 300 mm × 200 mm × 20 mm, was firmly fastened to a vertical wall, in the manner of Fig. 6.16, so that it projected a distance of 200 mm from the wall.

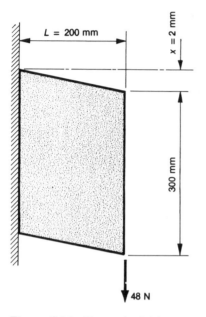

Figure 6.16 Example 6.14

It was found that when a downward load of 48 N was applied to the free vertical face, a vertical deflection of 2 mm was obtained as shown. Determine the modulus of rigidity of this sample of rubber.

Solution

$$\text{Shear stress, } \tau = \frac{\text{Shearing force}}{\text{Area (parallel to the force)}}$$

Area of any face parallel to the force is 300 mm × 20 mm, i.e. 6000 mm².

Hence
$$\tau = \frac{48}{6000} \left[\frac{N}{mm^2} \right] = 0.008 \text{ N/mm}^2 \text{ or } 0.008 \text{ MPa}$$

$$\text{Shear strain, } \phi = \frac{x}{L} = \frac{2}{200} \left[\frac{mm}{mm} \right] = 0.01$$

$$\text{Modulus of rigidity, } G = \frac{\tau}{\phi} = \frac{0.008}{0.01} \text{ MPa} = 0.8 \text{ MPa or } 800 \text{ kPa}$$

Answer: Modulus of rigidity of sample of rubber = 800 kPa

Exercise 6.1 – Review questions

1 A material which is subjected to an external pull is said to be in .... and the material is in a state of ....
2 A material which is subjected to an external thrust is said to be in .... and the material is in a state of ....
3 The force applied to a material which tends to make one section of the material to slide over an adjacent section is called ....
4 The stress induced in a material is determined by dividing the .... by the .... of the material.
5 The unit of stress is ....
6 If a material returns to its original length when a load is removed from it, it is said to be ....
7 The strain produced in a material is determined by dividing the .... by the ....
8 The symbol denoting direct stress is ....
9 The symbol denoting direct strain is ....
10 The symbol denoting shear stress is ....
11 The symbol denoting shear strain is ....
12 What kind of stress would the following components of a motor vehicle be subjected to when under normal operation?

(*a*) Cylinder head studs   (*i*) Cylinder head gaskets
(*b*) Connecting rods   (*j*) Brake rods
(*c*) Crankshafts   (*k*) Starter motor armature shafts
(*d*) Brake shoe rivets   (*l*) Gudgeon pins
(*e*) Flywheel bolts   (*m*) Valve pushrods
(*f*) Propeller shafts   (*n*) Fan belts
(*g*) Spring shackle pins   (*o*) The teeth on a gearwheel
(*h*) Kingpins   (*p*) Final drive axle half-shafts

13 What is meant by 'elasticity' in a material?
14 State Hooke's law.
15 Define the term 'Young's modulus of elasticity'.
16 Explain the term 'stiffness of a spring'.
17 Complete the following:

(*a*) $475 \, \text{N/m}^2 = \ldots\ldots \text{Pa}$
(*b*) $500 \, \text{MPa} = \ldots\ldots \text{N/mm}^2$
(*c*) $\ldots\ldots \text{kN/mm}^2 = 215 \, \text{GPa}$
(*d*) $162 \, \text{GN/m}^2 = \ldots\ldots \text{MPa}$

18 When a mild steel specimen is being tested to failure in tension the following terms are used:

(*a*) limit of proportionality;   (*b*) elastic limit;   (*c*) yield point;   (*d*) maximum load;   (*e*) point of fracture.

94

Sketch the general shape of the load–extension graph for mild steel, and on this graph indicate clearly the above terms.

19 Explain what is meant by the 'tensile strength' of a material.
20 State what you understand by 'factor of safety'.
21 Define the terms 'ductility' and 'brittleness'.
22 Sketch the form taken by stress–strain graphs during tensile tests to destruction for (*a*) a ductile material and (*b*) a brittle material.

Exercise 6.2 – Problems

1 A steel brake rod is subjected to a maximum tensile load of 2000 N. If the area resisting the load is 50 mm², calculate the tensile stress in the rod.

(WMAC/UEI)

2 A pushrod has a cross-sectional area of 20 mm². At a certain point when operating a valve the force in the rod is 1 kN. Determine the compressive stress in the rod.

(WMAC/UEI)

3 A piston has a force of 2 kN acting on the crown at top dead centre, and this force produces a compressive stress of 12.5 MPa in the connecting rod. Determine the cross-sectional area of the rod.

4 A force of 300 N is applied to a clutch pedal which has a leverage of 3 : 1 and operates the release arm by means of a cable. Calculate the stress in the cable if its cross-sectional area is 7.2 mm².

5 The bearing cap of a crankshaft main bearing is secured by two bolts which have a core diameter of 14 mm. Find the average stress in the bolts if the maximum force against the bearing cap is 18 kN.

(NWRAC/ULCI) (Modified)

6 A hollow cast-iron column has an outside diameter of 200 mm and a metal thickness of 25 mm. It carries a compressive stress of 16 MPa. Determine the load supported by the column.

7 A mild steel rod has to carry an axial pull of 40 kN. The maximum permissible stress is 120 MPa. Calculate a suitable diameter for the rod.

(WMAC/UEI) (Modified)

8 A handbrake lever has the effort applied 400 mm from the fulcrum. The brake actuating rod, which has a diameter of 7 mm, is attached at 80 mm from the fulcrum. Both forces act at right angles to the lever which is straight throughout its length. If the applied effort is 350 N, find the tensile stress in the rod.

(CGLI) (Modified)

9 At a certain instant during the stroke of a single-cylinder engine of 76 mm bore the cylinder pressure is 2 MPa. Calculate the resulting stress in each of the four cylinder-head studs, the core diameter of the studs being 9 mm.

(CGLI) (Modified)

10 A metal bar of length 2.5 m extends by 0.5 mm when a tensile force is applied to it. Calculate the tensile strain.

11 A compressive load causes a support to shorten by 0.06 mm. Calculate the original length of the support if the compressive strain is 0.000 04.

12 (a) A towing-bar, 50 mm diameter, carries a load which produces a tensile stress of 42 MPa. Determine the load, in kN.

(b) The bar is attached to a bracket held by four bolts. Determine the load in each bolt, in kN.

(c) If the area of the section of each bolt is 625 mm^2, determine the stress induced in each bolt, in MPa.

(NWRAC/ULCI) (Modified)

13 A specimen of steel of diameter 10 mm is subjected to a tensile load of 9 kN which causes a length of 100 mm to increase to 100.055 mm. Calculate

(a) the stress induced
(b) the strain for the steel
(c) Young's modulus of elasticity.

14 A steel rod of cross-sectional area 300 mm^2 is subjected to a tensile load of 45 kN. Calculate the extension produced on a length of 0.6 m if the value of Young's modulus of elasticity for steel is 200 GPa.

15 A steel rod is 3 m long and has a cross-sectional area of 400 mm^2. Determine the force, in kN, required to stretch the rod by 3 mm. Young's modulus for steel is 200 GPa.

(WMAC/UEI) (Modified)

16 A vertical steel wire, 4 m long and 2 mm diameter, carries a load of 450 N. Calculate:

(a) the stress;   (b) the strain;   (c) the extension of the wire.

(For steel, $E = 200$ GPa.)

17 A metal bar of thickness 16 mm and having a rectangular cross-section carries a load of 60 kN. Determine the minimum width of the bar to limit the maximum stress to 150 MPa.

The bar which is 1 m long extends by 0.75 mm when carrying the load of 60 kN. Determine the modulus of elasticity of the material of the bar.

18 In a laboratory experiment a wire of cross-sectional area 0.5 mm^2 and original length 2 m was subjected to increasing loads. The extension was measured for each load with the following results:

Load (N)	0	50	100	150	200	250	300
Extension (mm)	0	1	2	3	4	5	6

Plot graphs of load against extension and stress against strain, and state what may be deduced from their character. From one of these graphs, determine the value of Young's modulus of elasticity for the material of the wire.

19 The following results were obtained during a tensile test to destruction on a mild steel test piece of diameter 15.96 mm and 80 mm gauge length.

Extension for a load of 40 kN = 0.08 mm
Maximum load applied during test = 93 kN
Final length between gauge points = 106 mm
Diameter of test piece at fracture = 12.85 mm

From these results, determine:

(a) the modulus of elasticity for mild steel
(b) the tensile strength
(c) the percentage elongation
(d) the percentage reduction in area.

Note: A diameter of 15.96 mm gives a cross-sectional area of 200 mm^2.

20 The following results were obtained during a tensile test to destruction on a specimen of low carbon steel.

Diameter of specimen = 11.28 mm
Gauge length = 50 mm
Load at yield point = 26 kN
Maximum load on specimen = 47.5 kN
Final length at point of fracture = 67 mm
Diameter of specimen at fracture = 8.2 mm

From these results, determine the yield stress, the tensile strength, the percentage elongation, and the percentage reduction in area.

21 A steel tie-rod has a cross-sectional area of 300 mm^2 and is subjected to a tensile load of 27 kN. If the tensile strength of the steel used is 450 MPa, calculate the factor of safety at which the rod is worked.

22 A brake rod, 1.25 m long, is made from steel which has a modulus of elasticity of 200 GPa. Using a factor of safety of 6, calculate the minimum diameter of rod required to transmit a pull of 4000 N, the tensile strength of the material being 480 MPa. Determine also the extension of the rod when subjected to this pull.

23 A bolt having a diameter of 6 mm is subjected to a shearing force of 1.5 kN. Determine the shear stress in the bolt.

24 A spring shackle pin having a diameter of 25 mm is loaded so that the stress in it is 26 MPa. Determine the value of the shearing force on the pin.

25 Each brake lining of a heavy commercial vehicle is attached to its brake shoe by 16 rivets, each of diameter 7 mm. Calculate the shear stress in the rivets when the brakes are applied so that the

frictional force between the brake drum and each lining is 12 kN.

(CGLI) (Modified)

26   In the clevis joint shown in Fig. 6.13(a), the pin has a diameter of 7 mm and each of the rods which it connects has a diameter of 6 mm, the pull in each rod being 2 kN. Calculate:

(a) the tensile stress in the rods
(b) the shear stress in the pin.

27   An engine has a cylinder bore of 64 mm. The gudgeon pin has an outside diameter of 19 mm and an inside diameter of 13 mm, and the minimum cross-sectional area of the connecting rod is 320 mm². If the maximum cylinder pressure at top dead centre is 3300 kPa, determine:

(a) the shear stress in the gudgeon pin
(b) the maximum compressive stress in the rod.

(CGLI) (Modified)

Chapter 7

Vehicle suspension springs

7.1 Function and types of suspension springs

The function of a suspension spring is to reduce the velocity of the vertical displacement of a vehicle caused by irregularities of the road surface.

The steel suspension springs used on motor cars and commercial vehicles are of three kinds:

1. Laminated or 'semi-elliptic' leaf springs
2. Coil springs
3. Torsion bars.

Laminated springs are subjected to bending; so both tensile and compressive stresses will be induced in the material from which the plates or leaves are made. The nature of the stress induced in the material of coil and torsion bar springs, both of which are subjected to torsion, is one of shear.

7.2 Laminated or 'semi-elliptic' leaf springs

Laminated or *'semi-elliptic' leaf springs* are employed mainly for commercial vehicles and for the rear suspension of private cars. Figure 7.1 shows a semi-elliptic leaf spring incorporating a shock absorber.

Laminated or semi-elliptic leaf springs are made up from a number of spring steel strips assembled on a bolt at the centre, where they are attached to the axle casing or beam by two U-shaped stirrups or bolts.

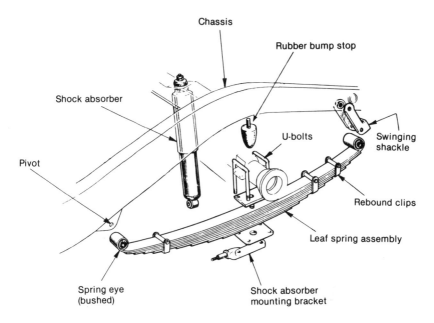

Figure 7.1 Typical semi-elliptic leaf spring incorporating a shock absorber

The leaves are graduated in length from the main leaf to ensure uniform stress throughout the spring. To prevent overloading of the main leaf during the return motion of the spring, the leaves are clamped together with rebound clips.

The main leaf has its ends rolled into eyes for attachment to the frame or body, one end being pivot mounted and the other shackled to allow for the increase in length of the spring as it flattens under load. To prevent direct contact of the hardened steel shackle pins with the spring, phosphor-bronze or rubber bushes are fitted in the spring eyes. The latter types of bush are now almost universal for the spring eye connections of laminated springs as these do not require lubrication, very rarely wear out, are silent, self-aligning and help to insulate road-wheel noise from the body.

The friction between the sliding leaves reduces flexibility but gives the springs self-damping properties, thus reducing the amount of work to be done by the shock absorber. However, spring squeak and wear make it necessary to reduce interleaf friction to a minimum. For this reason, synthetic rubber buttons are usually fitted at the tips of each leaf.

Action of leaf springs

Figure 7.2 shows, in schematic form, the shape taken up by the spring when the road wheel strikes a bump.

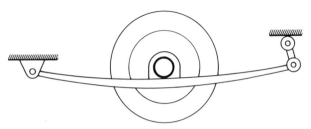

Figure 7.2   Spring deflection when the wheel strikes a bump

Figure 7.3 shows what happens to the spring and axle under rapid acceleration.

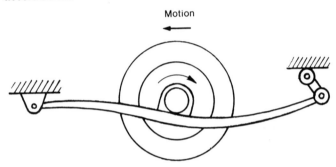

Figure 7.3   Action of spring during rapid acceleration

Figure 7.4 shows what happens to the spring and axle when the brakes are suddenly applied.

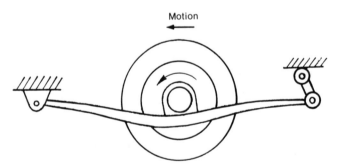

Figure 7.4   Action of spring when brake is suddenly applied

7.3 Coil springs

Coil springs are chiefly used with independent front and rear suspensions. They are made from spring steel wire wound in the form of a helix, which is twisted when the spring is compressed. Such springs are light and cheap and they can be easily accommodated in confined spaces. They can be made to have a lower rate and greater deflection (see Section 7.5) than a laminated spring, thus permitting a 'soft' ride.

Coil springs do not have the self-damping properties of laminated springs, so they must be used in conjunction with an effective shock absorber (see Fig. 7.5).

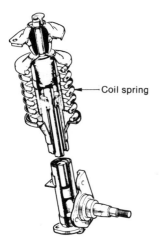

Coil spring

Figure 7.5 Strut-type independent front suspension

7.4 Torsion bars

Torsion bars are used with independent suspensions, their action being essentially the same as that which occurs in a coil spring.

A simple torsion bar suspension is shown in Fig. 7.6. One end of

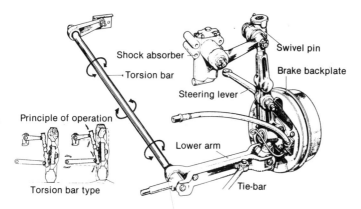

Figure 7.6 Torsion bar suspension

the bar is fixed to the frame member and the other end connected by a lever to the road wheel. Movement of the lever end by deflection of the wheel twists the torsion bar much as the wire in a coil spring is twisted under load.

Torsion bar springs provide a neat and compact design, although they are not as effective as coil springs as far as their action is concerned. In most cases, they are used in conjunction with the vehicle's main suspension springs to act as stabilizers.

7.5 Rate of springs

The *rate* or *stiffness* of a spring has already been defined in Section 6.4 as being the force required to produce unit deflection. The rate of a spring is measured in units such as N/mm or kN/mm.

Springs usually have a *constant rate*. This means that they are made to follow Hooke's law (see Section 6.3), so that the deflection produced when they are loaded will be directly proportional to the applied load (provided, of course, that they are not overstressed). If a constant rate spring is loaded and the deflection noted, the load–deflection graph will be a straight line, as shown in Fig. 7.7. The slope of this graph gives the rate of the spring.

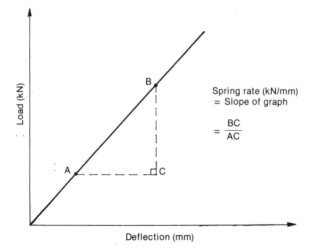

Spring rate (kN/mm)
= Slope of graph

$$= \frac{BC}{AC}$$

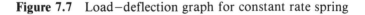

Figure 7.7 Load–deflection graph for constant rate spring

The rate of a leaf spring is dependent upon the following four factors:

1. Length of spring
2. Width of leaf

3. Thickness of leaf
4. Number of leaves.

If the lower leaves are assembled with their camber reversed, the spring rate will increase with greater loads. This is called a *progressive* or *variable rate* leaf spring.

Figure 7.8 shows a rear suspension system of a vehicle employing progressive rate leaf springs.

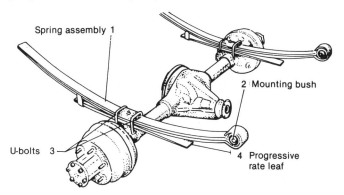

Figure 7.8   Rear suspension system employing progressive (or variable) rate springs

Figure 7.9 shows a load–deflection graph for a progressive or variable rate spring.

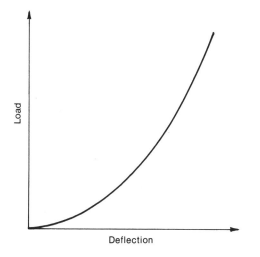

Figure 7.9   Load–deflection graph for a progressive (or variable) rate spring

Exercise 7.1 — Review questions

1 Complete the following statements.

   (*a*) A road spring is fitted to a motor vehicle in order to ....

   (*b*) One reason for fitting rebound clips to the leaves of laminated springs is ....

   (*c*) The purpose of a laminated leaf spring centre bolt is ....

   (*d*) Self-damping action of the laminated leaf spring is caused by ....

   (*e*) When under load, the coil spring in a front suspension unit is subjected to .... stress.

   (*f*) The rate or stiffness of a spring is ....

2 (*a*) Show by means of a sketch how the road spring of a rear wheel drive axle is attached to the rear axle and chassis.

   (*b*) Why is a swinging shackle necessary with a semi-elliptic leaf spring?

   (*c*) Show a drawing of a leaf spring when subjected to

      (*i*) braking force   (*ii*) accelerating force.

(WMAC/UEI)

3 State **three** advantages of fitting rubber bushes to the spring eyes of a laminated leaf spring in place of bronze bushes.

4 Figure 7.10 represents part of a transmission system.

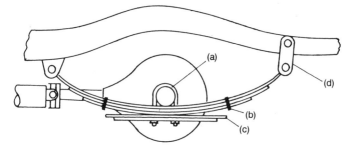

Figure 7.10

   (*a*) What name is given to this type of transmission?

   (*b*) What is the name and purpose of the parts labelled *a*, *b*, *c* and *d*?

(NWRAC/ULCI) (Modified)

5 Why are coil springs widely used on independent front suspension systems?

6 Give the reason why dampers are an essential part of independent front wheel suspensions using coil springs.

(CGLI)

7 What are the differences between the forces carried by a coil spring and a semi-elliptic leaf spring?

8 State **two** advantages of fitting torsion bars to the suspension of a motor vehicle in place of leaf springs.

(NWRAC/ULCI)

9 Select the correct answer in the following statement. The nature of the stress in a torsion bar spring is

(*a*) tensile
(*b*) compressive
(*c*) the same as that in a leaf spring
(*d*) shear.

10 State which of the following statements are true (T) or false (F), and correct where necessary.

(*a*) To obtain a 'soft' ride, a low-rate spring is necessary.
(*b*) For a variable rate leaf spring, the spring rate agrees with Hooke's law.
(*c*) The main stress is the same type in a torsion bar and a coil spring.
(*d*) When under load, a leaf spring will be subjected to both tensile and compressive stresses.
(*e*) One big advantage of using coil springs for independent front suspension systems is that they have self-damping properties.
(*f*) The front ends of the leaf springs on a commercial vehicle are attached to the chassis by spring clips.

11 What factors govern the stiffness or spring rate of a leaf spring?

(WMAC/UEI)

12 What is the difference between a constant rate spring and a progressive or variable rate spring?

13 Complete the table below giving the probable results that would be obtained when compressing a road spring to determine its stiffness and deflection. The results obtained would be expected to produce a straight line graph.

Load (kN)	0	2	4
Deflection (mm)	0		16

When a straight line graph is obtained the deflection is said to be .... to the load.

(WMAC/UEI)

14 Show by a sketch how the graph of Question 13 above would be modified if a progressive or variable rate spring were used.

Chapter 8

Forces acting at a point

8.1 Representation of a force

A force has the following characteristics:

(a) magnitude
(b) direction (line of action and sense)
(c) point of application.

A quantity which possesses both magnitude and direction is referred to as a *vector quantity*. Hence, force is a vector quantity and can be represented by a straight line drawn to scale from the point of application along the line of action of the force. An arrowhead is used to indicate the direction of the force.

8.2 Terms used in problems involving a number of forces acting at a point

In dealing with problems involving a number of forces acting at a point, the following terms are frequently used.

Equilibrium

When two or more forces act at a point and are so arranged to balance each other, the forces are said to be in *equilibrium*.

Resultant

The *resultant* of a number of forces acting at a point is that single force which would have the same effect if it replaced those forces.

Equilibrant

The *equilibrant* is a single force which, if added to a system of forces acting at a point, would produce equilibrium. In other words, the equilibrant will neutralize the other forces. It follows, therefore, that the equilibrant is equal in magnitude and direction, but opposite in sense to the resultant.

Coplanar forces

These are forces which are all acting in the same plane.

Concurrent forces

These are forces whose lines of action meet at the same point.

Note: When a number of coplanar forces acting on a body are in equilibrium, their lines of action must pass through a common point, i.e. the forces must be concurrent.

8.3 Parallelogram of forces

If two forces acting at a point are represented in magnitude and direction by the adjacent sides of a parallelogram, then their resultant will be represented in both magnitude and direction by the diagonal of the parallelogram drawn from that point.

The above statement is known as the *parallelogram of forces rule*, which is a graphical means of determining the resultant of two forces acting at a point. The method is illustrated by the following example.

Example 8.1

Two forces of 300 N and 500 N act at a point O and are inclined at 60° to each other. Determine, graphically, the magnitude and direction of the resultant force.

Solution

The diagram showing the magnitude and direction of the forces acting at the point O is given in Fig. 8.1(a). This diagram is referred to as the *space diagram*. The resultant of these forces is determined by constructing the *parallelogram of forces* shown in Fig. 8.1(b). This is drawn to a scale of 1 cm = 50 N as described below.

Draw OA 10 cm long to represent the 500 N force. Set off OB at an angle of 60° with OA, making it 6 cm long to represent the 300 N force. With centre A and radius OB draw an arc. With centre B and

108

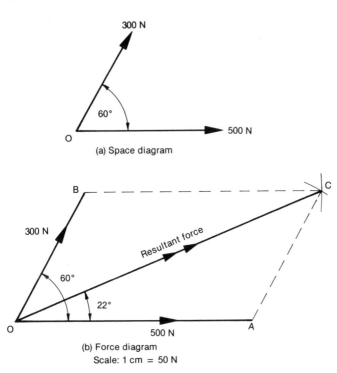

300 N

60°

O

500 N

(a) Space diagram

B

300 N

C

Resultant force

60°

22°

O

500 N

A

(b) Force diagram
Scale: 1 cm = 50 N

Figure 8.1 Parallelogram of forces – Example 8.1

radius OA draw another arc to intersect the first one at C. Join AC and BC to complete the parallelogram OACB, as shown. Now draw the diagonal OC. This represents the resultant force acting at O, its direction being from O towards C. Two arrowheads are inserted on OC to indicate that this vector is *not* a force, but is a single force that can replace the other two forces. By measurement, OC = 14 cm. Hence, since the scale used is 1 cm = 50 N, then:

Resultant force = 14 × 50 = 700 N
making an angle of 22° with OA

It should be noted that the *same* construction gives the equilibrant which has the same magnitude and direction as the resultant, but is of opposite sense, i.e. acting from C towards O.

8.4 Triangle of forces

If three coplanar forces acting at a point are in equilibrium, they can be represented in magnitude and direction by the sides of a triangle taken in order.

The above statement is known as the *triangle of forces rule*. It should be noted that the words 'taken in order' mean that the direction of the forces follow each other round each side of the triangle in either a clockwise or an anticlockwise order.

Suppose three forces, F_1, F_2 and F_3, acting at a point O, are in equilibrium and suppose the lines of action of these three forces to be as shown in the *space diagram*, Fig. 8.2(a).

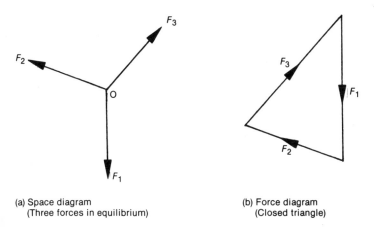

(a) Space diagram
   (Three forces in equilibrium)

(b) Force diagram
   (Closed triangle)

Figure 8.2 Triangle of forces

The corresponding *force (vector) diagram* is shown in Fig. 8.2(b) which must be drawn accurately to a suitable scale so that the sides of the triangle represent the magnitude and direction of the three forces. The sense of direction of each force is indicated by the arrowhead placed on the respective vector. Notice particularly that the force diagram has been drawn by taking the forces in a clockwise cyclic order around the point O.

8.5 Bow's notation

This convenient method of lettering the forces for reference purposes is particularly useful when there are three or more forces to be considered.

Capital letters are inserted in the spaces between the forces in the space diagram in a clockwise (or anti-clockwise) direction, as shown in Fig. 8.3(a). Each force can then be referred to by the letters in its adjacent spaces. In other words, force F_1 can be referred to as force AB, force F_2 as force BC, and force F_3 as force CA.

The vector of each force in the force diagram is labelled with its corresponding small letters on the two ends of the vector in the direction of the arrows. Thus forces AB, BC and CA are denoted by vectors *ab*, *bc* and *ca* respectively, as shown in Fig. 8.3(b).

110

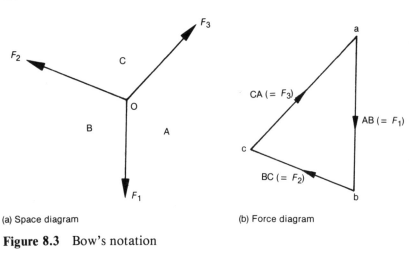

(a) Space diagram

(b) Force diagram

Figure 8.3 Bow's notation

Example 8.2

A load of 2000 N is suspended by two ropes, OX and OY, attached to a horizontal beam at X and Y, 1.8 m apart. If the ropes OX and OY make angles of 30° and 45° respectively with the beam, find graphically the tension in each rope when the system is in equilibrium.

Solution

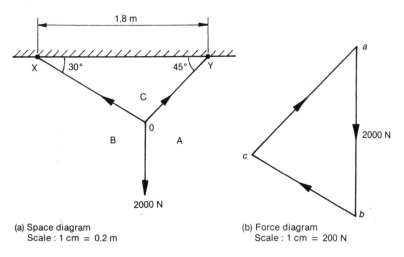

(a) Space diagram
Scale : 1 cm = 0.2 m

(b) Force diagram
Scale : 1 cm = 200 N

Figure 8.4 Triangle of forces — Example 8.2

The space diagram showing the load and the directions of the unknown forces (tensions) in the ropes is given in Fig. 8.4(a). This is drawn to a scale of 1 cm = 0.2 m, and the spaces between the forces around the junction O are lettered in accordance with Bow's notation.

The force diagram, Fig. 8.4(b), is drawn to a scale of 1 cm = 200 N and is constructed as follows:

Draw vector *ab* vertically and 10 cm long to represent the magnitude and direction of the force AB of 2000 N exerted by the load. Since the system is in equilibrium, the vector triangle of forces must close. Hence, from *b* draw a line parallel to the line of action of force BC, and from *a* draw another line parallel to the line of action of force CA so that the two lines meet at *c*. Insert arrowheads **in order** round the triangle, as shown.

The magnitude of the forces BC and CA (i.e. the tensions in the ropes OX and OY) can be found by measuring the sides *bc* and *ca*, respectively, of the vector triangle of forces and multiplying by the scale factor. By measurement, *bc* = 7.3 cm and *ca* = 9.0 cm. Thus:

Tension in rope OX = 7.3 × 200 = 1460 N
Tension in rope OY = 9.0 × 200 = 1800 N

Example 8.3

The pressure in an engine cylinder is 955 kPa when the crankshaft has rotated 45° from the top dead centre position. The bore and stroke are 80 mm each and the connecting rod length between centres is 120 mm. Construct the space and force diagrams to determine:

(*a*) the angle between the axis of the cylinder bore and the centre line of the connecting rod
(*b*) the force acting along the connecting rod
(*c*) the force between the thrust face of the piston and the cylinder wall.

Solution

The configuration diagram for the engine mechanism when the crank OA has turned 45° from the top dead centre position is drawn to scale in Fig. 8.5(a). The force P on the piston crown acts vertically downwards along the line of stroke; the thrust R in the connecting rod AB appears as an upward resisting force at its small end B; Q is the force between the thrust face of the piston and the cylinder wall, acting horizontally (i.e. at right angles to the line of stroke). The angle OBA is the inclination of the connecting rod to the cylinder bore centre line. By measurement, this angle is found to be approximately $13\frac{1}{2}°$.

Before constructing the force diagram, Fig. 8.5(b), it is first necessary to calculate the magnitude of the force P acting on the piston crown.

$$\begin{aligned} \text{Force } P &= \text{Pressure} \times \text{Area of cylinder bore} \\ &= 955 \times 10^3 \text{ [N/m}^2\text{]} \times \tfrac{1}{4}\pi \times 0.08^2 \text{ [m}^2\text{]} \\ &= 4800 \text{ N} \end{aligned}$$

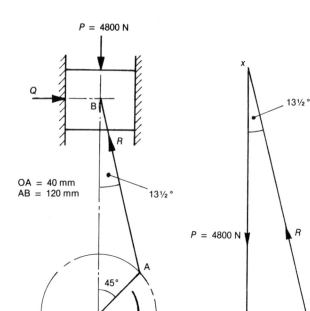

Figure 8.5 Triangle of forces – Example 8.3

Now draw a vertical line xy in Fig. 8.5(b) to represent P to a scale of, say, 1 cm = 400 N. The directions of yz and zx are known, and it is only necessary to draw lines parallel to Q and R from y and x, respectively, to meet at z to complete the force triangle xyz. By measurement, $yz = 2.9$ cm and $zx = 12.35$ cm. Thus:

Force $Q = 2.9 \times 400 = 1160$ N
Force $R = 12.35 \times 400 = 4940$ N

Example 8.4
A uniform trap-door, 2 m long and weighing 450 N, is shown in Fig. 8.6. It is hinged at one end and is supported when open by a rope over a pulley. When the door makes an angle of 30° to the floor, determine graphically the tension in the rope and the reaction at the hinge.

Solution
Draw the space diagram to a suitable scale, as shown in Fig. 8.7(a). The forces acting on the trap-door are:

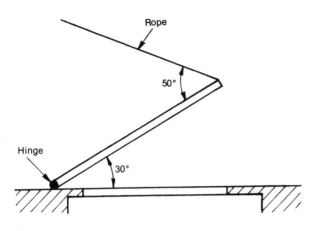

Figure 8.6 Trap-door – Example 8.4

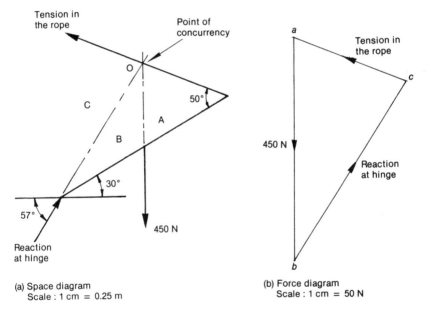

(a) Space diagram
Scale : 1 cm = 0.25 m

(b) Force diagram
Scale : 1 cm = 50 N

Figure 8.7 Triangle of forces – Example 8.4

(*i*) the weight 450 N vertically downwards at its mid-point
(*ii*) the tension in the supporting rope
(*iii*) the reaction at the hinge.

These three forces are in equilibrium and are concurrent (see Section 8.2). The point of concurrency, O, is determined by the intersection of the lines of action of forces (*i*) and (*ii*). Hence, the direction

114

of the hinge reaction is obtained by drawing a line from the hinge to the point O. Now, using Bow's notation, letter the spaces between the forces. Next draw to a suitable scale the force diagram, as shown in Fig. 8.7(b). By measurement bc = 8.7 cm and ca = 5.1 cm. Since the scale used here is 1 cm = 50 N, then:

Reaction at hinge = 8.7 × 50 = 435 N at 57° to the floor
Tension in the rope = 5.1 × 50 = 255 N

Example 8.5

A wheel and tyre assembly was balanced by having three small lead masses attached to the wheel rim. Two of the balances have masses of 55 g and 85 g respectively, and the angle between them is 120°. Assuming that radial force is proportional to the mass, determine, by the triangle of forces method, the magnitude and position of the third balance mass.

Solution

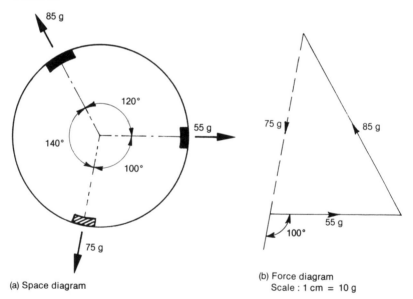

(a) Space diagram

(b) Force diagram
Scale : 1 cm = 10 g

Figure 8.8 Wheel balancing − Example 8.5

The space diagram is shown in Fig. 8.8(a). Using a scale of, say, 1 cm = 10 g, draw the force diagram of Fig. 8.8(b), as described in the previous examples. The magnitude of the third balance mass is represented by the dotted vector. This is found to be 75 g. Its position should be 100° from the 55 g mass and 140° from the 85 g mass, as shown in the space diagram, Fig. 8.8(a).

8.6 Polygon of forces

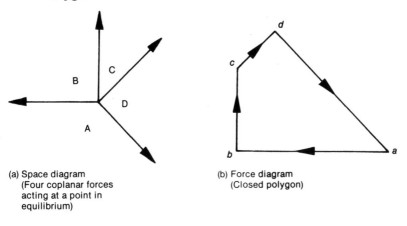

(a) Space diagram
(Four coplanar forces
acting at a point in
equilibrium)

(b) Force diagram
(Closed polygon)

Figure 8.9 Polygon of forces

The *polygon of forces rule* is an extension of the triangle of forces rule and can be expressed thus:

If four or more coplanar forces acting at a point are in equilibrium, they can be represented in magnitude and direction by the sides of a polygon taken in order (see Fig. 8.9).

If a system of several coplanar forces meets at a point and that system is not in equilibrium, then the polygon does not close and the force required to produce equilibrium in the system is represented by the vector which joins the open ends of the incomplete polygon. Thus, in Fig. 8.10(b), the equilibrant is represented by the vector $a'a$ (shown dotted), its direction being taken from a' to a. Note that the resultant of the force system is represented by the same vector, but its direction is from a to a'.

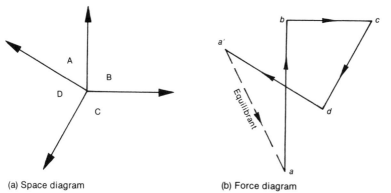

(a) Space diagram

(b) Force diagram

Figure 8.10 System of concurrent forces not in equilibrium

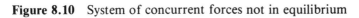

116

Example 8.6

Four coplanar forces act at a point as shown in Fig. 8.11(a). Determine their resultant in magnitude and direction.

(NWRAC/ULCI)

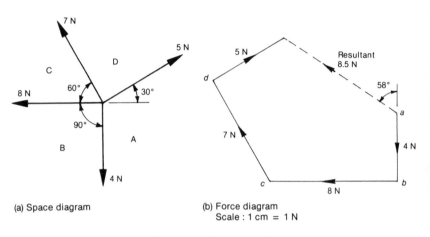

(a) Space diagram

(b) Force diagram
Scale : 1 cm = 1 N

Figure 8.11   Polygon of forces – Example 8.6

Solution

Using Bow's notation, put capital letters in the spaces between the forces in the space diagram, Fig. 8.11(a). Referring to the force diagram, Fig. 8.11(b), let 1 cm represent 1 N. Start by drawing vector *ab* 4 cm long, parallel to and in the same direction as force AB in the space diagram, Fig. 8.11(a). Continue by drawing, in the same order, vectors *bc* (8 cm long), *cd* (7 cm long) and *da'* (5 cm long) parallel to forces BC, CD and DA respectively, as shown. Join *aa'*. Then the vector *aa'*, taken in the sense from *a* to *a'*, represents the resultant force. By measurement, this is found to be 8.5 N acting in the direction 58° to the vertical, as shown in the force diagram, Fig. 8.11(b).

Example 8.7

Four members of a frame structure meet at a joint, as shown in Fig. 8.12(a). If the joint is in equilibrium, determine graphically the magnitude of the forces X and Y in the members shown.

(NWRAC/ULCI)

Solution

Fig. 8.12(a) is the space diagram lettered in accordance with Bow's notation. Since the joint is in equilibrium, the force diagram, Fig. 8.12(b), must be a closed polygon.

Using a scale of, say, 1 mm to 10 N, draw vector *ab* 90 mm long parallel to and in the same direction as the 900 N force in the space

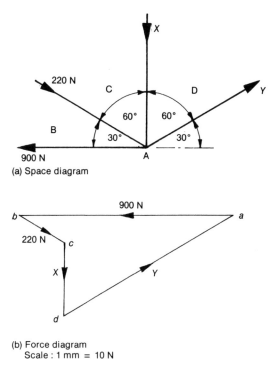

(a) Space diagram

(b) Force diagram
Scale : 1 mm = 10 N

Figure 8.12   Polygon of forces – Example 8.7

diagram. Next draw vector *bc* 22 mm long parallel to and in the same
direction as the 220 N force. From *c*, draw a line parallel to the direction of force *X* and from *a* draw another line parallel to the direction
of force *Y* so that the two lines meet at *d*. Then, vectors *cd* and *da*
will represent the magnitude and direction of forces *X* and *Y* respectively.
By measurement, *cd* = 30 mm and *da* = 82 mm. Thus:

Force $X = 30 \times 10 = 300\,\text{N}$
Force $Y = 82 \times 10 = 820\,\text{N}$

8.7   Resolution of a force into two components

A force acting at a point can be resolved into two components, these
being two forces that could replace the given force and have the same
effect on the point. It will be appreciated that to find the two components of a given force is the reverse process of finding the resultant of
two given forces. Although components in any two directions can be
found, the most useful are usually the *rectangular components*, i.e.
those which are at right angles to each other.

118

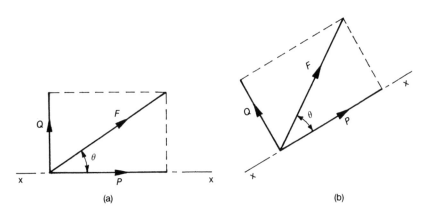

Figure 8.13 Resolution of a force into two rectangular components

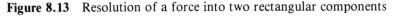

To find the rectangular component forces P and Q of a given force F acting at an angle θ to a line X–X (Fig. 8.13):

By elementary trigonometry,

$$\frac{P}{F} = \cos\theta, \qquad \therefore\ P = F\cos\theta$$

and $\quad \dfrac{Q}{F} = \sin\theta, \qquad \therefore\ Q = F\sin\theta$

$F\cos\theta$ is the component of force F parallel to X–X, and $F\sin\theta$ is the component of force F at right angles to X–X.

It should be noted that when the line X–X is horizontal, as in Fig. 8.13(a), the components P and Q are referred to as the horizontal and vertical components of the force F.

Example 8.8

At a certain instant a horizontal rope towing a vehicle makes an angle of 70° with the front axle. If the force in the tow rope is 1300 N, calculate:

(*a*) the effective force pulling the vehicle forward
(*b*) the force pulling the vehicle sideways.

(CGLI)

Solution

Force in tow rope, $F = 1300$ N

From Fig. 8.14:

(*a*) Effective force pulling the vehicle forward

$\quad = F\cos 20°$
$\quad = 1300 \times 0.9397 = 1222\,\text{N}$

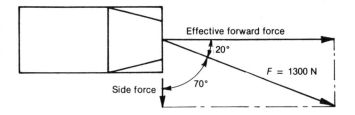

Figure 8.14 Example 8.8

(*b*) Force pulling the vehicle sideways

  = *F* sin 20°   [or *F* cos 70°]
  = 1300 × 0.342
  = 444.6 N

Answer: (*a*) 1222 N   (*b*) 444.6 N

8.8 Body resting on a smooth inclined plane

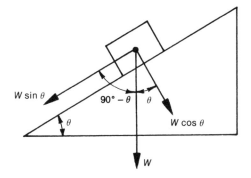

Figure 8.15 Body resting on a smooth inclined plane

When a body is resting on a smooth inclined plane, Fig. 8.15, the weight *W* of the body which acts vertically downwards under the influence of gravity can be resolved into two components at right angles. One of these components, *W* sin θ, acts parallel to and down the plane. The other component, *W* cos θ, acts at right angles to the plane, as shown.

It should be noted that the force parallel to the plane required to prevent the body sliding down the plane will be equal to *W* sin θ, and the normal reaction of the plane to the weight of the body will be equal to *W* cos θ.

Example 8.9

A motor vehicle has a mass of 1200 kg and stands on an incline of 1 in 8. Calculate:

(a) the force parallel to the road surface required to hold the vehicle stationary
(b) the normal reaction between the wheels and the road surface.

(Take the gravitational force on a mass of 1 kg to be 10 N.)

Solution

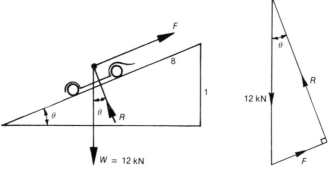

(a) Space diagram   (b) Force diagram

Figure 8.16 Vehicle resting on an inclined road – Example 8.9

Since the gravitational force exerted on a mass of 1 kg is 10 N, then:

Weight of vehicle, $W = 1200 \times 10$
$$= 12\,000\,N = 12\,kN$$

An incline (or a gradient) of 1 in 8 means that the road rises vertically by 1 m for every 8 m measured along the road surface.
From Fig. 8.16(a),

$\sin \theta = \frac{1}{8} = 0.1250$
$\therefore \quad \theta = 7.18°$

(a) Force F parallel to the road surface required to hold the vehicle stationary

$= W \sin 7.18°$
$= 12 \times 0.1250 = 1.5\,kN$

(b) Normal reaction R between the wheels and the road surface

$= W \cos 7.18°$
$= 12 \times 0.9920 = 11.9\,kN$

Answer: (a) 1.5 kN; (b) 11.9 kN

Exercise 8.1 – Review questions

1 (*a*) To define a force completely, three factors must be known. Name them.
   (*b*) How are these factors represented by a vector?
(EMEU)
2 Explain what is meant by the resultant of a number of forces acting at a point.
3 Explain what is meant by the equilibrant of a number of forces acting at a point.
4 Complete the following statements by inserting the missing word:

   (*a*) When three or more forces are all acting in the same plane, they are called .... forces.
   (*b*) When forces act at the same time and at the same point, they are called .... forces.
   (*c*) When a system of coplanar forces is balanced so that there is no resultant force, it is said to be in ....

5 Describe how the resultant of two non-parallel forces acting at a point may be determined graphically.
   What alteration is required to be made to the resultant in order that it may become the equilibrant of the two forces?
6 State the principle of the triangle of forces.
7 State the principle of the polygon of forces.
8 What is Bow's notation?
9 Explain what is meant by the resolution of a force into two components at right angles to each other.

Exercise 8.2 – Problems

1 Two connecting rods of a vee-engine are attached to the same crankpin. At a certain instant the angle between the two connecting rods, A and B, is 60°. The thrust along rod A is 22.5 kN and that along B is 8 kN. Determine, graphically, the magnitude and direction of the resultant force relative to rod A. Use a scale of 1 cm = 2.5 kN.
(WMAC/UEI)
2 An accident-damaged vehicle is trapped in a confined space making it necessary for it to be dragged out bodily. Two independent winches are required, pulling at right angles to each other. One acting from north to south exerts a pull of 2700 N, while the other acting from east to west exerts a pull of 1500 N. Find, graphically, the magnitude and direction of the resultant pull on the damaged vehicle.
(NWRAC/ULCI)
3 A load of 2000 N is suspended in the air by two steel ropes. If the

122

inclinations of the ropes to the vertical are 45° and 60° respectively, determine the tension in each rope.

4 An engine of total weight 1500 N hangs on a chain whose upper end is attached to an overhead support. A horizontal force exerted on the engine causes the chain to take up a position inclined at 30° to the vertical. What is the horizontal force and the force in the chain?

(EMEU) (Modified)

5 A chain AB is 2 m long and a hook is attached at a point C, 0.8 m from A. The ends A and B are fastened to two eyebolts in the same horizontal line, 1.6 m apart. If a load of 20 kN is suspended from the hook, determine the tension in each part of the chain.

6 A car is brought in with wheel wobble. During the check it is noticed that the near-side front wheel has a 60 g balance mass and a 30 g balance mass fitted to the wheel rim 120° apart, but a third mass is missing. Assuming that radial force is proportional to mass, find, by the triangle of forces, the magnitude of this mass and its position relative to the other masses to restore balance. The rim diameter is 0.4 m.

(CGLI) (Modified)

7 Three forces of magnitude 200 N, 145 N and 180 N respectively act at a point as shown in Fig. 8.17. Determine, by drawing the triangle of forces, the angles, measured in a clockwise direction from the 200 N force, at which the other two forces must act in order that the three forces shall be in equilibrium.

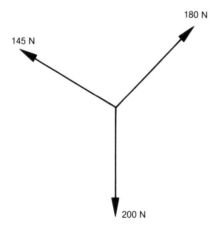

Figure 8.17

8 A vehicle has a mass of 1500 kg and rests on an incline of 18° to the horizontal. Calculate:

(a) the force required to be exerted by the brakes to keep the vehicle stationary (*b*) the normal reaction between the wheels and the road surface.

(Assume the gravitational force on a mass of 1 kg to be 10 N.)

9 A weight of 60 kN is suspended from the hook of a jib crane as shown in Fig. 8.18. Find, graphically, the magnitude of the forces in the jib and the tie.
Use a scale of 1 cm = 10 kN.

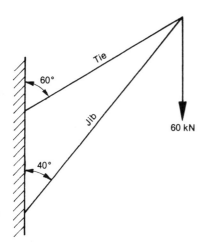

Figure 8.18 Jib crane

10 The wall crane shown in Fig. 8.19 consists of a horizontal jib AB supported by a tie-bar BC. If a mass of 450 kg is supported at B, find, graphically, the magnitude of the forces in the jib and the tie-bar.

(Assume the gravitational force on a mass of 1 kg to be 10 N.)

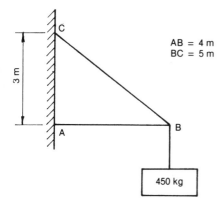

Figure 8.19 Wall crane

124

11 An engine has a stroke of 100 mm and a connecting rod length of
    200 mm between centres. The crank is 45° past top dead centre
    when the force on the piston is 5000 N. By means of a graphical
    solution, determine:

    (a) the angle between the axis of the bore and the centre line of
        the connecting rod
    (b) the force acting along the connecting rod
    (c) the force between the thrust face of the piston and the cylinder
        wall.

                                                              (EMEU)

12 Figure 8.20 shows a uniform bar resting with one end on a rough
    horizontal floor and supported by a smooth circular shaft. Gravity
    exerts on the bar a force of 800 N vertically downwards at its
    centre. Determine by a graphical method (a) the force F, (b) the
    reaction R and (c) the angle θ.
    (You are reminded that the lines of action of the three forces,
    continued if necessary, will meet at a point. A suitable scale for
    the force vector diagram is 20 mm = 100 N.)

                                                              (CGLI)

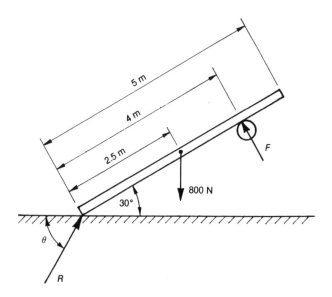

Figure 8.20

13 Determine, by constructing the polygon of forces, the magnitude
    and direction of the resultant for the system of concurrent coplanar
    forces shown in Fig. 8.21.

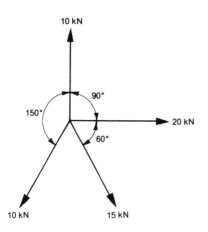

Figure 8.21

14 A clutch was balanced by having four masses placed on the clutch cover at the same radius. Three of the masses are 40 g, 50 g and 25 g respectively, and their angular positions from the vertical, in a clockwise direction, are 0°, 120° and 210° respectively.

Assuming that radial force is proportional to the mass, find, by applying the polygon of forces rule, the magnitude and position of the fourth mass. Use a scale of 10 mm = 5 g.

15 Four coplanar forces, AB, BC, CD and DA, of magnitude 40 N, 80 N, 50 N and 95 N respectively, act at a point O as shown in Fig. 8.22. Find, graphically, the magnitude and direction of their resultant. Use a scale of 1 cm = 10 N.

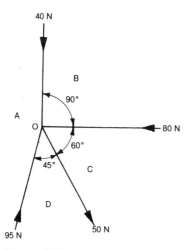

Figure 8.22

16 Find, graphically, the magnitude and direction of the resultant of four coplanar forces which are acting at a point on a body as follows:

Force W, 60 N acting horizontally to the left
Force X, 50 N inclined at 45° clockwise to force W
Force Y, 30 N inclined at 105° clockwise to force X
Force Z, 40 N inclined at 90° clockwise to force Y.

17 A point O is in equilibrium under the action of five coplanar forces as shown in Fig. 8.23. Find the magnitude of the two forces P and Q. Use a scale of 1 cm = 2 N.

(EMEU)

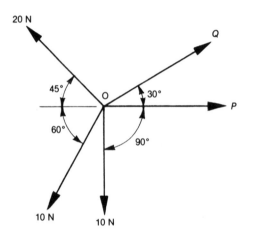

Figure 8.23

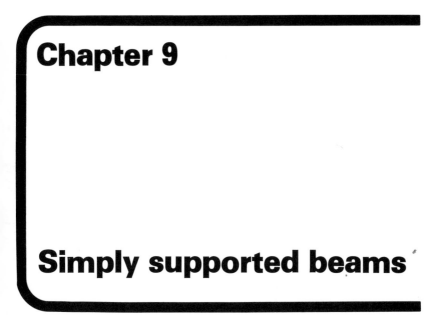

Chapter 9

Simply supported beams

9.1 Introduction

A *beam* is any structural member which is subjected to external forces along its length. Usually the beam is horizontal and the external forces vertical; these forces will consist of the *loads* applied to the beam and the *reactions* at the supports.

In general, the loads applied to a beam are the forces exerted by gravity on masses supported by the beam, and hence will act downwards. In this chapter, only loads acting at given points along the length of the beam are considered, called *concentrated* or *point loading*.

A *uniform beam* is one which has the same density of material and the same cross-sectional area throughout its length. The weight of a uniform beam is considered to act through its centre. It should be remarked that the weight of a beam is usually small compared with the loads it carries, and should therefore be neglected unless a definite value for it is given.

9.2 The moment of a force

The *moment* of a force is a measure of the turning effect of the force about a fixed point or *fulcrum*. It is equal to the product of the force and the perpendicular distance from the point to the line of action of the force.

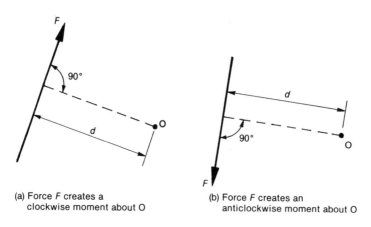

(a) Force F creates a
   clockwise moment about O

(b) Force F creates an
   anticlockwise moment about O

Figure 9.1 Turning effect of a force

Let a force F act at a perpendicular distance d from a fixed point O, as shown in Fig. 9.1(a) and (b). Then:

Moment of force $= Fd$ [9.1]

The unit of the moment of a force is the *newton metre* (N m).

The force can create either a *clockwise moment*, as in Fig. 9.1(a), or an *anticlockwise moment* about O, as in Fig. 9.1(b), depending on the direction of the force.

9.3   Equilibrium under the action of parallel forces

If a body is in equilibrium when acted upon by a number of parallel forces, then:

(*i*) the resultant force acting on the body is zero;
(*ii*) the algebraic sum of the moments of all the forces about a fixed point is zero.

Consider a uniform beam to be pivoted at its centre on a fulcrum. Suppose the beam is carrying point loads of W_1, W_2 and W_3 at distances d_1, d_2 and d_3 respectively from the fulcrum, as shown in Fig. 9.2.

Now, for the resultant force on the beam to be zero, the upward force provided by the reaction R at the fulcrum must equal the downward forces, i.e.

$R = W_1 + W_2 + W_3$

For the algebraic sum of the moments of the forces to be zero, the total anticlockwise moment produced by W_1 and W_2 about the fulcrum must equal the total clockwise moment produced by W_3 about the fulcrum. Thus, for equilibrium to be maintained,

$W_1 d_1 + W_2 d_2 = W_3 d_3$

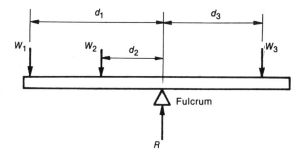

Figure 9.2

This condition can be stated as a *principle of moments*:

'When a body is in equilibrium under the action of a number of forces, the sum of the anticlockwise moments about a point is equal to the sum of the clockwise moments about the same point.'

Example 9.1

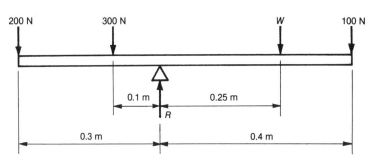

Figure 9.3   Example 9.1

A uniform horizontal lever is supported on a fulcrum and loaded as shown in Fig. 9.3. Calculate:

(*a*) the magnitude of the load W required to maintain equilibrium
(*b*) the magnitude of the reaction R at the support.

Neglect the mass of the lever.

Solution

(*a*) Taking moments about the support, and working throughout in units of N and m,

Total anticlockwise moment $= (200 \times 0.3) + (300 \times 0.1)$
$= 60 + 30 = 90\,\text{N m}$

Total clockwise moment $\quad = (W \times 0.25) + (100 \times 0.4)$
$= (0.25\,W + 40)\,\text{N m}$

For the lever to remain horizontal, the total anticlockwise moment about the support must equal the total clockwise moment about the support. Thus:

$$90 = 0.25\,W + 40$$

or $0.25\,W = 90 - 40$

and $W = \dfrac{50}{0.25} = 200\,\text{N}$

(b) At equilibrium, the resultant vertical force must be zero. Hence, the reaction at the support (acting upwards) must be equal to the sum of the loads (acting downwards), i.e.

$$R = 200 + 300 + 200 + 100 = 800\,\text{N}$$

Answer: (a) Magnitude of load $W = 200\,\text{N}$
            (b) Reaction at the support $= 800\,\text{N}$

Example 9.2

If the mass of the lever given in Example 9.1 is equivalent to a load of 100 N, what would then be the magnitude of the load W required for the lever to remain horizontal? Determine also the new value of the reaction R at the support.

Solution

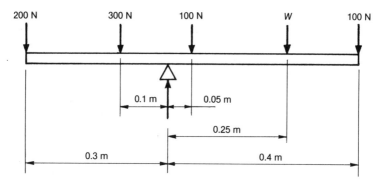

Figure 9.4   Example 9.2

The lever and its load is represented in Fig. 9.4. Since the lever is of uniform section, the force due to gravity on it is considered to act at the centre of its length, as shown.

Take moments about the support. It will be observed that the total anticlockwise moment is the same as in the previous example, i.e. 90 N m, but the conditions to the right of the fulcrum have changed.

Therefore,

Total clockwise moment = $(100 \times 0.05) + (0.25\,W + 40)$
$= (0.25\,W + 45)$ N m

Applying the principle of moments, for the lever to remain horizontal:

Total anticlockwise moment = Total clockwise moment

i.e. $\qquad\qquad 90 = 0.25\,W + 45$

so that $\qquad\qquad W = \dfrac{90 - 45}{0.25} = 180\,\text{N}$

At equilibrium, the resultant vertical force is zero. Thus:

Reaction R = Sum of loads
i.e. $\quad R = (200 + 300 + 100 + 180 + 100)$ N
$= 880$ N

Answer: Magnitude of $W = 180\,\text{N}$; Reaction $R = 880\,\text{N}$

9.4   Simply supported beams

A *simply supported beam* is one which rests on two knife-edge or roller supports and is free to move horizontally.

For a simply supported beam to be in equilibrium, both the conditions mentioned in Section 9.3 must be satisfied. The resultant force acting on the beam must be zero, and the algebraic sum of the moments about either of the supports must also be zero. These two facts enable the value of the reactions at the supports to be determined when the loading of the beam is known. The following examples illustrate the method used.

Example 9.3

The beam of a car lift is 4 m long and can be assumed to be simply supported at its ends A and B. It supports a vehicle which has a wheelbase (distance between front and rear axles) of 2.5 m and the front axle is at a distance of 0.5 m from A. If the load on the front axle is 5 kN and that on the rear axle is 8.5 kN, determine the reactions at the supports of the lift beam.

Solution

The lift beam and its load is represented in Fig. 9.5.

Let the reactions of the beam supports at A and B be R_A and R_B respectively. The magnitude of each reaction can now be determined by taking moments about one of the points of support. This procedure will prevent two unknown forces appearing in one equation.

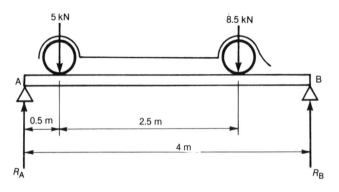

Figure 9.5 Simply supported beam – Example 9.3

To find reaction R_A at A

Take moments about B. (Reaction R_B will produce no moment about point B, since its line of action passes through this point.)

Total clockwise moment $= R_A \times 4 = 4R_A$ kN m
Total anticlockwise moment $= (5 \times 3.5) + (8.5 \times 1)$
$= 17.5 + 8.5 = 26$ kN m

For equilibrium,

Total clockwise moment $=$ Total anticlockwise moment
i.e. $4R_A = 26$
$\therefore$ $R_A = 6.5$ kN

To find reaction R_B at B

Take moments about A. (Reaction R_A will have no turning effect about A.)

Applying the principle of moments:

Anticlockwise moments about A $=$ Clockwise moments about A
i.e. $R_B \times 4 = (5 \times 0.5) + (8.5 \times 3)$
$4R_B = 2.5 + 25.5 = 28$
$\therefore$ $R_B = 7$ kN

Check: For equilibrium of vertical forces, the two reactions must equal the total load carried by the beam.

Hence $R_A + R_B = 6.5 + 7 = 13.5$ kN
and Sum of loads $= 5 + 8.5 = 13.5$ kN

Thus, the magnitude (and direction) of the reactions are correct.

Note: It will be observed that when the first reaction has been determined by taking moments, the second reaction could be found by subtracting the known reaction from the total load. Although there is slightly more work in the method shown above, it does provide a useful check.

Answer: $R_A = 6.5\,\text{kN}$; $R_B = 7\,\text{kN}$

Example 9.4

A uniform beam, 4 m long, is simply supported at two points A and B, point A being 0.5 m from the left-hand end and point B 1.5 m from the right-hand end. The beam carries loads of 600 N at the left-hand end, 800 N at its centre and 400 N at the right-hand end.

(*a*) Determine the magnitude of the support reactions at A and B.
(*b*) At what point should the load of 800 N be applied to make the support reactions equal?

Solution

(*a*) The system of forces acting on the beam is shown in Fig. 9.6.

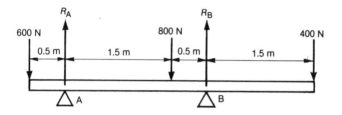

Figure 9.6   Simply supported beam − Example 9.4(*a*)

Taking moments about B, and working throughout in units of N and m, we get:

$$\text{Total clockwise moment} = (R_A \times 2) + (400 \times 1.5)$$
$$= (2R_A + 600)\,\text{N m}$$
$$\text{Total anticlockwise moment} = (600 \times 2.5) + (800 \times 0.5)$$
$$= 1500 + 400 = 1900\,\text{N m}$$

Since the resultant moment is zero, for equilibrium, these two totals are equal, and

$$2R_A + 600 = 1900$$

$$\therefore \qquad R_A = \frac{1900 - 600}{2} = 650\,\text{N}$$

Taking moments about A, and equating anticlockwise and clockwise moments, for equilibrium, gives:

$$(R_B \times 2) + (600 \times 0.5) = (800 \times 1.5) + (400 \times 3.5)$$
$$2R_B + 300 = 1200 + 1400$$
$$2R_B = 2600 - 300 = 2300$$
$$\therefore \qquad R_B = 1150\,\text{N}$$

134

As a check, $R_A + R_B = 650 + 1150 = 1800$ N, which equals the total load on the beam. Thus, the magnitude (and direction) of the reactions are correct.

(b) For the reactions at supports A and B to be equal,

$$R_A = R_B = \frac{1800}{2} = 900 \text{ N}$$

The beam and its loads are now as represented in Fig. 9.7 with the 800 N load moved nearer to A at a distance x metres from B.

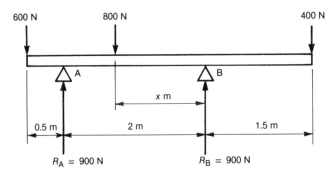

Figure 9.7 Example 9.4(b)

Taking moments about B, and equating anticlockwise and clockwise moments, for equilibrium, gives:

$$800x + (600 \times 2.5) = (900 \times 2) + (400 \times 1.5)$$
$$800x = 1800 + 600 - 1500$$
$$x = \frac{900}{800} = 1.125 \text{ m}$$

Hence, to make the support reactions equal, the load of 800 N should be applied at $1.125 + 1.5 = 2.625$ m from the right-hand end of the beam.

Answer: (a) $R_A = 650$ N, $R_B = 1150$ N
            (b) 2.625 m from right-hand end

Example 9.5

A bus chassis, 5.4 m long, consists of two side members and a number of cross members. Each side member can be considered as a beam, simply supported at two points A and B, 3.6 m apart, A being positioned 0.9 m from the front end of the frame and subjected to the following concentrated loads:

Engine support (front) 2 kN, engine support (rear) 2.5 kN, gearbox support 0.5 kN, and body W kN. The distances of these loads from the front end of the frame are respectively 0.6 m, 1.8 m, 2.4 m and 3 m. If the reaction at A is 8.5 kN, determine:

(a) the magnitude of the load W due to the vehicle body
(b) the magnitude of the support reaction at B.

Solution

Figure 9.8 is a diagrammatic representation of the loading.

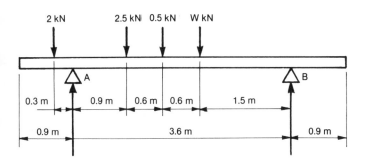

Figure 9.8   Example 9.5

(a) To determine the magnitude of W, take moments about B.

For equilibrium, the resultant moment must be zero. Thus:

Clockwise moments about B = Anticlockwise moments about B

$$(8.5 \times 3.6) = (2 \times 3.9) + (2.5 \times 2.7) + (0.5 \times 2.1)$$
$$+ (W \times 1.5)$$

i.e. $30.6 = 7.8 + 6.75 + 1.05 + 1.5\,W$

and $W = \dfrac{30.6 - 15.6}{1.5} = 10\,\text{kN}$

(b) For equilibrium of vertical forces, the resultant force on the beam must be zero.

Hence $R_A + R_B$ = Total downward forces
i.e. $8.5\,\text{kN} + R_B = (2 + 2.5 + 0.5 + 10)\,\text{kN}$
∴ $R_B = 15 - 8.5 = 6.5\,\text{kN}$

Answer: (a) Magnitude of $W = 10\,\text{kN}$
            (b) Reaction at B = 6.5 kN

Example 9.6

A uniform beam ABC is 6 m long and rests horizontally on two supports, A and B, which are 4 m apart. Point loads of 10 kN and 5 kN

136

are applied to the beam as shown in Fig. 9.9. Determine the magnitude of the load W applied at the end C which will cause the beam to just lift off support A.

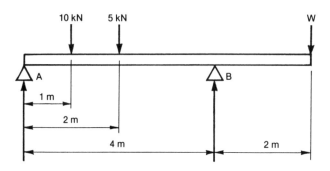

Figure 9.9 Example 9.6

Solution
When the beam is just lifting off support A, the reaction force at A is reduced to zero so that it is no longer supporting the beam. The beam then balances about support B. Hence:

Taking moments about B, and equating clockwise and anticlockwise moments, for equilibrium, gives:

$$W \times 2 = (5 \times 2) + (10 \times 3)$$
$$= 10 + 30 = 40$$
$$\therefore \quad W = 20 \, \text{kN}$$

Answer: Magnitude of W which will cause the beam to just lift off support A = 20 kN

9.5 Experimental determination of beam reactions

Object
To obtain the reactions at the supports of a loaded beam and compare them with the calculated values.

Apparatus
Some standard weights, a metre rule, and a wooden beam of uniform section supported horizontally at its ends on two 'clock-type' spring balances.

Procedure
Before placing any loads on the beam, adjust the spring balances so that they both read zero. This will eliminate the weight of the beam

itself. Now place two weights, W_1 and W_2, on the beam anywhere between the supports, as shown in Fig. 9.10. Note the spring balance readings; these will then be the observed values of the reactions, R_A at end A and R_B at end B. Measure the distances a, b and l. Repeat the experiment using different loads and distances and record the results. In each case, calculate the value of the reactions at the supports by the method described in Example 9.3. Compare the observed values with the calculated reactions.

The experiment can now be repeated using three or more weights. In each case check that

(*i*) the sum of the spring balance readings is equal to the sum of the loads
(*ii*) the sum of the clockwise moments about a support is equal to the sum of the anticlockwise moments about that support.

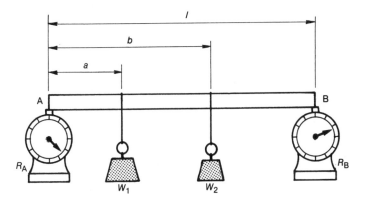

Figure 9.10 Experimental determination of beam reactions

Exercise 9.1 — Review questions

1 State what is meant by the 'moment of a force'.
2 The moment of a force is measured by the product of the force and . . . .
3 The unit of the moment of a force is the . . . .
4 State the two conditions necessary for the equilibrium of a body acted on by a number of parallel forces.

(CGLI)

5 Explain what is meant by a 'simply supported beam'.
6 For a simply supported beam to be in equilibrium, the sum of the . . . . moments about . . . . must be equal to the . . . . moments about . . . .
7 Describe an experiment for determining the reactions of a simply supported beam.

138

Exercise 9.2 — Problems

1 A uniform rod AB is 2 m long. The rod, which exerts a downward force of 60 N at its centre, is placed on a knife-edge support positioned 0.8 m from A. Determine the vertical downward force required at A to prevent rotation of the rod.

2 A uniform bar is resting on a single support and loaded as shown in Fig. 9.11. Determine the magnitude of the load W to be applied as shown if the bar is just to balance in a horizontal position about the support. Neglect the mass of the bar.

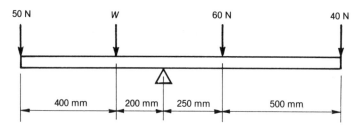

Figure 9.11

3 A motor vehicle has a wheelbase of 3 m. The load on the front axle is 12 kN and that on the rear axle is 16 kN. The vehicle rests on a simply supported bridge of span 7.5 m, the front axle being 1.5 m from the left-hand support. Calculate the magnitude of the reactions of the bridge supports.

(CGLI)

4 A uniform beam AB of length 6 m is simply supported at its ends. It carries point loads of 200 N, 400 N and 300 N at distances of 1.5 m, 3 m and 5 m respectively from end A. Determine the magnitude of the reactions at A and B.

5 A horizontal beam AB is 6 m long and is simply supported at A and B. Loads of 30 kN and 60 kN are carried at points 2 m and 4 m from A respectively.

(a) Find the magnitude of the reactions at A and B.
(b) If an extra load of 50 kN is to be added to the beam in such a position that the reactions at A and B are to be equal, what will these reactions then be, and at what distance from A must the 50 kN load be situated?

(CGLI) (Modified)

6 A chassis side member is 4.8 m long measured from the position of the front axle, the wheelbase is 3.6 m and the rear overhang is 1.2 m. The member can be considered as a beam simply supported at the position of the front and rear axles. It carries point loads of 10 kN and 30 kN at 0.6 m and 2.4 m respectively from the front

axle, and another point load of 20 kN at the rear end. Calculate
the value of the reactions at the front and rear axles.

7   A uniform beam AB of length 8 m is simply supported at its ends.
It carries point loads of 4 kN, 5 kN and 7 kN at the positions 2 m,
5 m and 7 m respectively from end A. If the reaction at end B is
13 kN, calculate (a) the force due to gravity on the beam, and
(b) the reaction at end A.

8   A uniform beam AB, 3 m long, is simply supported at its ends.
The force due to gravity on the beam is 2 kN and loads of 3 kN
and 5 kN are placed on the beam at distances of 0.5 m and 2.0 m
respectively from end A. Where must an additional load of 2 kN
be placed in order to make the support reactions equal?

(EMEU)

9   The beam of an overhead travelling crane in a workshop has a
span of 10 m, a mass of 3000 kg and is mounted on four wheels,
two at each end. A small crab hoist which has a mass of 250 kg
runs along the beam. A vehicle of mass 1000 kg is raised by the
hoist when at a distance of 3.8 m from the centre of the beam.
Calculate the load on each wheel on the main beam. You may
assume that the gravitational force acting on a mass of 1 kg is
10 N.

(NWRAC/ULCI) (Modified)

10 A motor-lorry frame can be considered as a beam 4.2 m long and
simply supported at two points, A and B, 3 m apart. The frame is
subjected to concentrated loads of 5 kN, 10 kN, 15 kN and 10 kN
as shown in Fig. 9.12. Calculate:

(a) the value of the support reactions at A and B
(b) the position at which the 15 kN load must be applied to make
the support reactions equal.

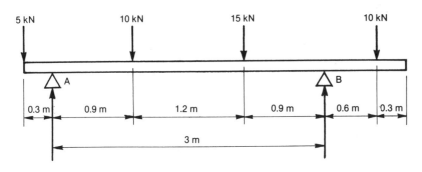

Figure 9.12

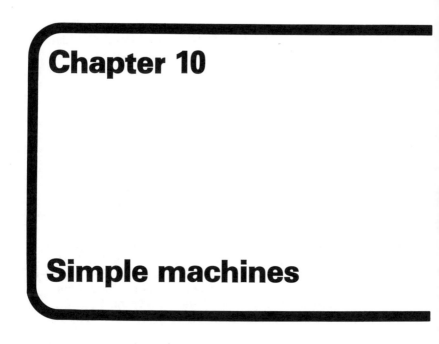

Chapter 10

Simple machines

10.1 Introduction

A simple machine is a device which enables a small force (the *effort*) acting at a point to overcome a large force (the *load*) acting at some other point.

Examples of simple machines are pulley systems, screw jacks, gear systems and levers. Vehicle gearboxes, rear axles and steering boxes are also types of machine, and these are dealt with in the next chapter.

10.2 Definitions of terms used in simple machine theory

The following terms are defined in simple machine theory.

Force ratio or mechanical advantage

A machine is usually designed so that the load is overcome by means of a considerably smaller effort.

The ratio of the load to the effort is called the *force ratio* or the *mechanical advantage* of the machine. Hence:

$$\text{Mechanical advantage (MA)} = \frac{\text{Load}}{\text{Effort}} \qquad [10.1]$$

Since mechanical advantage is a ratio of two forces, it has no units and is only a number which varies with the load.

Movement ratio or velocity ratio

The ratio of the distance moved by the effort to that moved by the load (in the same time) is called the *movement ratio* or the *velocity ratio* of the machine. Hence:

$$\text{Velocity ratio (VR)} = \frac{\text{Distance moved by effort}}{\text{Distance moved by load}} \qquad [10.2]$$

Since the units of both numerator and denominator are those of distance, velocity ratio is a dimensionless quantity.

The velocity ratio depends solely upon the construction of the machine, and is constant for any particular machine. It can be found experimentally simply by moving the machine and measuring the distances moved by the points of application of the effort and the load and dividing the former by the latter, or it can be determined by calculation from the relevant details or dimensions of the machine, which will be shown later in this chapter.

Efficiency of a machine

The *efficiency* of a machine is defined as the ratio of the useful work done by the machine to the actual work put into the machine. Thus:

$$\text{Efficiency} = \frac{\text{Work output}}{\text{Work input}} \qquad [10.3]$$

or

$$\text{Efficiency} = \frac{\text{Work done on load}}{\text{Work done by effort}} \qquad [10.4]$$

A useful relationship exists between mechanical advantage, velocity ratio and efficiency. Since work done = force × distance, then equation [10.4] becomes:

$$\text{Efficiency} = \frac{\text{Load} \times \text{Distance moved by load}}{\text{Effort} \times \text{Distance moved by effort}}$$

$$= \frac{\text{Load}}{\text{Effort}} \div \frac{\text{Distance moved by effort}}{\text{Distance moved by load}}$$

$$= \frac{\text{Mechanical advantage}}{\text{Velocity ratio}} \qquad [10.5]$$

The efficiency is usually stated as a percentage, and the above expression should therefore be multiplied by 100 to give a percentage value.

It should be noted that since the velocity ratio of a given machine is constant, the efficiency is directly proportional to the mechanical advantage.

For an *ideal* machine, i.e. a machine having no friction, the efficiency is unity or 100 per cent, so that the *ideal* mechanical advantage is equal to the velocity ratio. Hence:

$$Ideal\,\text{effort} = \frac{\text{Load}}{\text{Velocity ratio}} \qquad [10.6]$$

and therefore,

Effort to overcome friction at a particular load
= Actual effort − Ideal effort   [10.7]

However, no machine is ideal and some work must always be done to overcome friction and other resistances. The work output therefore is always less than the amount of work put into the machine and the efficiency can never reach 100 per cent. In some cases, the machine is specifically designed so that the efficiency is less than 50 per cent, to prevent overhauling (see also Section 10.4). The idea of an ideal or perfect machine is generally used for calculating friction and other losses.

Example 10.1

A hand-operated lifting machine in a repair shop raises an engine of mass 260 kg by means of an effort of 210 N at the handle. If the effort moves through a distance of 13.5 m in raising the engine 450 mm, calculate (*a*) the force ratio, (*b*) the movement ratio and (*c*) the efficiency of the machine.

(WMAC/UEI)(Modified)

Solution

(*a*) From equation [2.4], the load is a force of *mg* newtons, i.e.

$$260\ [\text{kg}]\ \times\ 9.81\ [\text{m/s}^2]\ =\ 2551\ \text{N}$$

Force ratio (i.e. mechanical advantage)

$$= \frac{\text{Load}}{\text{Effort}} = \frac{2551}{210}\left[\frac{\text{N}}{\text{N}}\right] = 12.15$$

(*b*) Movement ratio (i.e. velocity ratio)

$$= \frac{\text{Distance moved by effort}}{\text{Distance moved by load}}$$

$$= \frac{13.5\ \times\ 1000}{450}\left[\frac{\text{mm}}{\text{mm}}\right] = 30$$

(c) Efficiency (%) $= \dfrac{\text{Force ratio}}{\text{Movement ratio}} \times 100$

$$= \dfrac{12.15}{30} \times 100 = 40.5\%$$

Answer: (a) Force ratio = 12.15
  (b) Movement ratio = 30
  (c) Efficiency of machine = 40.5%

Example 10.2

Using the data given in Example 10.1, determine:

(a) the work done on the load in moving through a vertical distance of 600 mm
(b) the distance moved by the effort to move the load through 600 mm
(c) the work done against the resistances.

Solution

(a) Work done on load = Load × Distance moved by load
  = 2551 [N] × 0.6 [m]
  = 1531 J
(b) From equation [10.2],
  Distance moved by effort
  = Distance moved by load × Velocity ratio
  = 0.6 × 30 = 18 m
(c) Work done by effort = Effort × Distance moved by effort
  = 210 [N] × 18 [m]
  = 3780 J

∴ Work done against the resistances
= Work done by effort − Work done on load
= 3780 − 1531 = 2249 J

Answer: (a) Work done on load = 1531 J
  (b) Distance moved by effort = 18 m
  (c) Work done against the resistances = 2249 J

10.3 Relationship between load and effort — The law of a machine

If an experiment is carried out on a simple machine to find the effort (P) required to overcome a load (W) and a graph of P against W is plotted for various load values, then a straight line graph, similar to that shown in Fig. 10.1, would be obtained. The relationship between the effort P and the load W is therefore of the form:

$$P = aW + b \qquad [10.8]$$

where a and b are constants whose value depends on the particular machine concerned. This equation is called the *law of the machine*. After it has been determined by experiment, it can then be used to estimate the effort which would be required to raise any load on the machine.

The value of the constant b represents the effort required to overcome the frictional resistances when there is no load on the machine, and is the intercept on the effort-load graph. The value of the constant a is the slope of the effort–load graph (V/H in Fig. 10.1), and depends on the mechanical advantage of the machine.

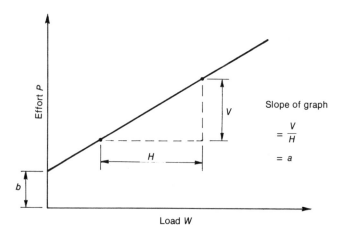

Figure 10.1   Effort–load graph for a simple machine

10.4   Limiting efficiency of a machine

The mechanical advantage of a machine varies with the load, but the velocity ratio is constant and cannot be altered without making a change to the arrangement of the machine. Since efficiency is obtained by dividing the mechanical advantage by the velocity ratio, it follows that efficiency will depend upon the load; in fact, it will be found to increase with increase of load. However, this increase in efficiency with load does not continue indefinitely, and a *limiting efficiency* is eventually reached. This is clearly illustrated by the efficiency–load graph of Fig. 10.2.

The limiting efficiency of a particular machine can be determined theoretically as follows.

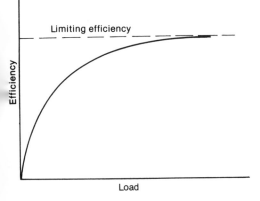

Figure 10.2 Typical efficiency–load graph for a simple machine

Mechanical advantage $= \dfrac{\text{Load } (W)}{\text{Effort } (P)}$

But from equation [10.8], effort $P = aW + b$

Hence $\text{MA} = \dfrac{W}{aW + b}$

Dividing numerator and denominator by W, gives:

$$\text{MA} = \dfrac{1}{a + (b/W)}$$

When W is large, b/W becomes small and therefore the mechanical advantage increases. When b/W becomes so small that it can be neglected, then the mechanical advantage reaches its maximum or 'limiting' value of $1/a$. The limiting value of the efficiency is then given by:

Limiting efficiency $= \dfrac{\text{Limiting mechanical advantage}}{\text{Velocity ratio}}$

$$= \dfrac{1}{a \times \text{VR}} \qquad\qquad [10.9]$$

If a lifting machine has an efficiency of less than 50 per cent, the load is self-sustaining, i.e. will not run back when the effort is removed.

Example 10.3

A lifting machine has a velocity ratio of 50. When tests were carried out on the machine, it was found that an effort of 180 N lifted a load of 2000 N while an effort of 300 N lifted a load of 5000 N.

Determine:

(a) the law of the machine, assuming it to be linear
(b) the effort, mechanical advantage and efficiency when lifting the maximum safe load of 10 000 N
(c) the limiting efficiency of the machine.

(CGLI)

Solution

(a) From equation [10.8], the law connecting the effort P and the load W is: $P = aW + b$.

$P = 180$ N when $W = 2000$ N, $\therefore 180 = 2000a + b$ [1]
$P = 300$ N when $W = 5000$ N, $\therefore 300 = 5000a + b$ [2]

To eliminate b, subtract equation [1] from [2], i.e.

$$300 = 5000a + b$$
$$180 = 2000a + b$$
$$120 = 3000a$$

$$\therefore \quad a = \frac{120}{3000} = 0.04$$

Substituting this result in equation [2], gives:

$$300 = (5000 \times 0.04) + b$$
$$\therefore \quad b = 300 - 200 = 100$$

Hence, the law of the machine is $P = 0.04W + 100$.

(b) When $W = 10\ 000$ N,

$$P = (0.04 \times 10\ 000) + 100$$
$$= 400 + 100 = 500 \text{ N}$$

Mechanical advantage $= \dfrac{\text{Load}}{\text{Effort}} = \dfrac{10\ 000}{500} \left[\dfrac{\text{N}}{\text{N}}\right] = 20$

Efficiency at this load $= \dfrac{\text{MA}}{\text{VR}}$ from equation [10.5]

$$= \frac{20}{50} = 0.4 \text{ or } 40\%$$

(c) Limiting efficiency $= \dfrac{1}{a \times \text{VR}}$ from equation [10.9]

$$= \dfrac{1}{0.04 \times 50} = 0.5 \text{ or } 50\%$$

Answer: (a)   The law of the machine is $P = 0.04W + 100$
(b)   Effort $= 500$ N, MA $= 20$. Efficiency $= 40\%$
(c)   Limiting efficiency $= 50\%$

Example 10.4

During an experiment on a lifting machine, the following values of the effort P to lift a load W were recorded:

Load, W (N)	500	1000	1500	2000	2500	3000	3500
Effort, P (N)	100	150	200	250	300	350	400

(a) Plot these values to show that the law of the machine is of the form $P = aW + b$, and determine suitable values for the constants a and b.

(b) For each load, calculate the mechanical advantage and the efficiency of the machine. Plot the graphs of mechanical advantage and efficiency on a base of load. The velocity ratio of the machine is 32.

Solution

(a) The effort–load graph is shown in Fig. 10.3. This is a straight line graph; therefore the law of the machine is of the form $P = aW + b$.

When the load W is zero, the effort required to overcome friction is 50 N. Hence, the value for the constant b is 50. The value for the constant a is obtained from the slope of the graph. Any two points A and B are therefore selected on the graph, and lines AC and BC are drawn parallel to the load and effort axes respectively as shown. Then:

$$\text{Slope of graph} = \frac{\text{BC}}{\text{AC}} = \frac{200}{2000}\left[\frac{\text{N}}{\text{N}}\right] = 0.1$$

That is, $a = 0.1$; therefore the law of the machine is $P = 0.1W + 50$.

(b) When effort P is 100 N and load $W = 500$ N:

$$\text{MA} = \frac{W}{P} = \frac{500}{100}\left[\frac{\text{N}}{\text{N}}\right] = 5$$

$$\text{Efficiency (\%)} = \frac{\text{MA}}{\text{VR}} \times 100 = \frac{5}{32} \times 100 = 15.6\%$$

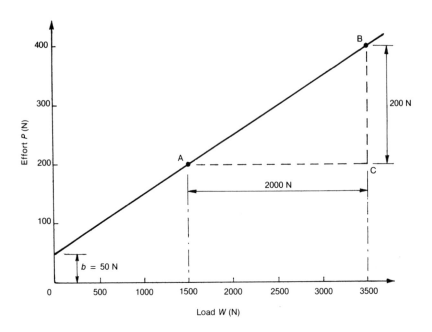

Figure 10.3 Effort–load graph – Example 10.4(*a*)

The values of the mechanical advantage and efficiency for each of the remaining loads are similarly calculated and tabulated below:

Load W (N)	0	500	1000	1500	2000	2500	3000	3500
Mechanical advantage	0	5	6.67	7.5	8	8.33	8.57	8.75
Efficiency (%)	0	15.6	20.8	23.4	25	26	26.8	27.3

These results are plotted on a base of load, as shown in Fig. 10.4.

10.5 Pulley systems

Figure 10.5 shows a *single-pulley system*. This is often used for the purpose of lifting a load in a more convenient manner by applying a *downwards* effort. The effort has to be slightly greater than the load to allow for friction in the pulley bearing and, therefore, the mechanical advantage is less than unity.

With this simple arrangement the velocity ratio is unity since the distance moved by the effort is equal to that through which the load moves in the same time.

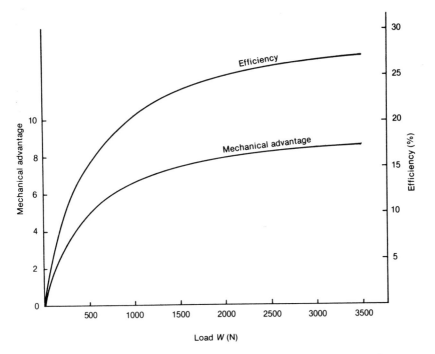

Figure 10.4 Graphs of mechanical advantage and efficiency against load — Example 10.4(*b*)

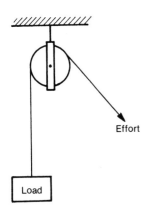

Figure 10.5 Single-pulley system

Pulley block systems are often arranged to give velocity ratios higher than unity. These consist of two blocks each with one or more pulleys mounted side by side on a common spindle. A single rope is used which passes round each pulley in turn. One end of the rope is fastened to either the upper fixed block or to the lower movable block, depending upon the number of pulleys used. The effort required to raise the load is applied at the free end of the rope, and the load is attached to the lower block.

One such arrangement is shown in Fig. 10.6. This is a *two-pulley system* so that each block is fitted with one pulley. If the load were raised by 1 m, each length of rope between the pulley blocks would have a slackness of 1 m. As there are *two* lengths of rope between the two blocks, the effort must move through a distance of 2 m in order to keep the rope taut. Hence the velocity ratio is 2.

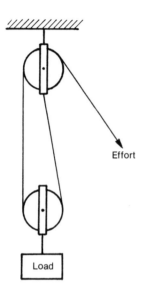

Figure 10.6   Two-pulley system

Let W be the load raised and P the effort required. If friction and the mass of the moving parts of the system are neglected, then, for an ideal machine,

$$\text{Work output} = \text{Work input}$$
i.e. Work done on load = Work done by effort
therefore $W \times 1 = P \times 2$

so that $\dfrac{W}{P} = 2 = \text{Mechanical advantage}$

Thus, the ideal mechanical advantage is 2. In practice, however, the actual mechanical advantage is less than 2, since extra effort must be applied to overcome friction in the two pulleys and the weight of the lower pulley block and rope.

A *three-pulley arrangement* is shown in Fig. 10.7. This has two pulleys fitted in the upper block and one pulley in the lower block. For clarity, the pulleys in the upper block are shown one above the other. In practice, however, they are side by side on the same spindle. In this case, there are *three* lengths of rope between the two blocks. Hence, for the load to move upwards by 1 m, these three lengths of rope must all shorten by 1 m, so that the effort must move through 3 m. Thus, the velocity ratio is now 3.

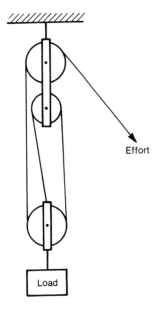

Effort

Load

Figure 10.7 Three-pulley system

The ideal mechanical advantage is also equal to 3. But, again, the actual mechanical advantage will always be less than the ideal value due to frictional losses and the mass of the moving parts.

It will be observed that the velocity ratio is equal to the number of pulleys used. Hence, in general, if n is the total number of pulleys used in the two pulley blocks, then the velocity ratio of the pulley system is n.

Example 10.5

A load of 1.26 kN is lifted by means of a pulley block system consisting of three pulleys in the upper block and two pulleys in the lower block. If the efficiency of the system at this load is 84 per cent, determine (*a*) the velocity ratio, (*b*) the mechanical advantage, (*c*) the effort required to lift the load and (*d*) the effort required to overcome the resistances.

Solution

(*a*) Velocity ratio   = Total number of pulleys in use
                      = 3 + 2 = 5

(*b*)   Efficiency (%) = $\dfrac{\text{Mechanical advantage (MA)}}{\text{Velocity ratio (VR)}} \times 100$

i.e. $84 = \dfrac{\text{MA} \times 100}{5}$

so that $\text{MA} = \dfrac{84 \times 5}{100} = 4.2$

(*c*) $\text{MA} = \dfrac{\text{Load}}{\text{Effort}}$ from equation [10.1]

∴ $\text{Effort} = \dfrac{\text{Load}}{\text{MA}} = \dfrac{1260}{4.2} = 300 \text{ N}$

(*d*)   Ideal effort $= \dfrac{\text{Load}}{\text{VR}}$ from equation [10.6]

                 $= \dfrac{1260}{5} = 252 \text{ N}$

∴ Effort required to overcome the resistances

= Actual effort − Ideal effort
= 300 − 252 = 48 N

Answer: (*a*)   VR = 5; (*b*) MA = 4.2
         (*c*)   Effort required to lift load = 300 N
         (*d*   Effort required to overcome resistances = 48 N

10.6   Weston differential pulley block

The *Weston differential pulley block* is usually chain operated and is shown diagrammatically in Fig. 10.8. This type of lifting machine gives high values of velocity ratio and is widely used in motor vehicle workshops for lifting engines and other units. It has the advantage of requiring a small length of chain in comparison with other pulley block arrangements.

In this machine, the upper block contains two pulleys of slightly different diameters rigidly connected together, while the lower movable block contains one pullley. An endless chain passes over the larger

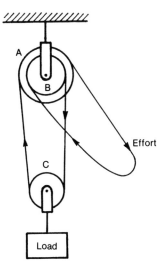

Figure 10.8 Weston differential pulley block

pulley A of the upper block, then under the movable pulley C and
finally over the smaller pulley B of the upper block.

Suppose the chain at which the effort is applied is pulled down so
that the pulleys in the upper block rotate once. Then, if D and d are
the diameters of these pulleys:

Distance moved by effort

= Length of chain moved off pulley A
= πD

Length of chain pulled up a pulley A = πD
Length of chain lowered off pulley B = πd
Net shortening of load chain = $\pi D - \pi d = \pi(D-d)$

Since the load is suspended from the loop of the chain, it follows that
it rises half this distance, i.e. $\tfrac{1}{2}\pi(D-d)$.

Now,

$$VR = \frac{\text{Distance moved by effort}}{\text{Distance moved by load}}$$

$$= \frac{\pi D}{\tfrac{1}{2}\pi(D-d)}$$

i.e. $VR = \dfrac{2D}{D-d}$ [10.10]

By making $(D-d)$ small, the velocity ratio can be made correspondingly large. As a chain is used instead of a rope, the pulleys may have either teeth or 'flats' cut into their grooves to fit the shape of the links of the chain. The diameters of the pulleys are proportional to the number of teeth or flats on each pulley. Hence, if N and n are the number of teeth or flats on the pulley A and B respectively, then:

$$VR = \frac{2N}{N-n} \qquad\qquad [10.11]$$

The efficiency of a Weston block is very low (less than 50 per cent) and, therefore, it does not overhaul or run backwards when the hand supplying the effort is withdrawn.

Example 10.6

The diameter of the small pulley of the compound block of a Weston differential chain block is 110 mm. When lifting a load of 2.4 kN the effort required is 250 N and the efficiency is 40 per cent. Find the diameter of the large pulley.

Solution

$$MA = \frac{Load}{Effort} = \frac{2400}{250}\left[\frac{N}{N}\right] = 9.6$$

$$VR = \frac{MA}{Efficiency} = \frac{9.6}{0.4} = 24$$

But from equation [10.10],

$$VR = \frac{2D}{D-d}$$

i.e. $24 = \dfrac{2D}{D-110}$

or
$$24(D-110) = 2D$$
$$24D - 2640 = 2D$$
$$22D = 2640$$
$$\therefore \qquad\qquad D = 120 \text{ mm}$$

Answer: Diameter of large pulley = 120 mm

10.7 The screw jack

The *screw jack* is a simple device, making use of a screw thread, for lifting heavy loads. The velocity ratio of a screw jack is usually fairly high and is designed to have an efficiency of less than 50 per cent, to prevent overhauling.

The jack consists of a screw mounted in an internally threaded body, as illustrated in Fig. 10.9. The effort is applied tangentially at the end of an arm or tommy bar, so that the screw is turned and the load rises.

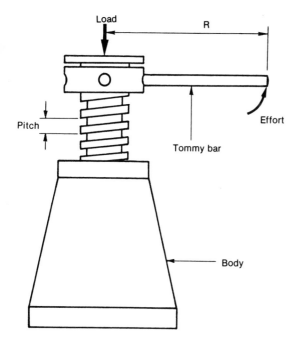

Figure 10.9   The screw jack

If the radius of the tommy bar is R, then, when the screw is turned through one revolution, the effort moves through a distance of $2\pi R$. At the same time, the load rises a distance equal to the *lead L* of the screw. (For a single-start thread the lead is equal to the pitch of the thread.) Hence, the velocity ratio of a screw jack is given by:

$$VR = \frac{2\pi R}{L} \qquad [10.12]$$

Note: The pitch is the distance between successive threads on a screw (see Fig. 10.9). For a screw thread having n starts, lead $= n \times$ pitch.

Example 10.7

A screw jack has a two-start thread of pitch 5 mm. An effort of 40 N is applied tangentially to the tommy bar, at a radius of 350 mm, to lift a load of 2200 N.

(a) Calculate the efficiency of the screw jack.

(b) Calculate the work done in overcoming friction when the load is raised a distance of 75 mm.

Solution

(a) For a two-start thread,

Lead of screw, $L = 2 \times$ Pitch $= 2 \times 5 = 10$ mm

$$\text{VR} = \frac{2\pi R}{L} \qquad \text{from equation [10.12]}$$

$$= \frac{2 \times 22 \times 350}{7 \times 10} \left[\frac{\text{mm}}{\text{mm}} \right] = 220$$

$$\text{MA} = \frac{\text{Load}}{\text{Effort}} = \frac{2200}{40} \left[\frac{\text{N}}{\text{N}} \right] = 55$$

$$\text{Efficiency (\%)} = \frac{\text{MA}}{\text{VR}} \times 100 = \frac{55 \times 100}{220} = 25\%$$

(b) Work done to raise the load by 75 mm

= Force $\times$ Vertical distance moved
= 2200 [N] $\times$ 0.075 [m] $=$ 165 J

This is the work output. Hence, from equation [10.3],

$$\text{Work input} = \frac{\text{Work output}}{\text{Efficiency}} = \frac{165}{0.25} = 660 \text{ J}$$

Now,
Work done in overcoming friction

= Work input − Work output
= 660 − 165 = 495 J

Answer: (a)   Efficiency of screw jack = 25%
  (b)   Work done in overcoming friction = 495 J

10.8   Levers

A *lever* is a simple machine which operates on the principle of moments. It is simply a rigid bar, straight or cranked, which can be turned about a pivot or fulcrum. The lever may be either one of three types or 'orders', depending on the relative positions of the fulcrum, the load and the effort. A lever of the first order has the fulcrum situated between the effort and the load, as shown in Fig. 10.10(a). A lever of the second order has the load placed between the fulcrum and the effort, as shown in Fig. 10.10(b). A lever of the third order has the effort applied between the fulcrum and the load, as shown in Fig. 10.10(c).

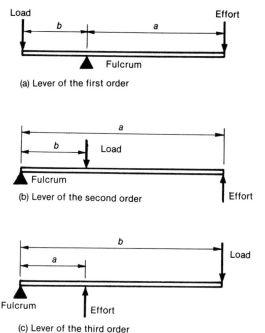

(a) Lever of the first order

(b) Lever of the second order

(c) Lever of the third order

Figure 10.10 Types or orders of lever

In all cases, if the lever is in equilibrium, the clockwise moment about the fulcrum is equal to the anticlockwise moment about the same point.

Effort × a = Load × b

i.e. $\dfrac{\text{Load}}{\text{Effort}} = \dfrac{a}{b}$ = Mechanical advantage

Now consider the lever system shown in Fig. 10.10(a). Suppose the lever is tilted clockwise through an angle θ radians, as shown in Fig. 10.11. Then the distance moved by the effort is the arc length BD, i.e. $a\theta$, and the distance moved by the load is the arc length AC, i.e. $b\theta$. Hence:

$$\text{Velocity ratio} = \frac{\text{Distance moved by effort}}{\text{Distance moved by load}}$$

$$= \frac{a\theta}{b\theta} = \frac{a}{b}$$

Thus, neglecting friction losses,

Mechanical advantage = Velocity ratio

$$= \frac{\text{Distance between effort and fulcrum}}{\text{Distance between load and fulcrum}}$$

In levers of the second order, the mechanical advantage is always greater than unity, whereas in levers of the third order the ratio is always less than unity; the object of using the latter type of lever is just convenience.

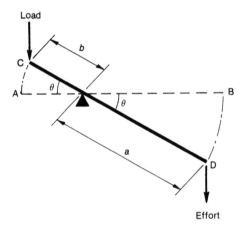

Figure 10.11 First order lever rotated through an angle θ radians

Example 10.8
A footbrake pedal is in the form of a lever as shown in Fig. 10.12. The distance from the fulcrum to the brake master cylinder rod connection is 60 mm, and from the fulcrum to the point where the driver's effort is applied is 400 mm. Neglecting friction, determine the force F in the master cylinder rod when the driver applies an effort of 360 N.

(WMAC/UEI)

Solution
Neglecting friction, and taking moments about the fulcrum, we get:

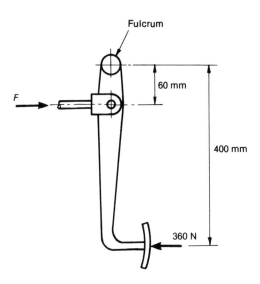

Figure 10.12 Footbrake pedal − Example 10.8

$F \times 60$ [mm] $= 360$ [N] $\times 400$ [mm]

$\therefore \qquad F = \dfrac{360 \times 400}{60} \left[\dfrac{N \times mm}{mm} \right]$

$\qquad\qquad = 2400 \text{ N} = 2.4 \text{ kN}$

Answer: Force *F* in master cylinder rod = 2.4 kN

10.9 Gear systems

Gear systems are used to transmit rotary motion and power from one shaft to another. A gearwheel has a number of specially shaped projections or 'teeth' around its periphery. These teeth mesh with a similar set of teeth on an adjacent gearwheel so that motion can be transferred from one wheel to the other without any slip taking place.

Figure 10.3 shows the general arrangement of two gearwheels A and B in mesh. If the power input is on gearwheel A, then this wheel is called a *driver gear* and wheel B a *follower* or *driven gear*.

Suppose there are 60 teeth on gearwheel A and 30 teeth on B. Then, when a total of 60 teeth have meshed together, wheel A will have made 60/60, or 1 revolution, and wheel B will have made 60/30, or 2 revolutions. The gearwheel having the smaller number of teeth rotates the faster of the two. It follows, therefore, that the rotational speeds of two gearwheels in mesh are inversely proportional to the numbers of teeth on the wheels.

Hence, if T_A, T_B = number of teeth on gearwheels A, B
and N_A, N_B = speed of rotation of gearwheels A, B

then

$$\frac{N_A}{N_B} = \frac{T_B}{T_A}$$ [10.13]

From equation [10.13], we may write:

$$\text{Velocity ratio} = \frac{\text{Speed of rotation of driver wheel}}{\text{Speed of rotation of driven wheel}}$$

$$= \frac{\text{Number of teeth on driven wheel}}{\text{Number of teeth on driver wheel}}$$

As applied to gearing, the term 'velocity ratio' is referred to as the 'gear ratio'.

Use of idler wheel

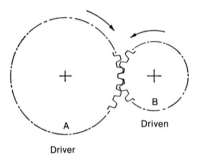

A   Driver

B   Driven

Figure 10.13 Two gearwheels in mesh. Wheels rotate in opposite directions

It will be observed from Fig. 10.13 that when two gearwheels are in mesh, the direction of rotation of one wheel is opposite to that of the other. If it is required that the driver and driven wheels should rotate in the same direction, an *idler wheel* C is placed between them, as shown in Fig. 10.14. The velocity ratio between wheels A and B will not be affected by the number of teeth on the idler wheel. This is shown below.

Let the number of teeth on the idler wheel be T_C and its speed of rotation be N_C.

Considering wheels A and C:

$$\frac{N_A}{N_C} = \frac{T_C}{T_A}, \text{ i.e. } N_C = N_A \times \frac{T_A}{T_C}$$ [10.14]

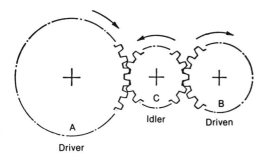

Figure 10.14 Use of idler wheel. The function of this wheel is to reverse the direction of rotation of the driven wheel

Considering wheels C and B:

$$\frac{N_C}{N_B} = \frac{T_B}{T_C}, \text{ i.e. } N_B = N_C \times \frac{T_C}{T_B} \qquad [10.15]$$

Substituting N_C from equation [10.14] in equation [10.15], gives:

$$N_B = N_A \times \frac{T_A}{T_C} \times \frac{T_C}{T_B} = N_A \times \frac{T_A}{T_B}$$

or $\dfrac{N_A}{N_B} = \dfrac{T_B}{T_A}$ which is same as equation [10.13]

That is, the velocity ratio between the driver wheel A and the driven wheel B is *independent* of the number of teeth on the idler wheel. The only function of this wheel is to make wheel B rotate in the same direction as wheel A (or to increase the centre distance of the shafts of A and B).

Compound gear trains

In a *single gear train* each gearwheel meshes directly with the next one. The simplest gearing of this type consists of two gearwheels only, as in Fig. 10.13. Next comes that with three gearwheels, as in Fig. 10.14. When two of the gearwheels in a train are fixed to the same shaft, such as B and C in Fig. 10.15, then the arrangement is known as a *compound gear train*. If the number of teeth on each wheel is known, the relationship between the speed of wheels A and D can be determined as follows.

For wheels A and B: $\dfrac{N_A}{N_B} = \dfrac{T_B}{T_A}$, i.e. $N_B = N_A \times \dfrac{T_A}{T_B}$

Wheels B and C are fixed to the same shaft, so that $N_C = N_B$.

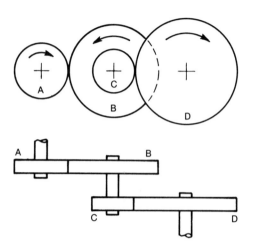

Figure 10.15 A compound gear train

For wheels C and D: $\dfrac{N_C}{N_D} = \dfrac{T_D}{T_C}$, i.e. $N_D = N_C \times \dfrac{T_C}{T_D}$

Substituting $N_C = N_B = N_A \times T_A/T_B$ from above, we get:

$$N_D = N_A \times \frac{T_A}{T_B} \times \frac{T_C}{T_D}$$

or $\qquad \dfrac{N_A}{N_D} = \dfrac{T_B}{T_A} \times \dfrac{T_D}{T_C}$ [10.16]

By inspection of the layout of Fig. 10.15, it will be observed that wheels A and C are driver gears while B and D are driven gears. Hence, from equation [10.16]:

Velocity or gear ratio $= \dfrac{\text{Product of teeth on driven gears}}{\text{Product of teeth on driver gears}}$

Example 10.9

A motor shaft, rotating at 1000 rev/min, has a gearwheel A with 30 teeth fixed to it. This meshes with a gearwheel B on another shaft which requires to rotate at 600 rev/min. Calculate the number of teeth on the second gearwheel.

Solution

Let T_A and T_B be the number of teeth and N_A and N_B the speed of rotation on the motor and shafting gearwheels respectively. Then, from equation [10.13]:

$$\frac{N_A}{N_B} = \frac{T_B}{T_A}$$

i.e. $T_B = \frac{N_A}{N_B} \times T_A = \frac{1000}{600} \times 30 = 50$ teeth

Answer: Number of teeth on gear wheel B = 50

Example 10.10

A double reduction set of gearing is as shown in Fig. 10.15. Wheel A is the driver gear, wheels B and C are fixed to the same shaft and wheel D is the final gear in the train. The number of teeth on each wheel is: A, 20 teeth; B, 50 teeth; C, 40 teeth; and D, 30 teeth.

(a) Determine the velocity ratio of the gearing system.
(b) Calculate the speed of rotation of wheel D when wheel A rotates at 1800 rev/min.

Solution

(a) From equation [10.16],

Velocity ratio = $\dfrac{\text{Product of teeth on driven gears}}{\text{Product of teeth on driver gears}}$

i.e. $VR = \dfrac{T_B \times T_D}{T_A \times T_C}$

$= \dfrac{50 \times 30}{20 \times 40} = 1.875$

(b) Again, from equation [10.16],

$VR = \dfrac{N_A}{N_D}$ where N refers to the speed of rotation

$\therefore N_D = \dfrac{N_A}{VR} = \dfrac{1800}{1.875} = 960$ rev/min

Answer: (a) VR of gearing system = 1.875
(b) Speed of rotation of wheel D = 960 rev/min

Exercise 10.1 – Review questions

1 The force ratio of a simple machine is given by $\dfrac{\cdots\cdots}{\cdots\cdots}$

164

2 The movement ratio of a simple machine is given by $\dfrac{\cdots\cdots}{\cdots\cdots}$

3 Explain what is meant by the efficiency of a machine.

4 Give reasons why the efficiency of a machine can never be 100 per cent.

5 Write down the relationship between mechanical advantage, velocity ratio and efficiency.

6 With regard to a lifting machine, complete the following expression:

$$\text{Limited efficiency} = \frac{\cdots\cdots}{\cdots\cdots}$$

7 For an ideal machine: Ideal effort $= \dfrac{\text{Load}}{\cdots\cdots}$

8 With regard to a simple machine, the relationship between the effort P and the load W is: $P = \cdots\cdots$

9 State and explain the conditions under which a simple lifting machine will overhaul, i.e. reverse under load.

10 Write down the formula for determining the velocity ratio of a Weston differential pulley block.

11 Write down the formula for determining the velocity ratio of a screw jack.

12 A lever is a simple machine which operates on the principle of $\cdots\cdots$

13 Give one example of each of the orders of lever.

14 Cross out the incorrect alternative so as to leave a correct statement:
When two gearwheels are in mesh their speed of rotation is *directly/inversely* proportional to their number of teeth.

15 If a driver gearwheel having 25 teeth is connected to a follower gear having 75 teeth, then for each revolution of the follower gear the driver gear makes $\cdots\cdots$ revolutions.

16 If an idler gear is interposed between two gears, what effect does it have on
(*a*) the direction of rotation
(*b*) the gear ratio of the two gears?

(NWRAC/ULCI)

17 With the aid of diagrams, distinguish between a simple gear train and a compound gear train.

Exercise 10.2 − Problems

1 In a chain-operated lifting gear the chain moves 4 m when lifting an engine through a vertical distance of 80 mm. The mass of the engine is equivalent to a force of 2 kN. If the steady pull exerted by the operator was 100 N, calculate:

(*a*) the movement ratio (velocity ratio)

(*b*) the force ratio (mechanical advantage)

(*c*) the efficiency of the machine.

2 A car lift has a movement ratio of 6 and can lift a mass of 900 kg when the effort is 2000 N. Calculate:

(*a*) the efficiency of the lift

(*b*) the effort required to overcome friction

(*c*) the work done against the resistances if the mass is raised 1.5 m.

(Assume a mass of 1 kg to have a weight of 10 N.)

3 When operated by an effort of 200 N a lifting machine has an efficiency of 40 per cent. If the velocity ratio is 80, calculate the load that can be lifted by this effort.

4 A machine on test required an effort of 142 N to raise a load of 2100 N, while an effort of 280 N lifted a load of 9000 N. The velocity ratio of the machine was 150. If the load−effort relationship is a straight line, what would be the probable effort required to raise a load of 6000 N and the efficiency at this load?

Show that the machine is self-sustaining (irreversible) for all loads.

5 A simple lifting machine has a velocity ratio of 24. On test it is found that an effort of 75 N will lift a load of 1100 N, and that an effort of 120 N will lift a load of 2000 N. Determine:

(*a*) the law of the machine, assuming it to be linear

(*b*) the effort and efficiency when lifting a load of 3000 N

(*c*) the limiting efficiency.

6 The following results were obtained in an experiment on a lifting machine:

Load W (N)	100	200	300	400	500
Effort P (N)	15	24	35	46	55

(*a*) Plot these results on a graph and deduce the law of the machine.

(*b*) Draw a graph of mechanical advantage against load.

7 In an experiment with a lifting machine having a velocity ratio of 30, the following results were obtained:

Load W (N)	200	400	600	800	1000	1200
Effort P (N)	24	39	52	65	80	94

Determine the efficiency at each load and then plot graphs having

load as the base to show the relationship between (a) load and effort and (b) load and efficiency.
Determine also the law of the machine.

8 An engine pulley block consists of three pulleys and is used to lift an engine which exerts a downward force of 1500 N. If friction absorbs 50 per cent of the effort required to raise the load, determine (a) the velocity ratio, (b) the effort applied, (c) the mechanical advantage and (d) the efficiency of the machine.

(NWRAC/ULCI)(Modified)

9 A load having a mass of 50 kg is lifted by applying an effort of 280 N to a four-pulley system. Determine:
(a) the efficiency of the machine
(b) the amount of work which must be done by the effort to lift the load through 1.5 m.
(Take $g = 9.8$ m/s^2.)

(CGLI)

10 A lifting machine consists of two pulley blocks, the upper block having three pulleys and the lower one having two. Calculate:
(a) the load which can be lifted by an effort of 150 N if the efficiency at this load is 80 per cent
(b) the work output if the load is raised a distance of 0.75 m.

11 In a Weston differential chain block, the chain wheel has 27 and 24 teeth respectively. Calculate the velocity ratio, mechanical advantage and efficiency when lifting a load of 1.89 kN if the effort required is 300 N.

12 The diameter of the large pulley of a set of differential pulley blocks is 140 mm. When lifting a load of 560 N the effort required is 50 N, and the efficiency is 40 per cent. Find the diameter of the small pulley.

13 A screw jack has a thread of 6 mm pitch. An effort of 80 N applied at a radius of 420 mm is just sufficient to move a load of 8.8 kN. Calculate:
(a) the efficiency of the jack
(b) the work done on the load to raise it by 50 mm
(c) the work done in overcoming friction when raising the load by 50 mm.

14 A screw jack has a two-start thread of 4 mm pitch and an operating lever 490 mm in length. If the efficiency of the jack is 40 per cent, calculate the load that can be raised when an effort of 50 N is applied to the end of the operating lever.

15 (a) A simple screw jack has a thread of lead 5 mm. If the effort is applied at an effective radius of 210 mm, determine the velocity ratio.
(b) It is found that the jack can lift a load W of 500 N when the effort P is 20 N, and that W is 1000 N when P is 30 N. Presuming that P and W are related by a law of the type $P =$

$aW + b$, determine, when the load is 1500 N, (*i*) the effort, (*ii*) the mechanical advantage and (*iii*) the efficiency of the jack.

(CGLI)

16 A lever AB is 0.8 m long and is pivoted at a point 0.2 m from A. An effort of 150 N is applied at B to overcome a load of 405 N acting at A.
   (*a*) Determine the velocity ratio, mechanical advantage and the efficiency of the lever.
   (*b*) If the lever were mounted on a frictionless pivot, what effort would be required to lift the load?

17 A footbrake pedal is straight and the distance from the pedal pad centre to the fulcrum is 200 mm. The brake rod is attached to the pedal at a distance of 50 mm from the fulcrum. Calculate the pull in the brake rod which is at 90° to the pedal when a force of 270 N is applied at right angles to the pedal pad.

(NWRAC/ULCI)

18 A shaft, rotating at 480 rev/min, has a gearwheel with 25 teeth fixed to it. This meshes with another gearwheel on a parallel shaft which has to rotate at 200 rev/min. Determine the number of teeth on the gearwheel of the second shaft.

19 Three gearwheels A, B and C on parallel shafts are in mesh. The number of teeth on each of the wheels is: A, 24 teeth; B, 72 teeth; and C, 96 teeth. If wheel A is rotating clockwise at 600 rev/min, determine:
   (*a*) the speed and direction of rotation of wheel B, (*b*) the speed and direction of rotation of wheel C. Show that the velocity ratio between wheels A and C is independent of the number of teeth on wheel B.

20 In a double-reduction gear train similar to that shown in Fig. 10.15, wheels A, B and C have 14, 30 and 16 teeth respectively. Determine the number of teeth on wheel D if it rotates at 560 rev/min when wheel A rotates at 2100 rev/min.

21 A compound gear train consists of an input gear A with 32 teeth which meshes with gear B having 20 teeth. Gearwheels B and C are attached to the same shaft. Gear C has 40 teeth and meshes with the output gear D having 16 teeth. Determine:
   (*a*) the velocity of the gear system
   (*b*) the speed of rotation of D when A is driven at 300 rev/min.

Chapter 11

Vehicle transmission and steering

11.1 Introduction

In this chapter we shall determine the gear ratio, torque ratio and efficiency of vehicle gearboxes, rear axles and steering boxes. We shall also
determine, without dismantling any of the components, the overall gear
ratio of a vehicle, and gearbox gear ratios in each gear.

   The vehicle transmission and steering components mentioned above
are all types of machine because they can modify and deliver the
energy they received into a form suitable for their particular functions.

Laboratory experiments

It is worth carrying out simple experiments in the laboratory on vehicle
gearboxes, rear axles and steering boxes to determine their force ratio
or torque ratio (see Section 11.6), movement ratio and efficiency. The
results given in the following example were obtained during an experiment of this kind carried out on a conventional gearbox, with second
gear engaged. The gearbox was supported on a stand and identical
pulleys were fitted on both the input and output shafts. When a
'weight' (this is the applied force or effort) was hung on the input shaft
it caused a load to be raised by the output shaft.

Example 11.1

A test gearbox was arranged with a pulley on the input shaft and
another pulley of the same diameter on the output shaft. With second

gear selected, it was found that a load of 40 N was raised 50 mm by applying an effort of 10 N moving through 250 mm. Calculate:

(a) the force ratio (or mechanical advantage)
(b) the movement ratio (or velocity ratio)
(c) the efficiency of the gearbox in second gear.

Solution

The arrangement is shown in Fig. 11.1.

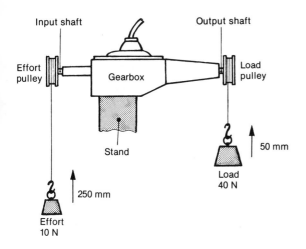

Figure 11.1 Determination of force ratio, movement ratio and mechanical efficiency of a gearbox − Example 11.1

(a) By equation [10.1],

$$\text{Force ratio} = \frac{\text{Load}}{\text{Effort}} = \frac{40}{10}\left[\frac{N}{N}\right] = 4$$

(b) By equation [10.2],

$$\text{Movement ratio} = \frac{\text{Distance moved by effort}}{\text{Distance moved by load}}$$

$$= \frac{250}{50}\left[\frac{mm}{mm}\right] = 5$$

(c) By equation [10.3],
Efficiency (%) of gearbox in second gear

$$= \frac{\text{Force ratio}}{\text{Movement ratio}} \times 100$$

$$= \frac{4}{5} \times 100 = 80\%$$

Answer: (*a*)   Force ratio = 4; (*b*) **Movement ratio = 5**
(*c*)   Efficiency of gearbox in second gear = 80%

11.2   Gearbox gear ratio

The gear ratios of a motor vehicle gearbox are generally obtained by compound gear trains (see Section 10.9). In its simplest form, a compound gear train, as used in a vehicle gearbox, is shown in Fig. 11.2. By inspection of this arrangement, it will be seen that A and C are driver gears and B and D are driven gears.

From equation [10.16], the gear (reduction) ratio of such an arrangement is calculated as follows:

$$\text{Gear ratio} = \frac{\text{Product of teeth on driven gears}}{\text{Product of teeth on driver gears}}$$

Example 11.2

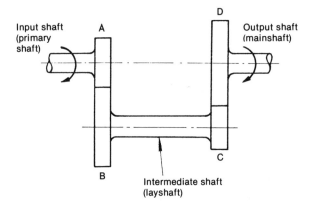

Figure 11.2   Compound gear train

A gearbox is driven in second gear. The layout is similar to that shown in Fig. 11.2 where the constant-mesh pinions A and B have 15 and 32 teeth respectively. The second gear pinion D on the mainshaft has 30 teeth and meshes with the layshaft gear C having 16 teeth. Calculate (*a*) the second gear ratio and (*b*) the propeller shaft speed for an engine speed of 4000 rev/min.

Solution

(*a*) Gearbox ratio in second gear

$$= \frac{\text{Product of teeth on driven gears}}{\text{Product of teeth on driver gears}}$$

$$= \frac{\text{Teeth on layshaft constant-mesh pinion B}}{\text{Teeth on input shaft pinion A}}$$

$$\times \frac{\text{Teeth on mainshaft second gear D}}{\text{Teeth on layshaft second gear C}}$$

$$= \frac{32}{15} \times \frac{30}{16} = 4 \text{ to } 1$$

(b) Propeller shaft speed $= \dfrac{\text{Engine speed}}{\text{Gear ratio}}$

$$= \frac{4000}{4} = 1000 \text{ rev/min}$$

Answer: (a)   Second gear ratio = 4 to 1
(b)   Propeller shaft speed = 1000 rev/min

11.3   Rear-axle ratio

When the rear axle of a motor vehicle is fitted with bevel gears, i.e. a crown wheel and pinion, the rear-axle or final-drive ratio is given by:

$$\text{Rear-axle ratio} = \frac{\text{No. of teeth on crown wheel}}{\text{No. of teeth on bevel pinion}} \qquad [11.1]$$

For heavy commercial vehicles where the rear-axle drive is usually of the worm and wheel type, the rear-axle ratio is given by:

$$\text{Rear-axle ratio} = \frac{\text{No. of teeth on worm wheel}}{\text{No. of starts on worm}} \qquad [11.2]$$

Example 11.3

The rear axle of a motor vehicle is fitted with a crown wheel which has 72 teeth and the corresponding bevel pinion has 17 teeth. Determine the rear-axle reduction ratio.

Solution

A simple bevel pinion and crown wheel arrangement is shown in Fig. 11.3.

$$\text{Rear-axle ratio} = \frac{\text{No. of teeth on crown wheel}}{\text{No. of teeth on bevel pinion}}$$

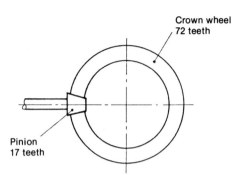

Figure 11.3 Rear drive layout (bevel pinion and crown wheel) –
Example 11.3

$$= \frac{72}{17} = 4.235 \text{ to } 1$$

Answer: Rear-axle reduction ratio = 4.235 to 1

Example 11.4

A four-start worm is driven by a propeller shaft at 2500 rev/min and
meshes with a worm wheel on the rear-axle shafts. The worm wheel has
21 teeth. Calculate the speed of the vehicle, in km/h if the effective
diameter of the road wheels is 0.7 m.

(WMAC/UEI)(Modified)

Solution
By equation [11.2],

$$\text{Rear-axle ratio} = \frac{\text{No. of teeth on worm wheel}}{\text{No. of starts on worm}}$$

$$= \frac{21}{4} = 5.25 \text{ to } 1$$

$$\text{Angular speed of road wheels} = \frac{\text{Propeller shaft speed}}{\text{Rear-axle ratio}}$$

$$= \frac{2500}{5.25} = 476 \text{ rev/min}$$

Linear speed of wheels = Angular speed × Circumference of wheels
= 476 × π × 0.7 m/min

$$= \frac{476 \times \pi \times 0.7 \times 60}{1000} = 62.83 \text{ km/h}$$

Neglecting slip between tyres and road, the vehicle road speed is equal to the linear speed of the driving wheels.

Answer: Speed of vehicle = 62.83 km/h

11.4 Overall gear ratio

The overall gear ratio is the product of the gearbox ratio and the rear-axle ratio, i.e.,

Overall gear ratio = Gearbox ratio × Rear-axle ratio   [11.3]

In the case of a normal arrangement without overdrive, the overall gear ratio in top gear (direct drive) is the same as the rear-axle reduction ratio.

Example 11.5

A vehicle has a third gear ratio of 1.5 to 1 and a rear-axle ratio of 4.5 to 1. Calculate (*a*) the overall gear ratio and (*b*) the number of revolutions made by the crown wheel per minute if the engine speed is 2700 rev/min.

Solution

(*a*) By equation [11.3],

Overall gear ratio = Gearbox ratio × Rear-axle ratio
= 1.5 × 4.5 = 6.75 to 1

(*b*) Number of revolutions made by the crown wheel per minute

$$= \frac{\text{Engine speed (rev/min)}}{\text{Overall gear ratio}} = \frac{2700}{6.75} = 400$$

Answer: (*a*)   Overall gear ratio = 6.75 to 1
   (*b*)   Revolutions made by crown wheel/min = 400

11.5 Practical determination of the gearbox and rear-axle ratios of a vehicle without dismantling any of these components

Procedure

1. Remove the engine sparking plugs and jack up *one* rear wheel just clear of the ground.
2. Put a chalk mark on the tyre of the jacked-up wheel and another one on the ground to line up with it.
3. Engage the top gear of the gearbox.

4. Using a starting handle, rotate the engine crankshaft until the jacked-up wheel has made *two* complete revolutions. At the same time, count the number of rotations made by the starting handle.
5. Assuming a top gear ratio of 1 to 1, the rear-axle ratio will be equal to the number of rotations made by the starting handle for two complete revolutions of the jacked-up rear wheel.
6. Now engage first gear and repeat procedure 4. This gives the overall gear ratio in first gear. The first gear ratio of the gearbox will then be found from equation [11.3] by dividing the overall gear ratio by the rear-axle ratio.
7. Repeat for the other gear ratios of the gearbox, including reverse, and proceed as in step 6.

It should be noted that while one driving wheel is jacked up and the other is stationary, the differential causes the jacked-up wheel to rotate at twice its normal rate. This is why it is necessary to consider two complete revolutions of the jacked-up rear wheel when finding the various gear ratios.

Example 11.6

The gear ratio of the final drive, being in doubt, is checked by jacking up one wheel and putting the gear lever in direct gear; the number of turns of the starting handle corresponding to 10 revolutions of the raised wheel is 25. What is the rear-axle ratio?

(CGLI)

Solution

For 10 revolutions of the raised wheel, the starting handle rotates 25 times; thus, for 2 revolutions of the raised wheel, the starting handle rotates 5 times. Hence, the rear-axle ratio is 5 to 1.

Alternatively, the rear-axle ratio can be determined as follows:

$$\text{Rear-axle ratio} = \frac{\text{No. of turns of starting handle} \times 2}{\text{No. of turns of jacked-up wheel}}$$

$$= \frac{25 \times 2}{10} = 5 \text{ to } 1$$

Answer: Rear-axle ratio = 5 to 1

Example 11.7

A car has one of its rear wheels jacked up clear of the ground. With top gear engaged, the engine is turned by hand and it is found to make 11 turns while the jacked-up rear wheel turns 4 times. With first gear engaged, 19 turns of the engine correspond to 2 turns of the road wheel. Assuming direct drive through the gearbox in top gear, calculate the rear-axle ratio and the first gear ratio of the gearbox.

(CGLI)

Solution

With top gear engaged,

$$\text{Rear-axle ratio} = \frac{\text{No. of turns of engine shaft} \times 2}{\text{No. of turns of jacked-up wheel}}$$

$$= \frac{11 \times 2}{4} = 5.5 \text{ to } 1$$

Similarly, with first gear engaged,

$$\text{Overall gear ratio} = \frac{\text{No. of turns of engine shaft} \times 2}{\text{No. of turns of jacked-up wheel}}$$

$$= \frac{19 \times 2}{2} = 19 \text{ to } 1$$

From equation [11.3],

$$\text{Gearbox ratio in first gear} = \frac{\text{Overall gear ratio}}{\text{Rear-axle ratio}}$$

$$= \frac{19}{5.5} = 3.455 \text{ to } 1$$

Answer: Rear-axle ratio = 5.5 to 1
First gear ratio of gearbox = 3.455 to 1

11.6 Torque ratio

As applied to gearing, the torque ratio is given by:

$$\text{Torque ratio} = \frac{\text{Output torque}}{\text{Input torque}} \qquad [11.4]$$

The torque acting on a pair of engaging gears is inversely proportional to their speeds of rotation. In other words, a decrease in speed in the output shaft of a gearbox is accompanied by an increase in torque, which is exactly what is required for driving heavy loads up hills, or moving a vehicle from rest.

If the efficiency is 100 per cent,

Input torque × Input speed = Output torque × Output speed

or $\dfrac{\text{Output torque}}{\text{Input torque}} = \dfrac{\text{Input speed}}{\text{Output speed}}$ [11.5]

so that, from equation [10.13], we may write:

Torque ratio = Speed ratio = Gear ratio [11.6]

In practice, however, there is always a certain amount of friction between the teeth of the gears and also in the bearings which support the shafts to which the gears are fixed, so that the value of the output torque for a given value of the input torque will be reduced. The efficiency of the gearing is then given by:

Efficiency (%) = $\dfrac{\text{Torque ratio}}{\text{Gear ratio}} \times 100$ [11.7]

Example 11.8

A gearbox has a reduction ratio of 5 to 1 when a certain gear is engaged. If the torque input to the gearbox is 70 N m, what torque will be available at the output shaft?
(Neglect frictional losses.)

Solution

Since frictional losses are neglected,

Torque ratio = Gear ratio = 5 to 1

From equation [11.4],

Torque on output shaft = Input torque × Torque ratio
= 70 × 5 = 350 N m

Answer: Torque on output shaft = 350 N m

Example 11.9

A motor vehicle gearbox has a first gear ratio of 3.75 to 1. The input shaft of the gearbox runs at 2400 rev/min with an input torque of 150 N m. The efficiency of the gearing is 80 per cent. Calculate (a) the speed of the output shaft and (b) the output torque.

Solution

(a) Speed of output shaft = $\dfrac{\text{Input speed}}{\text{Gear ratio}}$

$= \dfrac{2400}{3.75} = 640$ rev/min

(*b*) From equations [11.4] and [11.7],

Output torque = Input torque × Gear ratio × Efficiency

$$= 150 \times 3.75 \times \frac{80}{100} = 450 \text{ N m}$$

Answer: (*a*)   Speed of output shaft = 640 rev/min
   (*b*)   Output torque = 450 N m

Example 11.10

A motor vehicle gearbox on test, using a 2 to 1 ratio, gave the following results:

Input torque (N m)	50	100	150	250
Output torque (N m)	80	180	280	480

Plot a graph of input torque on a base of output torque and find the efficiency of the gearbox when the input torque is 200 N m.

(EMEU)(Modified)

Solution

The above values of input torque and output torque are plotted to give a straight line graph, as shown in Fig. 11.4.

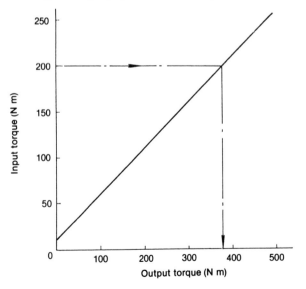

Figure 11.4   Example 11.10

From the graph, when the input torque is 200 N m, the output torque is 380 N m.

$$\text{Torque ratio} \ = \ \frac{\text{Output torque}}{\text{Input torque}} \ = \ \frac{380 \text{ N m}}{200 \text{ N m}} \ = \ 1.9 \text{ to } 1$$

$$\text{Efficiency (\%)} \ = \ \frac{\text{Torque ratio}}{\text{Gear ratio}} \times 100 \ = \ \frac{1.9}{2} \times 100 \ = \ 95\%$$

Answer: Efficiency when input torque is 200 N m $= 95\%$

Example 11.11
An engine develops a torque of 104 N m at 250 rev/min and drives through a gearbox having constant-mesh gears of 15 and 30 teeth respectively. The second gearwheel on the mainshaft has 36 teeth and the meshing pinion has 18 teeth. The rear-axle ratio is 5 to 1 and the effective radius of the tyres is 0.42 m. If the overall transmission efficiency is 85 per cent, calculate:

(*a*) the speed of the vehicle in second gear
(*b*) the torque in **each** half-shaft.

Solution
Second gear ratio of the gearbox

$$= \ \frac{\text{Product of number of teeth on driven gears}}{\text{Product of number of teeth on driver gears}}$$

$$= \ \frac{30 \times 36}{15 \times 18} \ = \ 4 \text{ to } 1$$

Overall gear ratio = Gearbox ratio × Rear-axle ratio
$$= 4 \times 5 = 20 \text{ to } 1$$

Speed of road wheels in second gear

$$= \ \frac{\text{Engine speed}}{\text{Overall gear ratio}} \ = \ \frac{2500}{20} \ = \ 125 \text{ rev/min}$$

Linear speed of road wheels

= Angular speed × Circumference
= 125 × 2π × 0.42 m/min

$$= \ \frac{125 \times 2\pi \times 0.42 \times 60}{1000} \ = \ 19.8 \text{ km/h}$$

Assuming no slip between the tyres and road, the vehicle speed is equal to the linear speed of the wheels.

Torque delivered to rear axle in second gear

= Engine torque × Overall gear ratio × Efficiency

$$= 104 \times 20 \times \frac{85}{100} = 1768 \text{ N m}$$

The differential divides the torque of the final drive equally between each axle half-shaft irrespective of the speed of the driving wheels. Hence,
Torque in each axle half-shaft when driving in second gear

$$= \frac{1768}{2} = 884 \text{ N m}$$

Answer: (*a*)   Speed of vehicle in second gear = 19.8 km/h
(*b*)   Torque in each half-shaft = 884 N m

11.7 Steering box calculations

The purpose of the steering box is to provide a gear reduction between the steering wheel and the front wheels, and so enable the driver to steer the vehicle with a relatively small effort applied to the steering wheel. The gear ratio is generally between 8 and 24 to 1, the actual value however is dependent upon the type and mass of the vehicle. Heavy vehicles usually require a high gear ratio to enable the driver to steer the vehicle with comparative ease, while light cars may require only three-quarters to one and a half turns of the steering wheel to move the front wheels from the straight ahead to the full lock position.

Gear ratio (or movement ratio)
If the number of turns of the steering wheel required to move the drop arm from the straight ahead to the position of full lock are known, then the gear ratio (or movement ratio) of the steering box can be calculated as follows:

Gear ratio of steering box

$$= \frac{360 \times \text{No. of turns of steering wheel}}{\text{No. of degrees turned through by drop arm}} \qquad [11.8]$$

If the steering gear is of the worm and wheel type, then the gear ratio of the steering box is calculated as follows:

Gear ratio of steering box

$$= \frac{\text{No. of teeth on worm wheel}}{\text{No. of starts on worm}} \qquad [11.9]$$

This is identical with equation [11.2] for rear-axle drives used on heavy commercial vehicles.

Example 11.12

Calculate the gear ratio of a steering box which required $1\frac{1}{4}$ turns of the steering wheel to move the drop arm through 30° from its central position to full lock in one direction.

Solution

$$\text{Gear ratio} = \frac{360 \times \text{No. of turns of steering wheel}}{\text{No. of degrees turned through by drop arm}}$$

$$= \frac{360 \times 1.25}{30} = 15 \text{ to } 1$$

Answer: Gear ratio of steering box = 15 to 1

Steering box torque

Let F = force exerted by each hand of driver on the steering wheel (N)

d = diameter of steering wheel (m)

G_s = gear ratio of steering box

E = efficiency of gearing

The torque T, in N m, transmitted to the drop-arm shaft is given by:

$$T = FdG_sE \qquad\qquad [11.10]$$

It will be noticed from this equation that the torque exerted through the steering wheel by the driver is multiplied by 10 to 20 times, or even more, depending on the actual value of the gear ratio of the steering mechanism, so that the vehicle can be steered with a small effort. However, the output torque will be slightly reduced by the inefficiency of the gearing because of friction.

Example 11.13

A steering box has a gear ratio of 16 to 1 and an efficiency of 85 per cent. Assuming the driver to exert a force of 60 N at the rim of a wheel 0.4 m in diameter, determine the torque on the drop-arm shaft.

Solution

Torque on drop-arm shaft

$$= FdG_sE \qquad \text{from equation [11.10]}$$

$$= 60 \text{ [N]} \times 0.4 \text{ [m]} \times 16 \times \frac{85}{100} = 326.4 \text{ N m}$$

Answer: Torque on drop-arm shaft = 326.4 N m

Example 11.14

The gear ratio of a steering box is 14 to 1. When the driver applies a force of 25 N with each hand on the steering wheel of 0.38 m diameter, the torque transmitted to the drop-arm shaft is 110 N m. Determine the percentage efficiency of the steering mechanism.

Solution

Torque applied to steering wheel = $F \times d$

where F = driver's force on steering wheel = 25 N

d = diameter of steering wheel = 0.38 m

$\therefore$ Torque applied to steering wheel = $25 \times 0.38 = 9.5$ N m

$$\text{Torque ratio} = \frac{\text{Output torque}}{\text{Input torque}} \quad \text{from equation [11.4]}$$

$$= \frac{\text{Torque transmitted to drop-arm shaft}}{\text{Torque applied to steering wheel}}$$

$$= \frac{110 \text{ N m}}{9.5 \text{ N m}} = 11.58$$

Efficiency of steering box (%)

$$= \frac{\text{Torque ratio}}{\text{Gear ratio}} \times 100 \quad \text{from equation [11.7]}$$

$$= \frac{11.58}{14} \times 100 = 82.71\%$$

Answer: Efficiency of steering box = 82.71%

Exercise 11.1 – Review questions

1 With the aid of a sketch, describe a laboratory experiment to determine the mechanical efficiency of a gearbox with first gear engaged. Assume the gearbox is mounted separately as a piece of laboratory equipment. Indicate in your answer any relevant formulae.

(WMAC/UEI)

2 Describe an experiment to determine the third gear ratio in a four-speed gearbox on a motor vehicle. No dismantling is necessary and a hydraulic jack and starting handle are available.

(WMAC/UEI)

3 Describe an experiment to determine the movement ratio between

the steering wheel and drop arm in a motor vehicle. State how the force ratio can be obtained.

(NWRAC/ULCI)

Exercise 11.2 — Problems

1 A test gearbox was fitted with identical pulleys on both the input and output shafts. In a particular gear a 48 N load was lifted 50 mm by an effort of 20 N moving through 150 mm. Calculate the following:
   (a) the force ratio (or mechanical advantage)
   (b) the movement ratio (or velocity ratio)
   (c) the mechanical efficiency.

(EMEU)

2 Figure 11.5 shows the basic layout of a four-speed constant-mesh gearbox with the numbers of the teeth shown on each gear. Calculate the first, second, third and fourth gear ratios of the gearbox.

(EMEU)

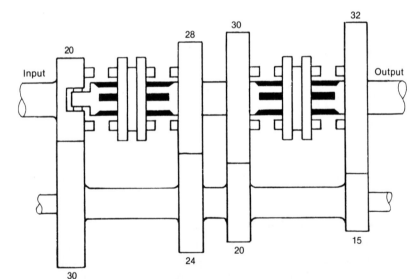

Figure 11.5 Layout of a four-speed constant-mesh gearbox

3 A gearbox is giving a speed reduction of 3 to 1 and in the final drive the crown wheel with 46 teeth is driven by a pinion with 6 teeth.

Calculate:

(*a*) the overall gear ratio

(*b*) the speed of the road wheels when the engine is running at 3450 rev/min.

4 The rear axle of a heavy commercial vehicle is fitted with a worm wheel which has 39 teeth, the corresponding worm has 6 starts. Determine the rear axle ratio.

5 In a gearbox the constant-mesh gears had 14 and 30 teeth respectively. The low gear on the mainshaft had 28 teeth and the meshing layshaft gear had 16 teeth. The rear-axle ratio was 4 to 1, the engine speed was 2000 rev/min and the road wheel diameter was 0.56 m. Calculate the road speed of the vehicle in this low gear.

(CGLI)

6 A gearbox provides a reduction of 4 to 1. What torque acts on the output shaft when the input torque is 70 N m? (Neglect frictional losses.)

(NWRAC/ULCI)

7 A front-engined rear-wheel drive vehicle has one rear wheel jacked up, top gear is engaged and the engine crankshaft rotates $2\frac{1}{2}$ times for one complete revolution of the jacked-up wheel. Calculate:

(*a*) the rear-axle ratio

(*b*) the torque on **each** axle half-shaft when driving in top gear with the engine transmitting a torque of 125 N m. State the assumption made.

(CGLI)

8 The torque of 120 N m is transmitted to a gearbox which has a ratio of 4.4 to 1 in its lowest gear and a mechanical efficiency of 90 per cent. Calculate the torque available at the gearbox output shaft.

(CGLI)

9 A vehicle with road wheels of 0.7 m effective diameter has a final-drive bevel wheel with 57 teeth, the bevel pinion driven by the propeller shaft having 14 teeth. Calculate the propeller shaft speed, in rev/min, when the vehicle travels at 48 km/h.

10 In a certain axle the final-drive ratio is 6.5 to 1. When the pinion is turned by a torque of 200 N m, it is found that the torque produced at the crown wheel is 1170 N m. Calculate (*a*) the torque ratio and (*b*) the percentage efficiency of the axle.

11 At an engine speed of 2550 rev/min a torque of 50 N m is applied to the gearbox. If the gearbox and final-drive ratios are 3.4 to 1 and 5 to 1 respectively, and the vehicle is travelling in a straight line, calculate:

(*a*) the speed of each road wheel

(*b*) the torque applied to each road wheel if the efficiency is 100 per cent.

184

12 Figure 11.6 shows an arrangement of gearwheels. The input shaft runs at 2000 rev/min with an input torque of 272 N m. The efficiency of the gearing is 90 per cent. Calculate:
(*a*) the speed of the output shaft in rev/min
(*b*) the output torque.

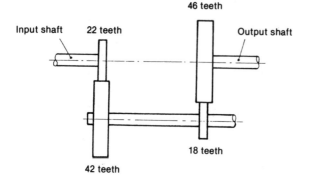

Figure 11.6

13 A car is jacked up to allow one rear wheel of the driving axle to be rotated. It is found by measurement that, for one revolution of the jacked-up wheel, the engine rotates 2.25 times when top gear (1 to 1) is engaged. The other gearbox forward ratios are: third, 2 to 1; second, 3 to 1; first, 4 to 1.
(*a*) Calculate (*i*) the final-drive ratio and (*ii*) the number of engine revolutions made for one revolution of the jacked-up wheel when each of the other forward gears is engaged in turn.
(*b*) If, when reverse gear is engaged, the engine does 10.125 turns for one revolution of the jacked-up wheel, what is the gearbox reverse ratio?

(CGLI)

14 When operated from lock to lock a steering wheel is turned $4\frac{1}{2}$ times while the steering drop arm swings through 81°. What is the gear ratio of the steering box?

(EMEU)

15 A steering box has an efficiency of 80 per cent. When the driver exerts a force of 70 N at the rim of the steering wheel of diameter 350 mm, the torque transmitted to the drop-arm shaft is 196 N m. Find the gear ratio of the steering box.

16 The following results were obtained from an experiment on a steering box of ratio 16 to 1.

Steering wheel Input torque (N m)	Drop arm Output torque (N m)
9	50
14	100
24	200
34	300

on a horizontal axis of output torque, plot graphs of both mechanical efficiency and input torque.

(EMEU)

Chapter 12

Temperature and quantity of heat

12.1 Temperature

Temperature is the term used to refer to the degree of hotness or coldness of a body. A body having a high temperature is said to be hot
while one having a low temperature is said to be cold. The fundamental SI unit of temperature is the *kelvin* (K) and the derived unit is the
degree celsius (°C).

12.2 Temperature scales

Temperature is measured either on the *Celsius scale* or on the *Kelvin
thermodynamic scale*. On the Celsius scale, the freezing point of water
is taken as zero (0 °C) and the point at which water boils under normal
atmospheric pressure is taken as 100 °C. It should be noted that in the
Celsius scale, the zero point was chosen to be that of melting ice. There
is, however, a certain degree of coldness beyond which no lower
temperature is possible. This occurs at -273.15 °C (in practice a value
of -273 °C is normally taken), and is called the *absolute zero of
temperature*.

The Kelvin scale is a theoretical scale based on the laws of thermo-
dynamics. It uses the absolute zero (-273 °C) for the beginning of the
scale instead of the arbitrary zero of the Celsius scale. A comparison of
Celsius and Kelvin temperature scales is given in Fig. 12.1. It will be
observed that a temperature interval is the same on both scales, i.e.

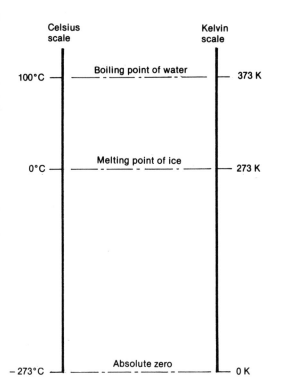

Figure 12.1 Comparison of Celsius and Kelvin temperature scales

1 °C = 1 K of temperature difference

It will also be observed that:

Kelvin temperature = Celsius temperature + 273
i.e.   K = °C + 273   [12.1]

It should be noted that thermodynamic or Kelvin temperature is often referred to as *absolute temperature*.

Example 12.1
The freezing point of alcohol at normal atmospheric pressure is − 115 °C. What is the corresponding temperature on the Kelvin scale?

Solution
Kelvin temperature = °C + 273
            = − 115 + 273 = 158 K

Answer: Freezing point of alcohol = 158 K

Example 12.2

The boiling point of oxygen at normal atmospheric pressure is 90 K. Convert this temperature into degrees celsius.

Solution

From equation [12.1],

Celsius temperature = Kelvin temperature − 273
= 90 − 273 = −183 °C

Answer: Boiling point of oxygen = −183 °C

12.3 Heat energy

When a body is capable of doing work it is said to possess energy. *Heat* is one form of energy and, therefore, it provides this capacity for doing work. Motor vehicle engines are forms of 'heat engines' in which the fuel is burnt to produce heat energy which is then converted into useful mechanical energy as the piston is driven down the cylinder.

Heat can be defined as that kind of energy which is transferred from one body to another when there is a temperature difference between them.

The amount or *quantity* of heat energy required to raise the temperature of a material depends upon the following three factors:

1. The mass of the material.
2. The rise in temperature of the material.
3. The type of the material.

This means that if equal masses of two different materials are heated through the same temperature rise, different amounts of heat energy will be required. For example, with equal masses of copper and lead at the same temperature, it is found that copper requires about three times the heat energy that is needed for lead to produce the same temperature rise for both masses.

12.4 Unit of heat energy

Since heat is a form of energy then, in common with all other types of energy, it is measured in *joules* (J). The joule is a small unit and in practice, kilojoules (kJ), or even megajoules (MJ), are often used as the unit of heat energy.

$1 \text{ MJ} = 10^3 \text{ kJ} = 10^6 \text{ J}$

12.5 Specific heat capacity

The quanity of heat required to raise the temperature of 1 kg of a substance by 1 K is called the *specific heat capacity* of the substance. This is denoted by c.

The basic unit for specific heat capacity is the *joule per kilogram kelvin* (J/kg K).

Such a multiple as kilojoule per kilogram kelvin (kJ/kg K) may also be used.

The quantity of heat given out or received by a substance is equal to the product of the mass of the substance, the specific heat capacity of the substance and its change in temperature.

Hence, if m = mass of substance, in kilograms
c = specific heat capacity, in J/kg K
δT = change in temperature, in kelvins
Q = quantity of heat given out or received, in joules
then $Q = m \times c \times \delta T$ [12.2]

Approximate values of the specific heat capacity for some common substances are given in Table 12.1.

Table 12.1 Approximate values of the specific heat capacity for some common substances

Substance	Specific heat capacity (J/kg K)	Substance	Specific heat capacity (J/kg K)
Lead	130	Cast iron	500
Mercury	140	Aluminium	900
Tin	230	Turpentine	1760
Brass	380	Petrol	1800
Zinc	385	Ice	2100
Copper	390	Paraffin oil	2150
Nickel	460	Alcohol	2500
Steel	480	Water	4190

Example 12.3

A 'hot-spot' used in the inlet manifold of a petrol engine has a mass of 0.15 kg. If the 'hot-spot' is heated from 10 °C to 160 °C, calculate the amount of heat energy absorbed by the metal if its specific heat capacity is 900 J/kg K.

Solution

Mass of 'hot-spot', m = 0.15 kg

Specific heat capacity of 'hot-spot', c = 900 J/kg K
Temperature rise = 160 − 10 = 150 °C or 150 K

Heat energy absorbed by 'hot-spot'

= Mass × Specific heat capacity × Temperature rise

i.e. $Q = m \times c \times \delta T$

$$= 0.15 \text{ [kg]} \times 900 \left[\frac{J}{\text{kg K}} \right] \times 150 \text{ [K]}$$

$$= 20\,250 \text{ J} = 20.25 \text{ kJ}$$

Answer: Heat energy absorbed by 'hot-spot' = 20.25 kJ

Example 12.4

Water in the cooling system of a motor vehicle circulates at the rate of
0.2 litre per second, and the temperature rises from 42 °C to 90 °C. If
the specific heat capacity of water is 4.2 kJ/kg K, calculate the amount
of heat energy absorbed by the cooling water per minute.
(Mass of 1 litre of water = 1 kg.)

Solution

Since 1 litre of water has a mass of 1 kg, then:
Mass of cooling water circulating per minute

$$= 0.2 \times 60 = 12 \text{ kg}$$
Temperature rise = 90 − 42 = 48 K

From equation [12.2],
Heat energy absorbed by cooling water per minute

= Mass × Specific heat capacity × Temperature rise

$$= 12 \times 4.2 \times 48 \left[\text{kg} \times \frac{\text{kJ}}{\text{kg K}} \times \text{K} \right]$$

$$= 2419 \text{ kJ}$$

Answer: Heat energy absorbed by cooling water = 2419 kJ/min

Example 12.5

A piece of metal of mass 10 kg absorbs 225 kJ of heat energy when its
temperature is raised from 15 °C to 60 °C. Find the specific heat capacity of the metal.

Solution

Heat energy absorbed by metal

$$\text{= Mass} \times \text{Specific heat capacity} \times \text{Temperature rise}$$

i.e. $\qquad Q = m \times c \times \delta T$

$\therefore 225 \times 10^3$ [J] $= 10$ [kg] $\times c \times (60 - 15)$ [K]

so that $\qquad c = \dfrac{225\ 000}{10 \times 45} \left[\dfrac{\text{J}}{\text{kg K}} \right] = 500 \text{ J/kg K}$

Answer: Specific heat capacity of metal $= 500$ J/kg K

Example 12.6

A furnace produces 30 MJ of heat energy per hour. How long will it take to heat 60 kg of steel from 20 °C to 200 °C? (Specific heat capacity of steel $= 0.48$ kJ/kg K.)

(NWRAC/ULCI)

Solution

Quantity of heat required to raise the temperature of the steel from 20 °C to 200 °C

$= \text{Mass} \times \text{Specific heat capacity} \times \text{Temperature rise}$

$= 60$ [kg] $\times 0.48$ [kJ/kg K] $\times (200 - 20)$ [K]

$= 60 \times 0.48 \times 180 = 5184$ kJ

Quantity of heat produced by furnace per minute

$= \dfrac{30 \times 10^3}{60} = 500$ kJ

Time taken to heat the steel

$= \dfrac{\text{Quantity of heat required}}{\text{Quantity of heat produced by furnace}}$

$= \dfrac{5184}{500} \left[\dfrac{\text{kJ}}{\text{kJ/min}} \right] = 10.37$ min

Answer: Time taken to heat the steel $= 10.37$ min

12.6 Heat energy transfer in mixtures

If a hot substance is mixed or brought into contact with a cold substance, heat energy will be transferred from the hot substance to the cold substance until both substances are ultimately at the same temperature. The final temperature of the mixture is always below the original temperature of the hotter substance and above that of the colder one. One of the substances is often a liquid; sometimes both substances are liquids.

The calculations on mixtures of hot and cold substances are based on the following principle:

Heat energy given up by hot substance
= Heat energy absorbed by cold substance

It is assumed that no loss of heat energy occurs to the surrounding air, but the heat energy given up or absorbed by the vessel containing the liquid should be taken into account.

Example 12.7

A steel component of mass 0.8 kg is to be hardened by being heated to 1050 °C and then plunged into an oil bath. The oil is contained in a steel tank of mass 2 kg and its initial temperature is 20 °C. Calculate the minimum mass of oil required in the tank if the final oil temperature must not exceed 50 °C. Neglect heat losses to the atmosphere.
(Specific heat capacity for steel = 0.48 kJ/kg K, and for oil = 1.60 kJ/kg K.)

(CGLI)

Solution (See Fig. 12.2)

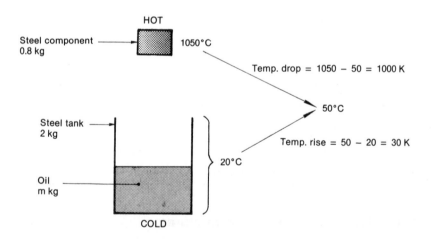

Figure 12.2   Example 12.7

Heat energy given up by component
= Mass × Specific heat capacity × Temperature fall
= 0.8 [kg] × 0.48 [kJ/kg K] × (1050 − 50) [K]
= 0.8 × 0.48 × 1000 = 384 kJ

Let *m* kilograms be the required mass of oil in the tank. Then:

Heat energy absorbed by oil
= Mass × Specific heat capacity × Temperature rise
= $m \times 1.6 \times (50-20)$
= $m \times 1.6 \times 30 = 48\,m$ kJ

Heat energy absorbed by steel tank
= Mass × Specific heat capacity × Temperature rise
= $2 \times 0.48 \times (50-20)$
= $2 \times 0.48 \times 30 = 28.8$ kJ

Neglecting heat energy losses to the atmosphere, we get:

Heat energy given up by component
      = Heat energy absorbed by oil and tank
i.e.   384   = $48m + 28.8$
   $48m$ = 355.2
∴ m = 7.4 kg

Answer: Minimum mass of oil required = 7.4 kg

Example 12.8

A steel component having a mass of 20 kg and a temperature of 700 °C is dropped into a tank containing 40 kg of water at 15 °C. Neglecting the heat energy absorbed by the tank and any loss of heat energy to the surrounding air, determine:

(*a*) the final temperature of the water
(*b*) the heat energy absorbed by the water.

(Take the specific heat capacities of steel and water as 0.48 kJ/kg K and 4.2 kJ/kg K respectively.)

Solution

(*a*) Let θ °C be the final temperature of the water. The final temperature of the steel component will also be θ °C. Hence:

Change in temperature of the water   = $(\theta - 15)$ K
Change in temperature of the component = $(700 - \theta)$ K

Working in units of kJ, kg and K, we get:

Heat energy given up by the component
= Mass × Specific heat capacity × Temperature fall
= $20 \times 0.48 \times (700 - \theta)$
= $6720 - 9.6\theta$ kJ   [1]

Heat energy absorbed by the water
= Mass × Specific heat capacity × Temperature rise
= $40 \times 4.2 \times (\theta - 15)$
= $164\theta - 2460$ kJ   [2]

Neglecting the heat energy absorbed by the tank and any loss of heat energy to the surrounding air, and equating [1] and [2], we get:

Heat energy given up by the component
= Heat energy absorbed by the water
i.e. $6720 - 9.6\theta = 164\theta - 2460$
so that $\qquad 173.6\theta = 9180$
$\therefore \qquad\qquad \theta = 52.88$ °C

(b) Substituting the value of θ in equation [2], we get:

Heat energy absorbed by the water
$= (164 \times 52.88) - 2460$
$= 8672 - 2460 = 6212$ kJ

Answer: (a) Final temperature of water = 52.88 °C
(b) Heat energy absorbed by water = 6212 kJ

Example 12.9

In an experiment to determine the specific heat capacity of copper, a specimen having a mass of 0.2 kg was transferred quickly from boiling water at 100 °C to a copper vessel of mass 0.3 kg, containing 0.25 kg of water at 21 °C. The final temperature reached by the copper and water was 26 °C. Calculate the value of the specific heat capacity of the copper.
The specific heat capacity of water may be taken as 4200 J/kg K.

Solution (See Fig. 12.3)

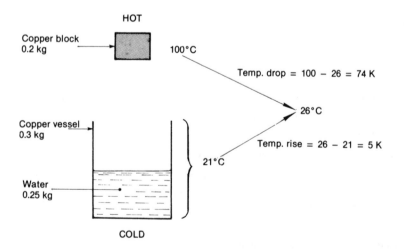

Figure 12.3 Example 12.9

Let c be the specific heat capacity of the copper in J/kg K. Then, working in units of J, kg and K:

Heat energy given up by the copper specimen
= Mass $\times$ Specific heat capacity $\times$ Temperature fall
= $0.2 \times c \times (100 - 26)$
= $0.2 \times c \times 74 = 14.8c$ J

Heat energy absorbed by water
= Mass $\times$ Specific heat capacity $\times$ Temperature rise
= $0.25 \times 4200 \times (26 - 21)$
= $0.25 \times 4200 \times 5 = 5250$ J

Heat energy absorbed by the copper vessel
= Mass $\times$ Specific heat capacity $\times$ Temperature rise
= $0.3 \times c \times (26 - 21)$
= $0.3 \times c \times 5 = 1.5c$ J

Assuming no loss of heat energy to the surroundings, we get:

Heat energy given up by the copper specimen
= Heat energy absorbed by water and vessel
i.e. $14.8c = 5250 + 1.5c$
so that $13.3c = 5250$
∴ $c = 394.7$ J/kg K

Answer: Specific heat capacity of copper = 395 J/kg K

Exercise 12.1 — Review questions

1 What is meant by the temperature of a body?
2 The SI unit of temperature is the ......
3 Name the two scales used in temperature measurement.
4 Complete the relationship: T K $= t$ °C $+$ ......
5 200 K is equivalent to ...... °C, and 60 °C is equivalent to ...... K.
6 Explain the term 'heat'.
7 The unit of heat energy is the ......
8 Describe briefly how heat energy is converted into work in a motor vehicle engine.
9 The amount of heat energy required to raise the temperature of a substance depends on
   (a) ......   (b) ......   (c) ......
10 Define the term 'specific heat capacity of a substance'.
11 Name the units and symbol used for specific heat capacity.
12 Describe briefly an experiment that you have carried out in the laboratory to determine the specific heat capacity of a metal by the method of mixtures.

In the following questions, select the correct answer.

13 The term used to indicate the hotness or coldness of a body is
   (*a*) kelvin   (*b*) degree celsius   (*c*) heat   (*d*) temperature
14 The absolute zero of temperature is equal to
   (*a*) 0 °C   (*b*) 273 °C   (*c*) − 273 °C   (*d*) 273 K
15 The freezing point of mercury at normal atmospheric pressure is
   − 39 °C. This temperature is equivalent to
   (*a*) − 39 K   (*b*) − 234 K   (*c*) 234 K   (*d*) 312 K
16 The temperature at the end of the compression stroke in a spark-
   ignition engine was found to be 528 K. This temperature is
   equivalent to
   (*a*) 255 °C   (*b*) 273 °C   (*c*) 528 °C   (*d*) 801 °C
17 During a heat treatment operation the temperature of a steel component was raised from 20 °C to 750 °C. The temperature rise
   expressed in kelvins is
   (*a*) 457 K   (*b*) 730 K   (*c*) 1003 K   (*d*) 273 K
18 Heat energy is measured in
   (*a*) degrees celsius   (*b*) kelvins   (*c*) joules   (*d*) kilograms
19 The unit of specific heat capacity is the
   (*a*) joule per kilogram   (*b*) joule   (*c*) kelvin
   (*d*) joule per kilogram kelvin
20 Which of the substances given below has the highest value of
   specific heat capacity?
   (*a*) cast iron   (*b*) brass   (*c*) aluminium   (*d*) petrol

Exercise 12.2 − Problems

Note: The mass of 1 litre of water is 1 kg.

1 Calculate the amount of heat energy required to raise the
   temperature of 3 kg of copper from 25 °C to 75 °C if the specific
   heat capacity is 390 J/kg K.
2 (*a*) 5 kg of water at 100 °C has the temperature reduced to 20 °C.
   How much heat energy is lost by the water during this process?
   The specific heat capacity of water is 4.2 kJ/kg K.
   (*b*) If 10 kg of fluid of specific heat capacity 2.4 kJ/kg K at 20 °C
   had received the same amount of heat energy as that lost by
   the water in (*a*) above, what would have been the final
   temperature of the fluid?
3 The liquid cooling system of an engine contains 12 litre of water.
   If its temperature is raised from 15 °C to 85 °C in 8 minutes,
   calculate the amount of heat energy absorbed by the water per
   minute, given that the specific heat capacity of water is
   4.2 kJ/kg K.
   (WMAC/UEI)(Modified)
4 A piece of metal of mass 12 kg absorbs 408 kJ of heat energy

when its temperature is raised from 15 °C to 100 °C. Find the specific heat capacity of the metal.

5 The lubricating oil from an engine flows through an oil cooler at the rate of 5.5 litre per minute. If the oil enters the cooler at a temperature of 82 °C and leaves the cooler to re-enter the engine at 10 °C, how much heat energy is extracted from the oil per second?
Specific heat capacity of the oil = 200 J/kg K
Mass of 1 litre of the oil   = 0.85 kg

6 The water cooling system of a certain vehicle contains 3.5 litre of water. Calculate the rise in water temperature if 1.14 MJ of heat energy are absorbed by the water cooling system in one minute. Assume no other losses and take the specific heat capacity of water as 4.2 kJ/kg K.

(CGLI)

7 A small furnace produces 15 MJ of heat energy per hour. How many minutes will it take to raise the temperature of 30 kg of copper from 20 °C to 220 °C?
The specific heat capacity of copper may be taken as 400 J/kg K.

(WMAC/UEI)

8 A heat energy loss of 1344 kJ/min from an engine to the cooling system causes a rise in temperature of 30 K in the water passing through the jackets. Calculate the rate of water circulation in litre per minute.
Specific heat capacity of water = 4.18 kJ/kg K

(CGLI)

9 The temperature of a piece of lead of mass 0.5 kg was raised to 100 °C. The lead was then transferred to a thin aluminium vessel containing 0.2 kg of water at 15 °C. If the final steady temperature after stirring was 21 °C, calculate the specific heat capacity of the lead. Neglect the heat energy absorbed by the vessel and take the specific heat capacity of water as 4.2 kJ/kg K.

10 A quantity of steel rivets are hardened by heating to 900 °C and plunging them into 400 kg of oil which is at a temperature of 25 °C. The temperature of the oil must not rise above 80 °C for this operation. Determine the maximum mass of the rivets that can be hardened under these conditions.
Specific heat capacity of steel = 0.49 kJ/kg K
Specific heat capacity of oil   = 2 kJ/kg K

(NWRAC/ULCI)

11 A steel component having a mass of 25 kg and a temperature of 650 °C is dropped into a tank containing 50 litre of water at 18 °C. Neglecting the heat lost to the tank and atmosphere, determine:
(a) the final temperature of the water
(b) the heat energy lost by the component.
Specific heat capacity of steel = 0.48 kJ/kg K
Specific heat capacity of water = 4.2 kJ/kg K

12 In an experiment to determine the specific heat capacity of iron, a piece of iron having a mass of 0.2 kg was heated to 99 °C and then transferred quickly to a copper vessel of mass 0.09 kg, containing 0.15 kg of water at 17 °C. The final temperature reached by the iron and water was 27 °C. What is the specific heat capacity of the iron?
Specific heat capacity of water   = 4.2 kJ/kg K
Specific heat capacity of copper = 0.4 kJ/kg K

13 During a heat treatment operation a steel component of mass 2.5 kg is heated to 770 °C and then plunged into oil which is at a temperature of 20 °C. If the final temperature of the oil is not to exceed 45 °C, calculate the minimum mass of oil that should be used. The specific heat capacity of steel is 460 J/kg K and that of the oil is 1850 J/kg K.

(WMAC/UEI)

14 An aluminium piston of mass 0.04 kg is heated to 200 °C and then quickly immersed in 0.18 kg of water contained in a copper vessel of mass 0.05 kg, the initial temperature of the water being 17 °C. If the final temperature of the mixture is 25 °C, determine the value of the specific heat capacity of the aluminium
Specific heat capacity of water   = 4200 J/kg K
Specific heat capacity of copper = 400 J/kg K

15 A 6 kg mass of stainless steel is left in a furnace until it attains the furnace temperature. The stainless steel is then withdrawn and quickly immersed in 8 litre of water contained in a vessel of mass 5 kg. The initial temperature of the water and vessel is 15 °C and the final temperature 85 °C. Assuming no losses, calculate the furnace temperature.
Specific heat capacity of stainless steel = 0.5 kJ/kg K
Specific heat capacity of water   = 4.2 kJ/kg K
Specific heat capacity of vessel   = 0.84 kJ/kg K

(NWRAC/ULCI)

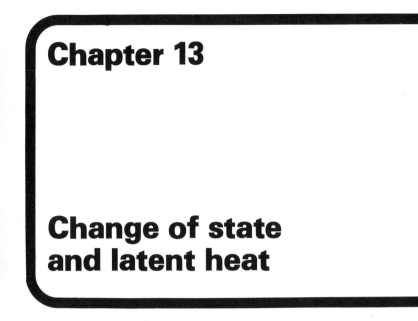

Chapter 13

Change of state and latent heat

13.1 Change of state

All substances, under suitable conditions of temperature and pressure, can exist in one of three states: solid, liquid, or gas. Many substances, however, can undergo a change of state if sufficient heat energy is either supplied to them or taken away from them. Water, for example, which is a liquid at normal temperatures, will solidify to form ice if cooled sufficiently, or will boil to form steam (gas) if heated sufficiently.

13.2 Sensible heat and latent heat

Sensible heat is that heat energy which produces a rise or fall in the temperature of a substance. It is called 'sensible' because the temperature change produced can be 'sensed' or detected, say, by a thermometer.

Hence, from equation [12.2],
Sensible heat

$$= \left(\begin{array}{c} \text{Mass of} \\ \text{substance} \end{array} \right) \times \left(\begin{array}{c} \text{Specific heat capacity} \\ \text{of substance} \end{array} \right) \times \left(\begin{array}{c} \text{Temperature} \\ \text{change} \end{array} \right)$$

Latent heat is the heat energy required to change the state of a substance without changing its temperature. The word 'latent' means 'hidden', since this heat energy is not apparent as far as indications on a thermometer are concerned (see graph of Fig. 13.1).

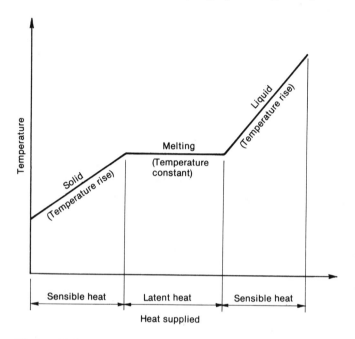

Figure 13.1

Latent heat is of two kinds:

1. That concerned in the change of state from a solid to a liquid (or vice versa), and is called *latent heat of fusion*.
2. That concerned in the change of state from a liquid to a vapour or gas (or vice versa), and is called *latent heat of vaporization*.

13.3 Melting points of solids

A solid is said to melt when it becomes a liquid.

The *melting point* of a substance is the temperature at which the change of state from solid to liquid occurs.

The melting points of some common substances are given in Table 13.1.

13.4 Freezing points of liquids

A liquid is said to *freeze* when it becomes a solid.

The *freezing point* of a substance is the temperature at which the

Table 13.1 Specific latent heat of fusion and melting point values for some common substances

Substance	Specific latent heat of fusion (kJ/kg)	Melting point (°C)
Lead	26	327
Tin	60	232
Zinc	102	419
Platinum	110	1770
Cast iron (white)	140	1135
Antimony	160	630
Copper	210	1083
Pure iron	270	1540
Ice	335	0
Aluminium	400	660
White metal	—	300–350
Brass	—	1030

change of state from liquid to solid occurs. It is equal in value to the melting point temperature of the substance.

Liquid cooling system

Water freezes at a temperature of 0 °C when exposed to normal atmospheric pressure, and has the peculiar behaviour to contract as it cools to 4 °C and then to expand as it cools further to 0 °C. Water alone, therefore, cannot be used in the cooling system of a motor vehicle as this will soon freeze when the vehicle is left idle in winter with consequent risk of cracking the radiator, cylinder block and head. One way of avoiding this is by using liquid additives in the cooling water which will lower its freezing temperature substantially. Ethylene glycol solutions combined with chemicals to prevent corrosion are widely used as *anti-freeze* solutions. An anti-freeze mixture does not have a sharply defined freezing point, but becomes slushy before it turns into solid ice.

The proportion of anti-freeze used depends upon the degree of protection required. In Great Britain, a coolant containing 25 per cent anti-freeze is usually sufficient as this protects the mixture down to − 12 °C before any slush forms, and the mixture will not freeze solid into ice until a temperature of − 26 °C is reached.

Electrolyte

The *electrolyte* used in a motor vehicle battery is a solution of concentrated sulphuric acid and distilled water. Neither acid nor anti-freeze should be added to prevent the battery freezing in cold weather. The

battery is best protected against freezing by maintaining it in a fully
charged condition. The freezing point of the electrolyte is about
− 62 °C for a fully charged battery, but is raised to about − 9 °C if the
battery is completely discharged.

Petrol and oil

Two other liquids used in the motor vehicle are *petrol* and *lubricating
oil*. These do not freeze above a temperature of about − 15 °C.

13.5 Specific latent heat of fusion

When a solid reaches its melting point temperature, further heating will
not increase the temperature of the substance until it has melted completely. Hence, all the heat energy given to the substance after the
melting point is reached goes to convert the substance from the solid
state to the liquid state. As already stated in Section 13.2, this heat
energy is called latent heat of fusion. (At the melting point, all the heat
supplied is used up as work as the molecules break away from one
another. Thus, no heat is available to increase the temperature.)

The reverse process by which a liquid changes into a solid is known
as *solidification* or *freezing*. (See also Section 13.4.)

When a substance changes its state from liquid to solid, all the latent
heat of fusion is given up before the liquid is completely solidified at
the same temperature.

The *specific latent heat of fusion* of a substance is defined as the
quantity of heat required to change 1 kg of the substance from the
solid state to the liquid state (or vice versa) without change of
temperature.

Specific latent heat of fusion is expressed in joules per kilogram
(J/kg) or, preferably, in kilojoules per kilogram (kJ/kg). For example,
if 335 kJ of heat energy are absorbed by 1 kg of ice at 0 °C in melting
into water at 0 °C, then the specific latent heat of fusion of ice is
335 kJ/kg.

The quantity of heat, Q, required to change a solid substance at its
melting point into liquid at the same temperature is given by:

$$Q = m \times L_f \qquad\qquad [13.1]$$

where m is the mass of the solid substance and L_f is its specific latent
heat of fusion.

The specific latent heats of fusion of some common substances are
included in Table 13.1.

Example 13.1

Calculate the heat energy required to melt, completely, 4 kg of a
copper alloy initially at a temperature of 80 °C.

Melting point of the alloy = 1080 °C.
Specific heat capacity of the alloy = 0.4 kJ/kg K
Specific latent heat of fusion of the alloy = 210 kJ/kg

Solution

From equation [12.2],
 Sensible heat required to raise the temperature of the copper alloy
from 80 °C to its melting point

= Mass × Specific heat capacity × Temperature rise from 80 °C to
 1080 °C
= 4 [kg] × 0.4 [kJ/kg K] × 1000 [K]
= 1600 kJ

(Remember that a temperature change of 1000 °C is exactly the same
as a temperature change of 1000 K. See Section 12.2.)

From equation [13.1],
 Latent heat required to melt the copper alloy at its melting point

= Mass × Specific latent heat of fusion
= 4 [kg] × 210 [kJ/kg]
= 840 kJ

Total heat energy required to melt the copper alloy

= Sensible heat + Latent heat
= 1600 + 840 = 2440 kJ

Answer: Total heat energy required = 2440 kJ

Example 13.2

A piece of ice, having a mass of 0.2 kg and an initial temperature of
0 °C, is immersed in a copper vessel of mass 0.3 kg and containing
0.5 kg of water at 35 °C. Calculate the final temperature when all the
ice has melted.
Assume no loss of heat energy.
Specific heat capacity of water = 4.2 kJ/kg K
Specific heat capacity of copper = 0.4 kJ/kg K
Specific latent heat of fusion of ice = 335 kJ/kg

Solution (see Fig. 13.2)

Let θ °C be the final temperature of the mixture. Then:
 Heat energy given up by the water

= Mass × Specific heat capacity × Temperature fall
= 0.5 [kg] × 4.2 [kJ/kg K] × $(35 - \theta)$ [K]
= $(73.5 - 2.1\theta)$ kJ

Heat energy given up by the copper vessel

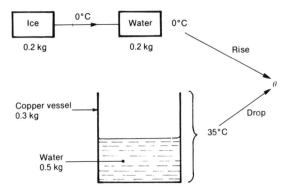

Figure 13.2 Example 13.2

= Mass × Specific heat capacity × Temperature fall
= 0.3 [kg] × 0.4 [kJ/kg K] × $(35 - \theta)$ [K]
= $(4.2 - 0.12\theta)$ kJ

Heat energy required to melt the ice

= Mass × Specific latent heat of fusion
= 0.2 [kg] × 335 [kJ/kg]
= 67 kJ

Heat energy required to raise the temperature of the melted ice (water) from 0 °C to θ °C

= Mass × Specific heat capacity × Temperature rise
= 0.2 [kg] × 4.2 [kJ/kg K] × θ [K]
= 0.84θ kJ

Now, assuming no heat energy losses,

Heat energy absorbed in melting the ice and heating to θ °C	=	Heat energy given up by the water and the copper vessel

i.e. $67 + 0.84\theta$ = $(73.5 - 2.1\theta) + (4.2 - 0.12\theta)$
so that 3.06θ =   10.7
∴ θ =   3.5 °C

Answer: Final temperature of the mixture = 3.5 °C

___

13.6   To determine the melting point of a substance from a cooling curve

We know that when a substance changes its state from solid to liquid by means of the application of heat the temperature remains constant during the process of melting, and that a similar result occurs during the reverse process of solidification. Hence, by plotting what is termed as a *cooling curve*, with simultaneous observations of temperature and time, we can determine from this curve the melting point of a substance with a fairly low melting point, e.g. naphthalene (melting point 78 °C). The experiment is carried out as described hereunder.

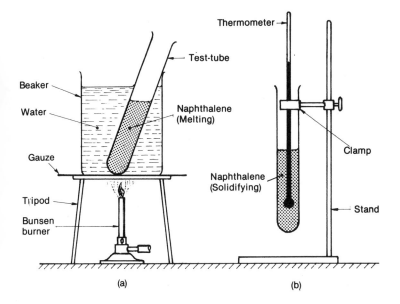

Figure 13.3 Determination of the melting point of naphthalene

A test-tube is half-filled with naphthalene and placed in a beaker of water. The water is heated to about 95 °C by a bunsen flame, see Fig. 13.3(a), until all the naphthalene has melted. The test-tube is then removed from the beaker and held vertically by a clamp and stand, as shown in Fig. 13.3(b). A thermometer is inserted in the liquid naphthalene and the temperature is recorded every minute until it has fallen to about 40 °C. It will be observed that when the freezing point (which is the same as the melting point) of naphthalene is reached, the temperature remains constant at around 78 °C until all the naphthalene has solidified. Thereafter, the temperature begins to fall again. The best way of illustrating these temperature changes is by plotting a graph of temperature against time. This should be similar to that shown in Fig. 13.4. The flat portion BC of the curve represents the period at which the naphthalene is giving up its latent heat as it changes its state from liquid to solid while the temperature remains constant. This particular temperature is the melting point (in this case about 78 °C).

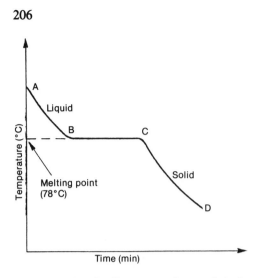

Figure 13.4   Cooling curve for naphthalene

13.7   Boiling of liquids

When heat is continually applied to a liquid, the temperature steadily rises until a value is reached at which the liquid vaporizes with no further rise in temperature. Bubbles of vapour form at the bottom of the liquid and rise to the surface, where they burst and escape to the air. The liquid is then *boiling* and the temperature attained is called the *boiling point* of the liquid.

Table 13.2 gives the boiling points of some common substances at normal atmospheric pressure. Note that petrol is composed of the lightest fuel fractions obtained from crude oil with boiling point temperatures ranging between 30 °C and 200 °C (see Section 16.13).

Table 13.2   Specific latent heat of vaporization and boiling point values for some common substances

Substance	Specific latent heat of vaporization (kJ/kg)	Boiling point (°C)
Mercury	280	357
Turpentine	290	156
Petrol	360	30–200
Benzene	400	80
Paraffin oil	610	280
Ethyl alcohol	850	79
Pure water	2260	100
Ethylene glycol	—	195

13.8 Specific latent heat of vaporization

Just as latent heat is absorbed when a substance changes its state from solid to liquid at the same temperature, so the same thing occurs when the change of state is from liquid to vapour or gas. In other words, when a liquid has been raised to its boiling point, it can only be vaporized by supplying a definite amount of heat energy to it. This heat energy is absorbed by the substance without any change of temperature occurring; it is used entirely for changing the state of the substance from liquid to vapour or gas. It has already been stated in Section 13.2 that this heat energy is called latent heat of vaporization.

The reverse process by which a vapour or gas changes into a liquid is known as *condensation*.

When a substance changes its state from a vapour or gas to a liquid, all the latent heat of vaporization is given up before the vapour or gas is completely condensed at the same temperature.

The *specific latent heat of vaporization* of a substance is defined as the quantity of heat required to change 1 kg of the substance from the liquid state to the gaseous state (or vice versa) without change of temperature.

For example, if 2260 kJ of heat energy are absorbed by 1 kg of water at 100 °C in changing to steam at 100 °C, then the specific latent heat of vaporization of water at normal atmospheric pressure is 2260 kJ/kg.

The quantity of heat, Q, required to change a liquid at its boiling point into a gas at the same temperature is given by:

$$Q = m \times L_v \qquad\qquad [13.2]$$

where m is the mass of the liquid and L_v is its specific latent heat of vaporization.

The specific latent heats of vaporization of a number of substances are included in Table 13.2.

Example 13.3

Find the mass of cooling water required to condense 5 kg of steam at atmospheric pressure and a temperature of 100 °C, and then to cool the resulting water to 60 °C, if the permissible rise in temperature of the cooling water is 30 K.

Specific heat capacity of water = 4.2 kJ/kg K
Specific latent heat of vaporization of steam = 2260 kJ/kg

Solution

Latent heat given up by the steam in condensing at 100 °C

= Mass × Specific latent heat of vaporization
= 5 [kg] × 2260 [kJ/kg]
= 11 300 kJ

Sensible heat given up by the condensed steam in cooling from 100 °C to 60 °C

= Mass × Specific heat capacity × Temperature fall
= 5 [kg] × 4.2 [kJ/kg K] × (100 − 60) [K]
= 840 kJ

Total heat given up by the steam and the water formed from it

= 11 300 + 840 kJ
= 12 140 kJ   [1]

This amount of heat energy is absorbed by the cooling water.
    Let m kg be the required mass of the cooling water. Then:

Heat absorbed by the cooling water
= Mass × Specific heat capacity × Temperature rise
= m × 4.2 × 30
= 126m kJ   [2]

Equating [1] and [2], we get:

    126m = 12 140
∴ m = 96.35 kg

Answer: Mass of cooling water required = 96.35 kg

Example 13.4

Calculate the amount of heat energy required to convert 0.5 kg of ice at − 20 °C into steam at 100 °C.

Specific latent heat of fusion of ice	= 335 kJ/kg
Specific latent heat of vaporization of water	= 2260 kJ/kg
Specific heat capacity of ice	= 2.1 kJ/kg K
Specific heat capacity of water	= 4.2 kJ/kg K

Solution

Working entirely in kJ, kg and temperature differences in K, we get:
    Sensible heat required to raise the temperature of 0.5 kg of ice from − 20 °C to freezing point (0 °C)

= Mass × Specific heat capacity × Temperature rise
= 0.5 × 2.1 × 20 = 21 kJ

    Latent heat required to convert 0.5 kg of ice at 0 °C into water at 0 °C

= Mass × Specific latent heat of fusion
= 0.5 × 335 = 167.5 kJ

    Sensible heat required to raise the temperature of 0.5 kg of water from 0°C to boiling point (100 °C)

= Mass × Specific heat capacity × Temperature rise
= 0.5 × 4.2 × 100 = 210 kJ

Latent heat required to convert 0.5 kg of water at 100 °C into steam at 100 °C

= Mass × Specific latent heat of vaporization
= 0.5 × 2260 = 1130 kJ

Total heat energy required to convert 0.5 kg of ice at − 20 °C into steam at 100 °C

= 21 + 167.5 + 210 + 1130 = 1528.5 kJ

Answer: Heat energy required = 1528.5 kJ

13.9 Effect of pressure on the boiling point of a liquid

The values given in Table 13.2 are the boiling points at normal atmospheric pressure, which is about 101.3 kPa (101.3 kN/m ^{2}) at sea level. If the pressure on the surface of a liquid is increased the temperature at which the liquid boils will be raised, and if the pressure is decreased, boiling will take place at a lower temperature.

The manner in which the boiling point of water increases with pressure is illustrated by the graph of Fig. 13.5.

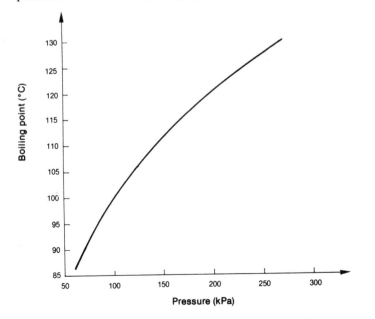

Figure 13.5   Variation of boiling point of water with pressure

The liquid cooling system of the modern motor car operates under pressure. The pressurized system raises the boiling point of the coolant and so provides a margin of safety when the vehicle is driven hard on a hot day or when it is driven in a mountainous region where the atmospheric pressure is lower than at sea level. For example, at a height of approximately 3000 m above sea level the pressure of the atmosphere is around 70 kPa, and if a vehicle were fitted with a radiator which is vented to the atmosphere, the coolant would boil at a temperature of 90 °C, which could result in excessive loss of the coolant.

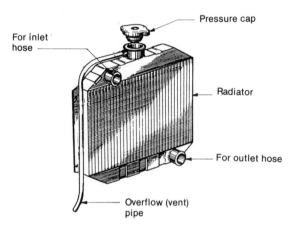

Figure 13.6   Pressurized cooling system

In a pressurized cooling system (see Fig. 13.6) the radiator is sealed with a pressure cap. This incorporates a spring-loaded valve which opens at a predetermined pressure, generally between 28 kPa and **90 kPa above atmospheric pressure. It will be observed from the** graph of Fig. 13.5 that an increase in pressure of 28 kPa raises the boiling point of the water by about 7 K, while an increase of 90 kPa will permit a rise of about 19 K before boiling occurs.

A small relief valve is also incorporated in the radiator cap. This operates in the reverse direction to the main valve and allows the pressure to drop to atmospheric value when the engine cools down, thus preventing the formation of a partial vacuum in the cooling system. The cap housing must have a vent pipe in it, so that water and steam can escape through this pipe in the event of overfilling or boiling.

Exercise 13.1 — Review questions

1   State what is meant by 'change of state'. Give **two** examples on a motor vehicle where the change of state is used to advantage.

2 Distinguish between 'sensible heat' and 'latent heat'.

3 Define the terms:
   (*a*) specific latent heat of fusion
   (*b*) specific latent heat of vaporization.

4 The units of the specific latent heats of fusion and vaporization are
   . . . . . .

5 The 'melting point' of a substance is . . . . . .

6 The 'freezing point' of a substance is . . . . . .

7 Complete the following statements.
   (*a*) Water is not left in the engine cooling system without anti-
   freeze solution in winter because . . . . . .
   (*b*) An anti-freeze solution will . . . . . . the freezing point of water
   in the cooling system.

(NWRAC/ULCI)

8 The 'boiling point' of a liquid is . . . . . .

9 Explain what is meant by 'condensation'.

10 State the effect of changes in pressure on the boiling point of a
liquid.

11 Show by means of a graph the relationship between the pressure
acting on the surface of water and its boiling temperature.

12 State the purpose of fitting a pressure cap to the header tank of the
cooling system of a motor vehicle and give the average pressure
range used.

13 State **two** advantages that the pressurized cooling system has when
compared with a system vented to the atmosphere.

14 Explain briefly the purpose of incorporating an overflow pipe (vent
pipe) in a motor vehicle liquid cooling system.

15 In the following statements regarding change of state there are
groups of three words within brackets. In each case, only **one** of
the words is correct. Underline the correct word.

When ice is heated sufficiently, it (solidifies, melts, condenses) and
becomes water. With further heating, it (melts, liquefies, boils) and
becomes steam. The reverse sequence occurs when steam is cooled.
The steam (condenses, vaporizes, freezes) to water which can be
(melted, frozen, liquefied) to produce ice.

16 The heat energy that produces a change in the temperature of a
substance is called
   (*a*) specific heat capacity   (*c*) latent heat
   (*b*) sensible heat   (*d*) hidden heat

17 The heat energy required to change the state of a substance
without changing its temperature is called
   (*a*) specific heat capacity   (*c*) latent heat
   (*b*) sensible heat   (*d*) thermal energy

18 Given that the specific latent heat of fusion of ice is 335 kJ/kg and
the specific heat capacity of water 4.2 kJ/kg K, the quantity of
heat required to change 2 kg of ice at 0 °C to water at 10 °C is
   (*a*) 84 kJ   (*b*) 670 kJ   (*c*) 754 kJ   (*d*) 3350 kJ

Exercise 13.2 — Problems

1 (a) Find the quantity of heat required to melt, completely, 5 kg of an aluminium alloy initially at 20 °C, given that, for the alloy: melting point = 660 °C; specific heat capacity = 900 J/kg K; specific latent heat of fusion = 400 kJ/kg.

  (b) If the heat is supplied to the aluminium alloy at the rate of 80 kJ/min, find:

     (i)   the time taken to bring the alloy to its melting point

     (ii) the additional time required to melt it.

2 0.2 kg of molten lead at its melting point of 327 °C is allowed to solidify at the same temperature and gives out 5200 J of heat energy. What is the specific latent heat of fusion of lead?

    If the specific heat capacity of lead is 130 J/kg K, how much additional heat energy does it give out in cooling to 27 °C?

3 Determine the amount of heat energy to be removed from 2 kg of water at 40 °C to produce ice at a temperature of −5 °C.

Specific latent heat of fusion of ice = 335 kJ/kg
Specific heat capacity of ice   = 2.1 kJ/kg K
Specific heat capacity of water   = 4.2 kJ/kg K

4 How much heat energy could be obtained from 5 kg of steam at atmospheric pressure if it were converted to water at 60 °C?

Specific latent heat of steam   = 2260 kJ/kg
Specific heat capacity of water = 4.2 kJ/kg K

(WMAC/UEI)

5 The liquid cooling system of a motor vehicle contains 12 litre of fresh water at a temperature of 20 °C. Calculate the quantity of heat required to evaporate one-tenth of the water at normal atmospheric pressure, given that the specific latent heat of vaporization of water is 2260 kJ/kg and the specific heat capacity of water is 4.2 kJ/kg K.

(Mass of 1 litre of water = 1 kg.)

6 Calculate the quantity of heat required to convert 2 kg of ice at −15 °C to steam at 100 °C. The specific latent heat of fusion of ice is 335 kJ/kg and the specific latent heat of vaporization of water is 2.26 MJ/kg. The specific heat capacity of ice is 2.1 kJ/kg K and the specific heat capacity of water is 4.2 kJ/kg K.

7 2 kg of steam at 100 °C are blown into a vessel containing 75 kg of water at 20 °C. Calculate the final temperature of the mixture. Neglect the heat energy absorbed by the vessel.

Specific heat capacity of water = 4.2 kJ/kg K
Specific latent heat of vaporization at 100 °C = 2260 kJ/kg

8 (a) Tin has a melting point of 232 °C, a specific heat capacity of 0.23 kJ/kg K and a specific latent heat of fusion of 60 kJ/kg. What quantity of heat is required to melt 20 kg of tin originally at 32 °C?

  (b) Steel has a specific heat capacity of 0.48 kJ/kg K. If 1.5 kg of steel at a temperature of 32 °C are plunged into the molten tin referred to in (a) above, what mass of tin solidifies when the steel and the tin both acquire a temperature of 232 °C?

(CGLI)(Modified)

9 Find the quantity of steam at atmospheric pressure that is required to change 0.2 kg of ice at −6 °C into water at 50 °C. The specific latent heat of vaporization of steam is 2260 kJ/kg and the specific latent heat of fusion of ice is 335 kJ/kg. The specific heat capacity of ice is 2.1 kJ/kg K and the specific heat capacity of water is 4.2 kJ/kg K.

(EMEU)

10 Steam of mass 0.5 kg and temperature 100 °C is condensed by passing it into 10 kg of water contained in a steel vessel of mass 4 kg. If the initial temperature of the water is 10 °C, calculate its final temperature. Assume that all the condensed steam is mixed with the water and that the water and container are at the same temperature. Neglect any heat losses to the atmosphere.
For water:
  Specific heat capacity = 4.2 kJ/kg K
  Specific latent heat of vaporization = 2260 kJ/kg
For steel:
  Specific heat capacity = 0.48 kJ/kg K

(CGLI)

11 The table below shows the results of various proportions of anti-freeze on the fluidity of the engine coolant over a range of temperatures.

Anti-freeze proportion by volume (%)	0	5	10	15	20	25	30
Temperature at which coolant starts to solidify (°C)	0	−1.5	−3	−5	−7.5	−10	−3.5
Temperature at which coolant solidifies (°C)	0	−4	−8	−14	−20.5	−28	−38

(a) Plot a graph of these results and draw smooth curves through both sets of plotted points.
(b) Determine from the graph:
   (i) the temperature at which the coolant solidifies for a mixture of 18 per cent anti-freeze
   (ii) the percentage of anti-freeze required to prevent solidification of the mixture down to −30 °C.
(c) State what is happening to the coolant between the upper and lower curves on the graph.

(CGLI)

Chapter 14

Expansion of solids and liquids

14.1 Effect of temperature change on solids and liquids

Most solids and liquids expand when they are heated and contract when they are cooled. Thus, the two effects of expansion and contraction depend on a change of temperature occurring.

In engineering practice, it is usual to consider the effect of temperature change on

(a) the linear dimensions of solid materials; this is known as *linear* expansion or contraction

(b) the volume of liquids; this is known as *cubical* or *volumetric* expansion or contraction.

14.2 Expansion and contraction of solids

An example of linear expansion and contraction is the shrinking of the starting ring gear on to the flywheel. The ring gear is bored so that its internal diameter, when cold, is slightly less than the diameter of the flywheel. The ring gear is then heated and the increased diameter enables it to be slipped over the rim of the flywheel. As the ring gear cools, its bore contracts, gripping the flywheel firmly.

Gudgeon pins are often fitted by dipping the aluminium alloy piston in hot water or oil, so as to expand the bore of the gudgeon pin boss.

It is worth noting that instead of heating and thus expanding the outer component, it is sometimes more convenient to contract the inner part by cooling it in some liquefied gas, e.g. liquid nitrogen. When the inner part returns to its original temperature, it expands and becomes a tight fit in the outer part. Motor vehicle components fitted in this manner are valve guides, valve seat inserts and cylinder liners.

14.3 Coefficient of linear expansion

The amount by which a material expands when heated is proportional to the original length and to the rise in temperature, but not all materials expand equally when heated through the same range of temperature. Aluminium, for example, expands about twice as much as steel; lead expands about three times as much as cast iron. How much a material actually expands when heated, or contracts when cooled, is measured by the *coefficient of linear expansion* which is defined as follows.

The *coefficient of linear expansion* of a material is the amount by which unit length (1 m, etc.) of the material changes when its temperature is changed by 1 K. This is represented by α (Greek letter 'alpha').

The coefficient of linear expansion of a material is found by experiment. From an inspection of Table 14.1, it can be seen that its value for copper is 17×10^{-6}/K. This means that 1 m of copper will become 1.000 017 m for a temperature rise of 1 K, or will become 0.999 983 m for a temperature fall of 1 K.

If L = the original length of the material
        α = the coefficient of linear expansion of the material
        δT = the change in temperature
        x = the change in length
then x $= L \times \alpha \times \delta T$ [14.1]

Also, from equation [14.1],
    Coefficient of linear expansion

$$= \frac{\text{Change in length}}{\text{Original length} \times \text{Change in temperature}}$$

i.e. $\alpha = \dfrac{x}{L \times \delta T}$ [14.2]

Table 14.1 gives average values of the coefficient of linear expansion for a number of different materials.

14.4 The bimetallic strip

The difference in the expansion of materials can easily be demonstrated by riveting together two equal strips of different materials, say, of

216

Table 14.1 Average values of coefficient of linear expansion

Material	Coefficient of linear expansion ($\alpha \times 10^{-6}$/K)
Invar	1
Antimony	10
Cast iron	10
Steel	12
Nickel	13
Copper	17
Bronze	18
Brass	19
Tin	21
Aluminium	24
Lead	29
Zinc	30

brass and steel, to form a *bimetallic strip* or *compound bar*, as shown in Fig. 14.1(a). When this bar is heated, it bends into an arc with the brass strip on the **outside** of the curve, as shown in Fig. 14.1(b). The brass strip therefore becomes longer than the steel strip, indicating that brass expands more than steel for the same temperature change.

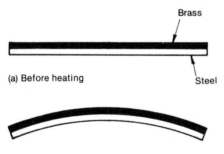

(a) Before heating

Brass

Steel

(b) After heating

Figure 14.1 Bimetallic strip

The bimetallic strip has many useful applications, such as, in automatic flashing units, in fuel gauges, in thermostats for controlling the temperature of furnaces and of hot-water storage tanks, etc.

Example 14.1

In an experiment to determine the coefficient of linear expansion of brass, a rod of this metal, 250 mm long, is found to expand by 0.39 mm when heated from 17 °C to 98 °C. Determine the value for the coefficient of linear expansion of brass.

Solution

Increase in temperature, $\delta T = 98 - 17 = 81$ K
Increase in length, x $= 0.39$ mm
Original length, L $= 250$ mm

$$\text{Coefficient of linear expansion} = \frac{\text{Increase in length}}{\text{Original length} \times \text{Rise in temperature}}$$

i.e. $$\alpha = \frac{x}{L \times \delta T}$$

$$= \frac{0.39}{250 \times 81} \left[\frac{\text{mm}}{\text{mm} \times \text{K}} \right]$$

$$= 0.000\ 019\ 26/\text{K}$$

or $$\alpha = 19.26 \times 10^{-6}/\text{K}$$

Answer: Coefficient of linear expansion of brass $= 19.26 \times 10^{-6}/\text{K}$

Example 14.2

An exhaust front pipe is 1.5 m long at 20 °C. What will be its length when its temperature is raised to 370 °C?
The coefficient of linear expansion of the steel used is $12 \times 10^{-6}/\text{K}$.

Solution

Increase in length = Original length × Coefficient of expansion
$\qquad\qquad\qquad\qquad$ × Temperature rise
i.e. $\qquad x = L \times a \times \delta T$
$\qquad\qquad\quad = 1.5\ [\text{m}] \times 12 \times 10^{-6}\ [/\text{K}] \times (370-20)\ [\text{K}]$
$\qquad\qquad\quad = 1.5 \times 12 \times 10^{-6} \times 350$ m
$\qquad\qquad\quad = 0.0063$ m

Length of pipe at 370 °C = Original length + Expansion
$\qquad\qquad\qquad\qquad\qquad\ = 1.5 + 0.0063 = 1.5063$ m

Answer: Length of pipe at 370 °C $= 1.5063$ m

Example 14.3

The outside diameter of a steel cylinder liner is 85 mm at a temperature of 15 °C. In order that it can be fitted to the cylinder block, it was necessary to cool the liner to -55 °C by using liquefied gas. Calculate the decrease in outside diameter of the liner at this lower temperature. Coefficient of linear expansion of steel $= 12 \times 10^{-6}/\text{K}$.

Solution

Temperature interval between 15 °C and −55 °C

= 15 + 55 = 70 °C or 70 K

From equation [14.1],
Decrease in outside diameter

= Original diameter × Coefficient of expansion × Temperature fall

$$= 85 \times 12 \times 10^{-6} \times 70 \left[\frac{mm \times K}{K} \right]$$

= 0.0714 mm

Answer: Decrease in outside diameter = 0.0714 mm

Example 14.4

A starter ring gear is heated so that it can be fitted over a flywheel. If the inside diameter of the ring gear is 254 mm and the outside diameter of the flywheel is 254.6 mm, calculate the temperature to which the ring gear must be raised from its initial temperature of 20 °C. Allow a working clearance of 0.15 mm for the contraction which takes place during fitting.

Coefficient of linear expansion of steel = 12×10^{-6}/K

(CGLI)

Solution

Total increase in diameter of ring gear

= (254.6 − 254) mm + Working clearance
= 0.6 + 0.15 = 0.75 mm

But from equation [14.1],

Total increase in diameter
= Original diameter × Coefficient of expansion × Temperature rise
i.e. 0.75 [mm] = 254 [mm] × 12×10^{-6} [/K] × δT

$$\therefore \qquad \delta T = \frac{0.75 \times 10^6}{254 \times 12} = 246 \text{ K or } 246 \text{ °C (of temperature rise)}$$

Temperature to which ring gear must be raised

= Initial temperature + Temperature rise
= 20 °C + 246 °C
= 266 °C

Answer: Temperature required = 266 °C

Example 14.5

Two rods, one of aluminium and the other of copper, are both 500 mm long at 20 °C. If they are allowed to expand freely, what will be their difference in length at 100 °C?
Coefficients of linear expansion are:

Aluminum (α_A) = 24 × 10⁻⁶/K; Copper (α_C) = 17 × 10⁻⁶/K

Solution

Difference in length at 100 °C

$$
\begin{aligned}
&= (L \times \alpha_A \times \delta T) - (L \times \alpha_C \times \delta T) \\
&= L \times \delta T \times (\alpha_A - \alpha_C) \\
&= 500 \times (100 - 20) \times (24 \times 10^{-6} - 17 \times 10^{-6}) \\
&= 500 \times 80 \times 7 \times 10^{-6} \\
&= 0.28 \text{ mm}
\end{aligned}
$$

Answer: Difference in length at 100 °C = 0.28 mm

Example 14.6

A cast-iron cylinder and its mating aluminium alloy piston have a nominal diameter of 100 mm. At 20 °C the diametral clearance between the piston and the cylinder bore is 0.5 mm. What will be the diametral clearance when both attain a working temperature of 300 °C?
Coefficients of linear expansion are:
Aluminium alloy = 22 × 10⁻⁶/K; cast iron = 10 × 10⁻⁶/K

Solution

Note: In order to make problems of this type easy to solve, the calculations are usually based on the nominal size, i.e. the size which is assumed common for the two mating parts.

Temperature rise = 300 − 20 = 280 K

Working in units of mm and K, then, for a nominal diameter of 100 mm:

Difference in diameter between piston and cylinder bore for a temperature rise of 280 K

$$
\begin{aligned}
&= 100 \times 280 \times 10^{-6} (22 - 10) \\
&= 0.336 \text{ mm}
\end{aligned}
$$

The aluminium expands more than the cast iron, and hence the clearance between piston and cylinder at 300 °C is decreased.

$$
\begin{aligned}
\therefore \text{ New clearance} &= \text{Clearance at 20 °C} - 0.336 \text{ mm} \\
&= 0.500 - 0.336 = 0.164 \text{ mm}
\end{aligned}
$$

Answer: Diametral clearance at 300 °C = 0.164 mm

14.5 Coefficient of superficial expansion

In dealing with expansion in two directions, i.e. length and breadth (Fig. 14.2), it will be observed that a change in *area* takes place.

Figure 14.2 Superficial expansion

The amount by which unit area (1 m^2, etc.) of a material changes when its temperature is changed by 1 K is called the *coefficient of superficial expansion*, and is represented by β (Greek letter 'beta').

For all practical purposes, the coefficient of superficial expansion for a given material is twice its linear coefficient, i.e. $\beta = 2\alpha$.

14.6 Coefficient of cubical expansion

When the temperature of a solid material is changed, expansion or contraction takes place in all directions so that a change in *volume* is experienced (Fig. 14.3).

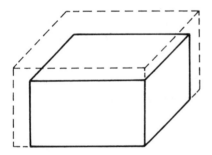

Figure 14.3 Cubical expansion

The amount by which unit volume (1 m^3, etc.) of a material changes when its temperature is changed by 1 K is called the *coefficient of cubical or volumetric expansion*, and is represented by γ (Greek letter 'gamma').

For all practical purposes, the coefficient of cubical expansion for a given material is three times its linear coefficient, i.e. $\gamma = 3\alpha$.

Example 14.7

An aluminium alloy piston is machined to a diameter of 80 mm and the temperature during this operation is 20 °C. Calculate the increase in area of the piston top when the piston reaches 270 °C under engine running conditions. Assume that the coefficient of linear expansion for aluminium alloy is 22×10^{-6}/K.

Solution

Area of piston top at lower temperature
$= \frac{1}{4}\pi \times 80^2 = 5027$ mm^2

Coefficient of superficial expansion, $\beta = 2\alpha$
$$= 2 \times 22 \times 10^{-6}\text{/K}$$

Temperature rise $= 270 - 20 = 250$ K

Increase in area of the piston top at the higher temperature
$=$ Original area $\times$ Coefficient of superficial expansion
   $\times$ Temperature rise
$= 5027 \times 2 \times 22 \times 10^{-6} \times 250 = 55.3$ mm^2

Answer: Increase in area of piston top $= 55.3$ mm^2

14.7 Expansion and contraction of liquids

Unlike solids, liquids have no fixed length or surface area but always take up the shape of their container. Hence, in the case of liquids, only volumetric change need be considered.

Let V = original volume of a liquid
γ = the coefficient of cubical expansion of the liquid
δT = the change in temperature

then:

Change in volume of the liquid $= V \times \gamma \times \delta T$ [14.3]

    It should be noted that the containing vessel will also expand. Hence, the apparent change in volume is the difference between the change in the volume of the liquid and that of the containing vessel.
    Average values of the coefficient of cubical expansion for some common liquids are given in Table 14.2.

Example 14.8

A copper tank is filled with 1200 litre of petrol at 8 °C. What volume of petrol would overflow when the temperature rises to 13 °C?

Coefficient of linear expansion of copper = 17×10^{-6}/K
Coefficient of cubical expansion of petrol = 125×10^{-5}/K

222

Table 14.2 Average values of coefficient of cubical expansion

Liquid	Coefficient of cubical expansion ($\gamma \times 10^{-5}$/K)
Ethyl alcohol	110
Glycerine	53
Mercury	18
Petrol	125
Turpentine	105
Water	45

Solution

Petrol:

Increase in volume = $V \times \gamma \times \delta T$ from equation [14.3]
where V = 1200 litre, γ = 125 $\times$ 10^{-5}/K
and δT = 13 − 8 = 5 K

$\therefore$ Increase in volume = 1200 $\times$ 125 $\times$ 10^{-5} $\times$ 5 = 7.5 litre

Copper tank:

Increase in volume = $V \times \gamma \times \delta T$
where V = 1200 litre, $\gamma = 3\alpha$ = 3 $\times$ 17 $\times$ 10^{-6}/K
and δT = 13 − 8 = 5 K

$\therefore$ Increase in volume = 1200 $\times$ 3 $\times$ 17 $\times$ 10^{-6} $\times$ 5 = 0.306 litre
Hence,

Volume of petrol that will overflow at 13 °C
= 7.5 − 0.306 = 7.194 litre

Answer: Volume of petrol that will overflow = 7.194 litre

Exercise 14.1 − Review questions

1 Most solids and liquids ...... when heated and ...... when cooled.
2 State what is meant by the coefficient of linear expansion of a material.
3 The symbol denoting the coefficient of linear expansion is ......
4 Briefly describe a typical experiment to demonstrate expansion and contraction of a metal.
5 Briefly describe an experiment that you have carried out in the laboratory to determine the coefficient of linear expansion of a metal rod. Make a neat sketch of the apparatus used.

6 If a steel gudgeon pin is a tight fit in an aluminium alloy piston at room temperature, state the probable reason for the pin becoming a loose fit when both pin and piston have their temperatures raised to 100 °C.

(NWRAC/ULCI)

7 Name three examples in a motor vehicle where clearance must be allowed for expansion due to heat.

(WMAC/UEI)

8 Describe briefly the procedure involved in fitting the following components:
(a) gudgeon pin to piston and connecting rod
(b) a valve seat insert into an aluminium alloy cylinder head.

9 The amount by which unit area of a material expands when the temperature is raised by 1 K is called the ......

10 β is the symbol for ......

11 Define the coefficient of cubical expansion.

12 What is the symbol used for the coefficient of cubical expansion?

13 Complete the following:
(a) $\beta = 2 \times$ ......   (b) $\gamma = 3 \times$ ......

14 Name two vehicle components where allowance is made for volumetric expansion.

(NWRAC/ULCI)

15 Describe an experiment to show that liquids expand when heated and contract when cooled. Make a sketch of the apparatus used and state the conclusions drawn from the experiment.

(NWRAC/ULCI)

Exercise 14.2 – Problems

1 In an experiment to determine the coefficient of linear expansion of copper, a rod of this metal, 400 mm long, is found to expand 0.56 mm when heated from 16 °C to 100 °C. Determine the coefficient of linear expansion of copper.

2 An overhead exhaust valve is 130 mm long at 15 °C. Under running conditions the average temperature of the valve is 105 °C. If the coefficient of linear expansion for the valve material is 0.000 012/K, calculate the increase in length.

(NWRAC/ULCI)(Modified)

3 The internal diameter of a cast-iron brake drum is 200 mm. When the brake is applied for a short period of time, the temperature of the drum increases by 180 K. Calculate the internal diameter of the drum at the new temperature.
Coefficient of linear expansion of cast iron = 10×10^{-6}/K.

4 A bearing is held in place on a semi-floating half-shaft, 40 mm diameter, by shrinking on a steel collar. When both components are at 20 °C the internal diameter of the collar is 0.2 mm smaller than the shaft diameter. Determine the minimum temperature to

which the collar must be heated to just slide down the shaft.
Coefficient of linear expansion of steel = 12×10^{-6}/K.

5 The effective length of the pushrod of an overhead valve engine is given as 250 mm at 9 °C. At its average working temperature of 105 °C, its length has increased to 250.288 mm. Calculate the coefficient of linear expansion for the pushrod material.

6 An aluminium piston is 50 mm diameter at 300 °C. If the temperature is raised to 500 °C, what will be the diameter if the coefficient of linear expansion is 25.2×10^{-6}/K?

(WMAC/UEI)

7 An exhaust pipe increases in length by 5.85 mm when its temperature is raised from 15 °C to 215 °C. If the coefficient of linear expansion of the metal used is 0.000 011 7/K, what was the original length of the pipe?

8 A steel girder is 10 m long at -10 °C. Find the change in length if its temperature is increased to 30 °C.
Coefficient of linear expansion of steel is 11×10^{-6}/K.

(EMEU)

9 If a flywheel starter ring gear is 400 mm diameter and it is required to shrink it on to a flywheel rim of 400.5 mm diameter, determine the temperature to which the ring gear must be raised. Assume an initial temperature of 10 °C and a coefficient of linear expansion of 0.000 011/K. Allow an additional 0.625 mm expansion as a working margin.

(WMAC/UEI)

10 A steel shaft runs in a bronze bush. The nominal diameter is 80 mm and, at room temperature of 20 °C, the diametral clearance is 0.05 mm. Calculate the diametral clearance at the working temperature of 80 °C. The coefficients of linear expansion for steel and bronze are 12×10^{-6}/K and 19.5×10^{-6}/K respectively.

(CGLI)

11 The interference fit between a cast-iron cylinder liner and an aluminium alloy cylinder block at 100 °C is 0.05 mm. If the coefficient of linear expansion of the 100 mm diameter liner is 0.000 01/K and for the cylinder block 0.000 015/K, find the difference in size at 0 °C.

(EMEU)

12 A piston and gudgeon pin have a clearance fit of 0.025 mm at 150 °C. The gudgeon pin is 20 mm diameter at 0 °C, and the interference fit between piston and pin at this temperature (0 °C) is 0.005 mm. If the coefficient of linear expansion of the pin material is 0.000 01/K, calculate the coefficient of linear expansion for the piston material.

(EMEU)

13 A 25 mm diameter cast-iron valve seat insert has an interference fit of 0.01 mm in an aluminium alloy cylinder head, at a temperature of 250 °C. Determine the fit at 20 °C if the coefficient of linear

expansion for the cast iron is 0.000 01/K and for the cylinder head 0.000 02/K.

(EMEU)

14 A cast-iron valve seat has to be fitted into an aluminium alloy cylinder head, with an interference fit at 20 °C of 0.05 mm. The seat has a nominal outside diameter of 50 mm. Determine:

(a) the temperature to which the cylinder head has to be raised in order to produce an increase in seat recess diameter of 0.05 mm

(b) the interference fit between head and fitted seat at 120 °C.

The coefficient of linear expansion of the iron is 0.000 015/K and for the aluminium 0.000 02/K.

(EMEU)

15 An aluminium alloy piston has a diameter of 100 mm at a temperature of 18 °C. When the piston is working in the cylinder, its average temperature is 350 °C. Calculate the increase in area of the piston top at the higher temperature. Coefficient of linear expansion for aluminium alloy is 23×10^{-6}/K.

16 A rectangular block of copper measures 150 mm $\times$ 100 mm $\times$ 40 mm at 10 °C. When heated to 85 °C its volume increases by 2295 mm³. What is the coefficient of linear expansion of copper?

17 A vehicle engine that has recently had its radiator topped-up with water is left running for 6 minutes. At the end of this time it is found to require 0.4 litre of water in order to replace that lost through the overflow pipe. If the initial temperature of the water was 15 °C, and the total capacity of the engine cooling system is 11 litre, calculate the final temperature of the water.

Coefficient of volumetric expansion of water = 45×10^{-5}/K.

(WMAC/UEI)

18 The mercury contained in a certain thermometer has a volume of 500 mm³ at 5 °C. What is the increase in volume when the temperature is raised to 80 °C? Assume the coefficient of cubic expansion of mercury to be 18×10^{-5}/K.

19 80 000 mm³ of methyl alcohol having a coefficient of volumetric expansion of 120×10^{-5}/K is contained in an aluminium container that it just fills at -10 °C. Calculate the volume of alcohol that would overflow when the temperature rises to 40 °C. Take the coefficient of linear expansion of aluminium to be equal to 24×10^{-6}/K.

Chapter 15

The gas laws

15.1 Introduction

The internal combustion engine aspirates air into which a measured quantity of fuel is introduced. This fuel mixture is burnt in the cylinder of the engine in such a way that it produces high-pressure, high-temperature gases which can be made to expand and do work by pushing a piston in the cylinder. It is therefore essential to make a study of the behaviour of gases, since the amount of work done depends fundamentally upon obtaining the best possible 'performance' from the gases in the cylinder of the engine.

Certain important laws governing the behaviour of perfect gases under varying conditions of temperature and pressure have been established from experimental results. It is upon these laws that our ideal considerations are based, since the laws apply very closely to actual gases such as exist in the cylinders of a motor vehicle engine.

15.2 Pressure of a gas

Any quantity of a gas, if placed into a vessel of larger volume than itself, will at once fill every part of the vessel. The rapidly moving molecules of the gas continually collide with the walls of its container and produce forces distributed all over the inside of the vessel (see Fig. 15.1). The amount of the force exerted on unit area of the surface of the container is defined as the *pressure* of the gas.

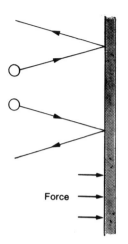

Figure 15.1 Pressure of a gas

The unit of pressure is the *newton per square metre* (N/m^2). This unit has a special name, the *pascal* (symbol Pa). Note that the name pascal is also given to the unit of stress (see Section 6.1). For high pressures, it is more convenient to express the pressure in kilopascals (kPa), or in megapascals (MPa).

An alternative unit of pressure in the *bar*, where:

1 bar $= 10^5$ Pa $= 100$ kPa

The bar is a convenient practical unit, being very nearly equal to one standard atmosphere (101.325 kPa $=$ 1.013 25 bar), and is widely used.

15.3 Atmospheric pressure

The earth is surrounded by an atmosphere which extends about 320 km above its surface. This atmosphere exerts a pressure due to the mass of air above the surface of the earth. At sea level atmospheric pressure is about 101.3 kPa (101.3 kN/m^2 or 1.013 bar). Atmospheric pressure decreases with altitude; at a height of approximately 3000 m, for instance, it is about 70 kPa or 700 mbar.

Atmospheric pressure varies slightly from day to day and is recorded by means of a *barometer* in which the height of a column of mercury is used as a measure of the pressure. A simple mercury barometer can be constructed in the laboratory as described below.

Take a glass tube about 1 m long and closed at one end. Fill the tube to the top with clean mercury, taking care to remove all air bubbles. Close the open end with the forefinger, invert the tube, and then lower it carefully until the open end is well below the free surface of some mercury in a bowl (Fig. 15.2). It will be observed that, on removing the finger, the column of mercury in the tube falls until it is just supported by the atmospheric pressure outside. It follows therefore that the atmospheric pressure acting on the free surface of the mercury in the bowl can be measured in terms of the height h of the column of mercury in the tube. Now place a metre rule carefully against the tube and measure the height h as accurately as possible. It will be somewhere about 760 mm. The space A above the mercury in the tube is almost a vacuum, as it contains only a very small amount of mercury vapour.

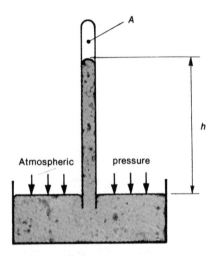

Figure 15.2 Simple mercury barometer

Since Hg is the chemical symbol for mercury then, if a mercury barometer stands at 760 mm, this would be written 760 mmHg.

The *Fortin barometer* uses the above principle to enable the atmospheric pressure to be recorded accurately. In addition to the mercury column, a scale and reservoir level adjusting screw are fitted.

15.4 Gauge pressure and absolute pressure

Most pressure gauges are constructed to indicate the pressure of a gas inside a closed vessel **above** that of the atmosphere. When such a gauge reads 'zero', this does not mean that there is a perfect vacuum in the vessel but that the pressure inside it is equal to atmospheric pressure.

Pressure as indicated by the ordinary gauge is called *gauge pressure*. The total or *absolute pressure* is the pressure above that of a perfect vacuum, i.e. the sum of the gauge and atmospheric pressures. In other words,

Absolute pressure = Gauge pressure + Atmospheric pressure

Example 15.1

The pressure in a motor vehicle tyre is checked and found to be 172 kPa by tyre gauge. What is the absolute pressure in kPa and in bar?
(Take the atmospheric pressure to be 101.3 kPa.)

Solution

Absolute pressure = Gauge pressure + Atmospheric pressure
$$= 172 + 101.3$$
$$= 273.3 \text{ kPa}$$
$$= 2.733 \text{ bar (since 1 bar} = 100 \text{ kPa)}$$

Answer: Absolute pressure = 273.3 kPa or 2.733 bar

15.5 Pressure gauges

The manometer

This type of gauge is useful for measuring small differences in pressure. It consists of a simple U-tube containing liquid, usually water or mercury. One end of the tube is open to the atmosphere and the other end is connected to the vessel containing gas under pressure. When the pressure of the gas inside the vessel is greater than the pressure of the atmosphere, the liquid will rise in the open-ended limb of the tube and fall in the other, as shown in Fig. 15.3. The difference

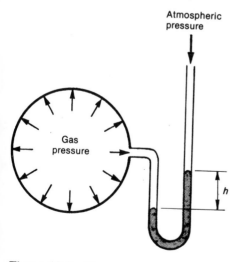

Figure 15.3   The manometer

230

in levels of the liquid in the tube (*h* mm of liquid) registers the pressure inside the vessel. This, of course, is the gauge pressure. The actual or absolute pressure will be equal to the pressure of the atmosphere plus the gauge pressure.

The Bourdon pressure gauge

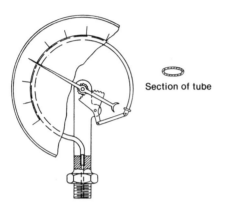

Section of tube

Figure 15.4   The Bourdon pressure gauge

For measuring great pressures above atmospheric, it is usual to employ a *Bourdon* type of pressure gauge (Fig. 15.4). This consists essentially of a phosphor-bronze tube of elliptical cross-section and bent into an arc of a circle. The free end of the tube is sealed and is connected by means of a short link to a small toothed sector. This sector gears with a pinion fitted to the pointer spindle. When subjected to internal pressure, the tube tends to become straight and causes the free end to move in proportion to the gas pressure. This movement is amplified by the action of the sector and pinion which, in turn, causes the pointer to rotate over a scale from which the pressure can be read.

As in the case of the manometer, it must not be forgotten that the Bourdon pressure gauge measures the gauge pressure. The atmospheric pressure must therefore be added to this gauge pressure in order to determine the absolute pressure of the gas.

Example 15.2

A mercury manometer connected to a tank containing gas indicates a gauge pressure of 138 mmHg. If the barometer reads 752 mmHg, determine the absolute pressure inside the tank.

Solution
Absolute pressure inside the tank

= Gauge pressure + Atmospheric pressure

$= 138 + 752 = 890$ mmHg

Answer: Absolute pressure of gas $= 890$ mmHg

Example 15.3

A Bourdon pressure gauge indicates a pressure of 500 kPa. Determine the absolute pressure, in kPa, if the barometer shows an atmospheric pressure of 985 mbar.

Solution

Atmospheric pressure $= 985$ mbar
$= 0.985$ bar
$= 98.5$ kPa (since 1 bar $= 100$ kPa)

Absolute pressure $=$ Gauge pressure $+$ Atmospheric pressure
$= 500 + 98.5 = 598.5$ kPa

Answer: Absolute pressure $= 598.5$ kPa

15.6 Vacuum gauges

Pressure gauges used for measuring pressures **below** atmospheric pressure are called *vacuum gauges*. These are usually graduated in millimetres of mercury (mmHg) and work on the same principle as the Bourdon pressure gauge. A reading of 760 mmHg on a vacuum gauge indicates a perfect vacuum (i.e. zero absolute pressure). Zero on the gauge indicates atmospheric pressure. A reading of, say, 300 mmHg is referred to as 300 mm of vacuum and would correspond to an absolute pressure of $760 - 300 = 460$ mmHg.

Vacuum gauges are often used by service mechanics for diagnosing engine faults, or to make the adjustments necessary for obtaining the best possible engine performance. The amount of partial vacuum or *depression* in an engine manifold and its effects on a vacuum gauge will give an indication of the engine's mechanical condition and whether the valves, ignition timing and carburettor settings are correct.

15.7 Relationship between pressure and volume of a gas: Boyle's law

Boyle's law gives the relationship between pressure and volume of a quantity of gas under **constant temperature** conditions. It states that:

'The absolute pressure of a given mass of gas varies inversely as its volume when the temperature of the gas remains constant.'

Thus, if the absolute pressure of a given mass of gas is doubled, its

232

volume is halved, or if the absolute pressure is halved, the volume will be doubled.

Hence, if p = absolute pressure of gas
and V = volume of gas

then, Boyle's law may be expressed as follows:

$$p \propto \frac{1}{V}$$

$$\therefore \quad p = \frac{1}{V} \times C$$

or $\quad pV = C$, a constant $\hspace{2cm}$ [15.1]

If the absolute pressure p is plotted against the volume V, the curve shown in Fig. 15.5 will be obtained. This is called a *rectangular hyperbola*.

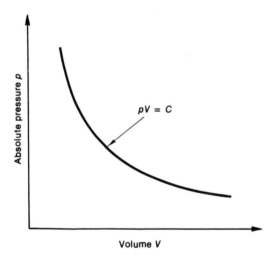

Figure 15.5

If suffix 1 denotes the initial state and suffix 2 the final state of a given mass of gas, then, since pV = a constant, we may write:

$$p_1 V_1 = p_2 V_2 \hspace{3cm} \bullet \; [15.2]$$

If now another graph is drawn of absolute pressure against the reciprocal of the volume, i.e. of p against $1/V$, this second graph (Fig. 15.6) will be a straight line passing through the origin, thus showing that the absolute pressure p is directly proportional to $1/V$.

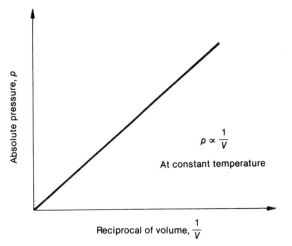

$p \propto \dfrac{1}{V}$

At constant temperature

Reciprocal of volume, $\dfrac{1}{V}$

Figure 15.6

It is important to note that in any calculations involving Boyle's law and other gas laws, it is the *absolute pressure* and **not** the gauge pressure that must be used.

Example 15.4
A volume of 0.5 m³ of air at a gauge pressure of 1500 kPa (15 bar) is allowed to expand in a cylinder until the volume is 2 m³. If the temperature remains constant, what is the new gauge pressure?

Assume the atmospheric pressure to be 100 kPa (1 bar).

Solution
Initial pressure $= p_1 = 1500 + 100 = 1600$ kPa abs
Final pressure $= p_2 = ?$
Initial volume $= V_1 = 0.5$ m³
Final volume $= V_2 = 2$ m³

Since the temperature remains constant, the expansion is according to Boyle's law. Thus:

$$p_1 V_1 = p_2 V_2 \quad \text{from equation [15.2]}$$

$$\therefore \quad p_2 = \frac{p_1 V_1}{V_2} = \frac{1600 \times 0.5}{2} = 400 \text{ kPa abs}$$

i.e.
   New gauge pressure $= 400 - 100 = 300$ kPa

Answer: New gauge pressure $= 300$ kPa (or 3 bar)

Example 15.5

A quantity of gas occupies a volume of 5 m³ at a pressure of 140 kPa absolute. It is then compressed at constant temperature until its pressure is 560 kPa absolute. Determine the volume of the gas at the end of the compression.

Solution

Initial pressure $= p_1 = 140$ kPa abs
Final pressure $= p_2 = 560$ kPa abs
Initial volume $= V_1 = 5$ m³
Final volume $= V_2 = ?$

Since the temperature of the gas remains constant, compression must take place according to Boyle's law. Thus:

$$p_1 V_1 = p_2 V_2$$

$$\therefore \quad V_2 = \frac{p_1 V_1}{p_2} = \frac{140 \times 5}{560} = 1.25 \text{ m}^3$$

Answer: Volume of gas at end of compression $= 1.25$ m³

15.8 Relationship between volume and temperature of a gas: Charles' law

Charles' law gives the relationship between volume and temperature of a quantity of gas when the **pressure is kept constant**. It states that:

'The volume of a given mass of gas varies directly as it thermo-dynamic or absolute temperature when the pressure is kept constant'.

Thus, at double the absolute temperature, the volume of a given mass of gas is doubled; at three times the absolute temperature, the volume is trebled, and so on.

Hence, if $\quad V = $ volume of gas
and $\quad\quad T = $ absolute temperature of gas

then, Charles' law may be expressed as follows:

$$V \propto T$$
$$\therefore \quad V = T \times C$$
$$\text{or} \quad \frac{V}{T} = C, \text{a constant} \quad\quad\quad [15.3]$$

If suffix 1 denotes the initial state and suffix 2 the final state of a given mass of gas, then, since $V/T = $ a constant, we may write:

$$\frac{V_1}{T_1} = \frac{V_2}{T_2} \quad\quad\quad\quad [15.4]$$

It should here be emphasized that in problems dealing with the gas laws, all temperatures must be converted to absolute temperatures. Thus, if θ is the temperature of the gas in degrees celsius and T the absolute temperature in kelvins, then by equation [12.1]:

$$T\,\text{K} = \theta\,°\text{C} + 273$$

Example 15.6

A given mass of gas occupies a volume of 200 litre at a temperature of 27 °C. What would the volume of this mass of gas be at (a) 90 °C, and (b) at -30 °C, under the same pressure conditions?

Solution

(a) $V_1 = 200$ litre $T_1 = 27 + 273 = 300$ K
    $V_2 = ?$ $T_2 = 90 + 273 = 363$ K

Since the pressure of the gas remains unaltered, the change must follow Charles' law. Thus:

$$\frac{V_1}{T_1} = \frac{V_2}{T_2} \qquad \text{from equation [15.4]}$$

$$\therefore V_2 = \frac{V_1 T_2}{T_1} = \frac{200 \times 363}{300} = 242 \text{ litre}$$

(b) $V_1 = 200$ litre $T_1 = 300$ K
    $V_3 = ?$ $T_3 = -30 + 273 = 243$ K

Again, since the pressure of the gas remains unaltered, the change must follow Charles' law. Thus, applying equation [15.3] to this case, we get:

$$\frac{V_1}{T_1} = \frac{V_3}{T_3}$$

$$\therefore V_3 = \frac{V_1 T_3}{T_1} = \frac{200 \times 243}{300} = 162 \text{ litre}$$

Answer: (a) Volume of gas at 90 °C $= 242$ litre
           (b) Volume of gas at -30 °C $= 162$ litre

Example 15.7

A quantity of gas at a temperature of 15 °C is heated at constant pressure until its volume is doubled. What will be the final temperature of the gas?

Solution

$V_1 = V_1$ $T_1 = 15 + 273 = 288$ K
$V_2 = 2V_1$ $T_2 = ?$

Since the gas is heated at constant pressure, the expansion must follow Charles' law. Thus:

$$\frac{V_1}{T_1} = \frac{V_2}{T_2}$$

$$\therefore \quad T_2 = \frac{T_1 V_2}{V_1} = \frac{288 \times 2V_1}{V_1} = 576 \text{ K}$$

i.e. Final temperature of gas $= 576 - 273 = 303 \text{ }°C$

Answer: Final temperature of gas $= 303 \text{ }°C$

15.9 Combination of Boyle's and Charles' laws: The general gas equation

A given mass of gas may undergo simultaneous changes in pressure, volume and temperature. When this change occurs in the state of the gas, neither Boyle's law, which assumes constant temperature, nor Charles' law, which assumes alteration of temperature with constant pressure, can be applied. However, this change of state may be regarded as taking place in two stages:

(1) a change according to Boyle's law; and
(2) a change according to Charles' law.

The resulting change will then be according to the laws of Boyle and Charles combined.

Let the state of a given mass of gas change from the initial conditions of pressure p_1, volume V_1 and temperature T_1, Fig. 15.7(a), to the final conditions of pressure p_2, volume V_2 and temperature T_2, Fig. 15.7(c). It is possible to imagine the final conditions to be arrived at in two stages as described below.

Stage 1
A change in pressure from p_1 to p_2 at constant temperature T_1. The volume will change from V_1 to some intermediate value V_A, Fig. 15.7(b). Since the temperature remains constant, the change is according to Boyle's law. Thus:

$$p_1 V_1 = p_2 V_A$$

$$\therefore \quad V_A = \frac{p_1 V_1}{p_2} \qquad\qquad [15.5]$$

Stage 2
A change in temperature from T_1 to T_2 at constant pressure p_2. The

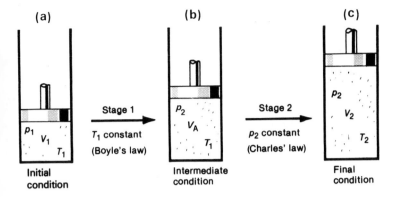

Figure 15.7 Boyle's and Charles' laws

volume will change from V_A to the final volume V_2. Since the pressure remains constant, the change is according to Charles' law. Thus:

$$\frac{V_A}{T_1} = \frac{V_2}{T_2}$$

$$\therefore \quad V_A = \frac{V_2 T_1}{T_2} \tag{15.6}$$

Hence, equating the values of V_A from equations [15.5] and [15.6], we get:

$$\frac{p_1 V_1}{p_2} = \frac{V_2 T_1}{T_2}$$

or $\quad \dfrac{p_1 V_1}{T_1} = \dfrac{p_2 V_2}{T_2}$ [15.7]

This equation, which is a combination of Boyle's and Charles' laws, is known as the *general gas equation*. It may be expressed in the form:

$$\frac{pV}{T} = C, \text{a constant} \tag{15.8}$$

The general gas equation is very useful in making calculations of changes in the conditions of a quantity of gas in the cylinder of an internal combustion engine.

Remember that in any calculations involving the gas laws, **absolute** pressures and temperatures must be used.

Example 15.8
At the commencement of compression a cylinder contains 480 cm³ of gas at a pressure of 96 kPa absolute and temperature 100 °C. At the

end of compression the volume is 80 cm³ and the pressure 725 kPa absolute. What will be the temperature at the end of compression?

Solution

p_1 = 96 kPa abs p_2 = 725 kPa abs
V_1 = 480 cm³ V_2 = 80 cm³
T_1 = 100 + 273 = 337 K T_2 = ?

Now, using the general gas equation [15.7], we get:

$$\frac{p_1 V_1}{T_1} = \frac{p_2 V_2}{T_2}$$

$$\therefore \quad T_2 = \frac{p_2 V_2 T_1}{p_1 V_1} = \frac{725 \times 80 \times 373}{96 \times 480} = 469.5 \text{ K}$$

i.e.
Temperature at end of compression = 469.5 − 273 = 196.5 °C

Answer: Temperature at end of compression = 196.5 °C

15.10   Standard temperature and pressure (STP)

It is often necessary, for reference purposes, to reduce the volume of a gas to some standard conditions. These conditions are known as *standard temperature and pressure*, usually abbreviated to STP, and are taken to refer to a temperature of 0 °C (273 K) and normal atmospheric pressure of 101.325 kPa (1.013 25 bar) or 760 mmHg.

The general gas equation is used in reducing a quantity of gas to STP. The following example will illustrate this procedure.

Example 15.9

A quantity of gas at a pressure of 720 mmHg and a temperature of 17 °C occupies a volume of 2.4 litre. Reduce the volume of the gas to STP.

Solution

Let suffix 1 denote the original conditions of the gas and suffix 2 its conditions at STP. Then:

p_1 = 720 mmHg p_2 = 760 mmHg
V_1 = 2.4 litre V_2 = ?
T_1 = 17 + 273 = 290 K T_2 = 0 °C = 273 K

Using the general gas equation [15.7], we get:

$$\frac{p_1 V_1}{T_1} = \frac{p_2 V_2}{T_2}$$

$$\therefore \qquad V_2 = \frac{p_1 V_1 T_2}{p_2 T_1} = \frac{720 \times 2.4 \times 273}{760 \times 290} = 2.14 \text{ litre}$$

Answer: Volume of gas at STP = 2.14 litre

15.11 Relationship between pressure and temperature of a gas at constant volume: Pressure law

From the general gas equation [15.7], if the volume is kept constant, i.e. if $V_1 = V_2$, then equation [15.7] becomes:

$$\frac{p_1}{T_1} = \frac{p_2}{T_2} \qquad\qquad\qquad [15.9]$$

Equation [15.9] shows that:

'The pressure of a given mass of gas varies directly as its thermodynamic or absolute temperature when the volume is kept constant.'

This is exactly analogous with the volume change with temperature at constant pressure, and can therefore be applied to pressure changes at constant volume in a similar manner to the volume changes at constant pressure.

Example 15.10
When the pressure in a car tyre was checked at a temperature of 12 °C, the tyre gauge showed a reading of 1.75 bar. What would be the tyre gauge reading when the temperature had increased to 38 °C, assuming the volume of air in the tyre to be constant.
(Take the atmospheric pressure to be 1.01 bar.)

Solution
$p_1 = 1.75 + 1.01 = 2.76$ bar abs $\qquad T_1 = 12 + 273 = 285$ K
$p_2 = ?$ $\qquad\qquad\qquad\qquad\qquad\qquad T_2 = 38 + 273 = 311$ K

Since the volume of the air in the tyre is assumed to remain constant, then $V_1 = V_2$, so that:

$$\frac{p_1}{T_1} = \frac{p_1}{T_2} \qquad \text{from equation } [15.9]$$

$$p_2 = \frac{p_1 T_2}{T_1} = \frac{2.76 \times 311}{285} = 3.01 \text{ bar abs}$$

∴ Tyre gauge reading = 3.01 − 1.01 = 2.0 bar

Answer: Tyre gauge reading at 38 °C = 2.0 bar

15.12 Compression ratio

The *compression ratio* (*r*) of an engine is the ratio between the total volume of the cylinder when the piston is at bottom dead centre to the volume of the clearance space when the piston is at top dead centre.

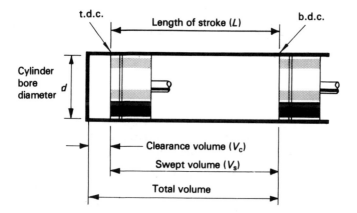

Figure 15.8

Consider the piston and cylinder of Fig. 15.8. The *bore* of the cylinder is the internal diameter of the cylinder. The *stroke* is the distance moved by the piston between top dead centre (t.d.c.) and bottom dead centre (b.d.c.) positions, and is equal to twice the crank radius.

The *swept volume* (V_s) of the cylinder is the volume swept out by the piston during a single stroke. Hence, if d is the cylinder bore diameter and L is the length of the stroke, then:

Swept volume, V_s = Area of cylinder bore × Length of stroke

i.e.
$$V_s = \frac{\pi d^2}{4} \times L \qquad [15.10]$$

It should be noted that the *capacity* of any engine is the sum of the swept volumes of all its cylinders.

The *clearance volume* (V_c) is the volume enclosed between the piston crown and the cylinder head when the piston is at top dead centre.

Now, total volume of the cylinder when the piston is at bottom dead centre

= Clearance volume + Swept volume

$= V_c + V_s$

Hence:

$$\text{Compression ratio, } r = \frac{V_c + V_s}{V_c} \qquad [15.11]$$

The thermal efficiency of an internal combustion engine (see Section 18.13) depends upon the compression ratio; the higher the compression ratio, the higher the efficiency.

In the design of all types of internal combustion engines, every effort is made to use as high a compression ratio as possible, but the highest value for the compression ratio will depend on practical considerations. In the case of a petrol engine, in which a mixture of petrol vapour and air is compressed in the combustion chamber, a very high compression ratio will cause the mixture to ignite spontaneously and violently (this phenomenon is known as *detonation*), resulting in the loss of power and possible damage to the engine. With petrol engines, therefore, the compression ratio is usually limited to about 10 to 1.

In the case of a compression-ignition engine, since air alone is contained in the cylinder during the compression stroke, the problem of detonation does not arise. Consequently, compression ratios of up to about 25 to 1 can be used. Higher values, however, will cause pressures above practical possibilities.

Example 15.11

A six-cylinder engine has a bore of 70 mm and a stroke of 80 mm. If the clearance volume of one cylinder is 42 000 mm^3, calculate:

(a) the compression ratio of the engine
(b) the capacity of the engine, in litre.

(1 litre $= 10^6$ mm^3.)

Solution

(a) Swept volume, V_s = Area of bore × Length of stroke

$$= \frac{\pi}{4} \times 70^2 \times 80 = 308\ 000 \text{ mm}^3$$

Clearance volume, $V_c = 42\ 000$ mm^3

$$\text{Compression ratio} \quad = \frac{V_c + V_s}{V_c}$$

$$= \frac{42\,000 + 308\,000}{42\,000} \left[\frac{mm^3}{mm^3}\right]$$

$$= \frac{350\,000}{42\,000} = 8.33 \text{ to } 1$$

(b) Engine capacity

= Swept volume of 1 cylinder × No. of cylinders
= 308 000 × 6
= 1 848 000 mm³
= 1.848 litre (since 1 litre = 10^6 mm³)

Answer: (a) Compression ratio = 8.33 to 1
       (b) Engine capacity = 1.85 litre

Example 15.12

The compression ratio of a compression-ignition engine is 12 to 1, the bore diameter is 110 mm and the stroke is 140 mm. Calculate the clearance volume of the engine.

(CGLI)

Solution

Swept volume, V_s = Area of bore × Length of stroke
           = $\frac{1}{4}\pi \times 110^2 \times 140 = 1\,331\,000$ mm³

Now,

Compression ratio, $r = \dfrac{V_c + V_s}{V_c} = 1 + \dfrac{V_s}{V_c}$

or $\qquad\qquad r - 1 = \dfrac{V_s}{V_c}$

i.e. $\qquad\qquad 11 = \dfrac{1\,331\,000}{V_c}$

so that $\qquad V_c = \dfrac{1\,331\,000}{11} = 121\,000$ mm³

Answer: Clearance volume = 121 000 mm³

Example 15.13

The piston of an engine sweeps out a volume of 475 cm³. If the clearance volume at the top of the stroke is 96 cm³, calculate the compression ratio.

At the end of the suction stroke the cylinder is full of mixture at a

pressure of 3.3 kPa below atmospheric. Assuming the temperature to remain constant, calculate the pressure at the end of the compression stroke.
(Assume the atmospheric pressure to be 101.3 kPa.)

(CGLI)(Modified)

Solution

Volume of mixture at commencement of compression,

V_1 = Clearance volume (V_c) + Swept volume (V_s)
   = 96 + 475 = 571 cm^3

Volume of mixture at end of compression,

V_2 = Clearance volume (V_c) = 96 cm^3

Hence, from equation [15.11],

$$\text{Compression ratio}, r = \frac{V_1}{V_2} \qquad\qquad [15.12]$$

$$= \frac{571}{96} \left[\frac{cm^3}{cm^3} \right] = 5.95 \text{ to } 1$$

Now since the pressure at the commencement of the compression stroke is 3.3 kPa **below** atmospheric, then:

Initial absolute pressure (p_1)
= Atmospheric pressure − Gauge pressure
= 101.3 − 3.3 = 98 kPa

Since the temperature remains constant, the mixture is compressed in accordance with Boyle's law. Thus:

$$p_1 V_1 = p_2 V_2$$

$$\therefore \quad p_2 = p_1 \times \frac{V_1}{V_2} = p_1 \times r$$

$$= 98 \times 5.95 = 583 \text{ kPa abs}$$

Answer: Compression ratio = 5.95 to 1
         Pressure at end of compression = 583 kPa abs

Example 15.14

The compression ratio of an engine is 9 to 1, the pressure at the commencement of the compression stroke is 110 kPa abs and the temperature is 115 °C. Calculate the absolute pressure at the end of the compression stroke if the temperature has risen to 180 °C.

Solution

$T_1 = 115 + 273 = 399 \text{ K}$ p_1 110 kPa abs
$T_2 = 180 + 273 = 453 \text{ K}$ $p_2 = ?$

Compression ratio, $r = \dfrac{V_1}{V_2} = 9$

By the general gas equation [15.7],

$$\frac{p_1 V_1}{T_1} = \frac{p_2 V_2}{T_2}$$

$$\therefore \quad p_2 = \frac{p_1 T_2}{T_1} \times \frac{V_1}{V_2} = \frac{p_1 T_2}{T_1} \times r$$

$$= \frac{110 \times 453 \times 9}{388} = 1153 \text{ kPa abs}$$

Answer: Pressure at end of compression = 1153 kPa abs

Example 15.15

A compression-ignition engine has a compression ratio of 16 to 1 and the air pressure at the commencement of the compression stroke is 85 kPa abs, the temperature being 47 °C. Calculate the temperature at the end of the compression stroke when the pressure is 3400 kPa abs.

Solution

$p_1 = 85 \text{ kPa abs}$ $T_1 = 47 + 273 = 320 \text{ K}$
$p_2 = 3400 \text{ kPa abs}$ $T_2 = ?$

Compression ratio, $r = \dfrac{V_1}{V_2} = 16$

Now $\dfrac{p_1 V_1}{T_1} = \dfrac{p_2 V_2}{T_2}$

$$\therefore \quad T_2 = \frac{p_2 T_1}{p_1} \times \frac{V_2}{V_1} = \frac{p_2 T_1}{p_1} \times \frac{1}{r}$$

$$= \frac{3400 \times 320}{85 \times 16} = 800 \text{ K}$$

i.e. Temperature at end of compression = 800 − 273 = 527 °C

Answer: Final temperature = 527 °C

Exercise 15.1 – Review questions

1 The unit of pressure is ......
2 A given mass of gas is enclosed in a vessel. Explain briefly how the pressure measured at the wall of the vessel is produced by the gas molecules.
3 What do you understand by the term 'atmospheric pressure'?
4 Distinguish between 'gauge pressure' and 'absolute pressure'.
5 What is meant by 'standard temperature and pressure'?
6 A pressure of 1 bar = ... kPa.
7 An instrument which measures small pressures above atmospheric is called ......
8 An instrument which measures great pressures above atmospheric is called ......
9 An instrument which measures pressures below atmospheric is called ......
10 State Boyle's law.
11 Describe a laboratory experiment to verify Boyle's law. Include a sketch of the apparatus used.
12 State Charles' law.
13 Describe a laboratory experiment to verify Charles' law. Include a sketch of the apparatus used.
14 What is meant by the 'absolute or thermodynamic temperature' of a gas?
15 Explain the meaning of 'absolute zero of temperature'.
16 The general gas equation is obtained by combining ...... law and ...... law.
17 The relationship between the absolute pressure (p), the absolute temperature (T) and the volume (V) of a given mass of gas is ......
18 State the law which indicates how the absolute pressure of a given mass of gas varies with its thermodynamic temperature when the volume is kept constant.
19 An increase in the temperature of a gas at constant volume will cause the pressure to ......

(NWRAC/ULCI)

20 Explain what you understand by the 'compression ratio' of an engine.
21 (a) Describe how the compression ratio of an engine is calculated.
   (b) Knowing the compression ratio of an engine, state how the compression pressure can be calculated approximately.

(NWRAC/ULCI)

Exercise 15.2 – Problems

1 A quantity of gas has an initial absolute pressure of 300 kPa and volume 0.14 m³. It is then expanded in accordance with Boyle's

law until its volume becomes 0.7 m³. Determine the final pressure of the gas.

2 A quantity of gas has an initial volume of 586 cm³ and a temperature of 20 °C. It is then expanded in accordance with Charles' law until its volume becomes 880 cm³. Determine the final absolute temperature of the gas.

3 A mass of gas has an initial absolute pressure of 100 kPa and a temperature of 18 °C. The temperature of the gas is then increased to 600 °C while the volume remains constant. Determine the final pressure of the gas.

4 In the compression stroke of a diesel engine, 3 litre of air at an absolute pressure of 93 kPa and a temperature of 45 °C are compressed to an absolute pressure of 2900 kPa and a temperature of 690 °C. If the compression follows the law pV/T = constant, calculate the volume of the air at the end of the compression.

5 A quantity of gas occupies a volume of 0.056 m³ at a gauge pressure of 13 bar and a temperature of 27 °C. The gas is allowed to expand until the gauge pressure has fallen to 7.4 bar, the temperature also falling to 15 °C. What is the new volume of the gas?
If the temperature then increases to 38 °C without change in volume, what will be the new gauge pressure?
(The atmospheric pressure is assumed to be 1 bar.)

6 The volume of air in a car tyre is 12.7 litre when the pressure gauge reading is 1.9 bar and the temperature is 18 °C. If the temperature of the air in the tyre rises to 72 °C, what will be the new pressure gauge reading
(a) assuming the volume of the air in the tyre to be constant
(b) if the volume increases to 13 litre?
(Atmospheric pressure = 1.01 bar.)

7 A quantity of air is compressed in a cylinder to one-fifth of its original volume. The absolute pressure is initially 108 kPa and the temperature during compression rises from 288 K to 400 K. What is the pressure of the compressed air?
If this air is now allowed to expand at constant temperature to its original volume, what will be the new pressure.
(WMAC/UEI)(Modified)

8 A quantity of gas has an initial absolute pressure of 1.4 MPa and a volume of 840 cm³. The gas is then expanded until the absolute pressure becomes 280 kPa. What is the new volume of the gas
(a) if the temperature remains constant
(b) if the temperature subsequently changes from 27 °C to 10 °C at the constant pressure of 280 kPa absolute?

9 (a) Air at a pressure of 105 kPa absolute and a temperature of 15 °C is compressed to 2.8 MPa absolute. Its volume is one-twelfth of its original volume.
Calculate the final temperature of the air.

(*b*) What would have been the final temperature and pressure if the compression had occurred in accordance with Boyle's law?

(WMAC/UEI)(Modified)

10 The compression ratio of a petrol engine is 8 to 1 and the pressure at the commencement of the compression stroke is 100 kPa absolute, the temperature being 47 °C. Calculate the temperature at the end of the compression stroke when the pressure is 1.5 MPa absolute.

11 A six-cylinder engine has a bore of 100 mm and a stroke of 140 mm. Calculate:
(*a*) the swept volume of one cylinder, in cm^3
(*b*) the capacity of the engine, in litre.
(1 litre = 1000 cm^3.)

12 A compression-ignition engine has a bore and stroke of 100 mm and 112 mm respectively, and a clearance volume of 63 000 mm^3. Calculate the compression ratio.

(NWRAC/ULCI)

13 Calculate the clearance volume of a compression-ignition engine. The bore is 105 mm, the stroke is 120 mm and the compression ratio is 16 to 1.

(CGLI)

14 A four-cylinder, four-stroke engine has a compression ratio of 8.5 to 1 when using a clearance volume of 66.4 cm^3. Calculate:
(*a*) the swept volume of the cylinder
(*b*) the bore diameter when the stroke is 77 mm.

(WMAC/UEI)

15 The combusion chamber of an overhead valve engine is hemispherical, the radius being equal to that of the bore radius. The bore and stroke are 80 mm and 140 mm respectively. Assuming that the piston just reaches the hemisphere, calculate the swept volume of the cylinder and the compression ratio.

(CGLI)

16 The compression ratio of a six-cylinder 'square' engine, of capacity 2.25 litre, is 8.5 to 1. Determine:
(*a*) the cylinder bore diameter
(*b*) the thickness of metal that would have to be removed from the top face of the cylinder block to increase the compression ratio to 9 to 1.
(*Note*: For a 'square' engine the bore is equal to the stroke. 1 litre = 10^6 mm^3.)

(CGLI)(Modified)

17 (*a*) A compression-ignition engine has a bore of 140 mm and a stroke of 122 mm. The clearance volume is 128 cm^3. Calculate the compression ratio of the engine.
(*b*) In the above engine, the air pressure at the commencement of the compression stroke is 100 kPa absolute and the temperature is 35 °C. Calculate the temperature at the end of

the compression stroke when the pressure is 4 MPa absolute.

(CGLI)

18 Determine the compression ratio in a diesel-type engine in which the temperature of the air in the cylinder is raised by compression from 15 °C to 527 °C, the absolute pressure rising at the same time from 105 kPa to 3.5 MPa.

(EMEU)(Modified)

19 A compression-ignition engine has a compression ratio of 17 to 1. The temperature at the beginning of compression is 40 °C and at the end of compression is 450 °C. If the pressure in the cylinder at bottom dead centre is 100 kPa absolute, calculate the pressure in the cylinder when the piston has reached top dead centre.

(WMAC/UEI)

20 The air pressure at the commencement of the compression stroke in a cylinder of a compression-ignition engine is 1 bar absolute, the temperature is 25 °C and the air has a volume of 1.7 litre. The compression ratio of the engine is 16 to 1. Calculate the air temperature at the end of the compression stroke, the pressure having risen to 42 bar absolute.

If this compressed air then expands to twice its volume but its pressure remains constant, calculate the temperature of the air at the end of this expansion.

(CGLI)(Modified)

21 An engine cylinder has a bore diameter of 76 mm and a piston stroke of 102 mm. With the piston at the bottom of its stroke, the cylinder and combustion space contain air at an absolute pressure of 85 kPa and a temperature of 20 °C. The air is then compressed by the piston until, at the top of its stroke, the absolute pressure has risen to 3.4 MPa and the temperature to 400 °C. Calculate the compression ratio of the engine.

Chapter 16

Fuels and combustion

16.1 Introduction

Fuels are substances composed mainly of carbon and hydrogen and
may appear in the solid, liquid or gaseous form. Examples of these are
given below:

Solid	Liquid	Gaseous
Coal	Petrol	Natural gas (methane)
Wood	Kerosene	Coal gas
Anthracite	Diesel oil	Producer gas
Coke	Benzole	Blast furnace gas
Peat	Alcohol	Hydrogen

Fuels employed in the operation of internal combustion engines used
in motor vehicles are of liquid form.

Every fuel has a heat energy content which is released when the fuel
burns or when *combustion* takes place.

16.2 Elements, compounds and mixtures

Elements are substances that cannot be split up into two or more
simpler substances. There are just over 100 different elements, and

some of the more commonly occurring are: iron, copper, aluminium, lead, zinc, tin, gold, silver, mercury, oxygen, hydrogen, nitrogen, carbon and sulphur.

Compounds are formed by combining two or more elements in such a manner that a chemical change takes place. The properties of a compound are completely different from those of its constituent elements. For example, water is a compound which, in its natural state, is a liquid. This is quite a different property from the elements hydrogen and oxygen from which water is made. Both these elements are gases in their natural state.

Mixtures are obtained by mixing together two or more elements or compounds **without** any chemical change taking place. Air is a mixture containing mainly nitrogen and oxygen. Brass is a mixture or *alloy* of the metals copper and zinc.

The main difference between compounds and mixtures may be summarized as follows:

Compounds	Mixtures
The constituents are held together by a chemical force, and can never be separated by purely physical means.	The constituents are not held together by any force, and can be easily separated by physical means.
On the formation of a compound a new substance is made; it does not resemble its constituents.	No new substance is formed in a mixture; it always resembles its constituents.
Heat energy is generally evolved on the formation of a compound.	Heat energy is not normally evolved when a mixture is made.
Elements always combine to form a compound in a fixed and definite proportion.	The constituent substances of a mixture can be mixed in any proportion.

16.3 The atom and relative atomic mass

The *atom* is defined as the smallest particle of an element which can take part in a chemical change. All atoms of one element are of the same kind, but are different from those of other elements.

Every atom has a mass, but this is very small and in most instances the mass of an atom is quoted relative to that of another atom. The *relative atomic mass* of an element is the number of times the mass of its atom is heavier than one-twelfth of an atom of carbon.

The relative atomic masses of elements encountered in combustion equations are given in Table 16.1. Note that an atom of each element is denoted by a chemical symbol, e.g. H represents **one** atom of hydrogen.

Table 16.1 Relative atomic masses

Element	Chemical symbol	Relative atomic mass
Hydrogen	H	1
Carbon	C	12
Nitrogen	N	14
Oxygen	O	16
Sulphur	S	32

16.4 The molecule and relative molecular mass

Although the atom is the smallest quantity of an element, it does not always exist on its own. In many instances, two or more atoms of an element combine to form a stable particle, known as a *molecule*. The *molecule* may be defined as the smallest particle of a substance which can exist independently and still retain the characteristics of that substance.

Carbon exists as a **single** atom and is therefore represented by C. Four atoms of carbon, for example, are represented by 4C. Nitrogen exists as a molecule composed of **two** atoms, and this is represented by N_2 and **not** by 2N. The latter means two separate atoms of nitrogen. Four molecules of nitrogen, for example, are represented by $4N_2$.

The *relative molecular mass* of a molecule is the sum total of the relative atomic masses of the atoms making up the molecule of a substance. For example, the relative molecular mass of nitrogen (N_2) is $2 \times 14 = 28$. Also, the molecule of carbon dioxide (CO_2) consists of one atom of carbon (relative atomic mass 12) and two atoms of oxygen (relative atomic mass 16). Hence, the relative molecular mass of carbon dioxide is $12 + (2 \times 16) = 44$.

Table 16.2 gives a list of relative molecular masses and molecular symbols for some elements and compounds. Notice particularly that the molecular symbol for a compound shows the constituents of which it is made and shows also the number of atoms of each element present.

16.5 Combustion

Combustion is a chemical combination taking place between a combustible fuel and oxygen, heat energy being evolved during the process. Combustion can only occur if

Table 16.2 Relative molecular masses

Substance	Molecular symbol	Relative molecular mass
Element		
Hydrogen	H_2	2
Carbon	C	12
Nitrogen	N_2	28
Oxygen	O_2	32
Sulphur	S	32
Compound		
Water or steam	H_2O	18
Carbon monoxide	CO	28
Carbon dioxide	CO_2	44
Sulphur dioxide	SO_2	64
Methane	CH_4	16

(*a*) the self-ignition temperature of the fuel is first reached
(*b*) there is a suitable proportion of oxygen to fuel.

All the oxygen necessary for the combustion process is obtained from the air, which is a simple mixture of two chief gases, nitrogen and oxygen. Other gases, together with some water vapour, are also present but only in very small quantities and, for most combustion purposes, air may be regarded as consisting entirely of oxygen and nitrogen in the proportions

By mass: 23% oxygen and 77% nitrogen
By volume: 21% oxygen and 79% nitrogen

Nitrogen is an inactive gas; it plays no useful part in the combustion process and passes out with the exhaust gases.

16.6 Combustion equations

When combustion takes place, the elements of the fuel combine with oxygen and new chemical compounds, called the products of combustion (or simply products), are produced. The chemical process of combustion is written out in the form of equations. In any such equation, the following rules are applied:

1. The total number of atoms of each kind should be the same on both sides of the equation.
2. Before combustion takes place, each separate element should exist as a complete molecule.

The application of these rules to the combustion of carbon, hydrogen and sulphur will now be shown in the following sections of this chapter.

16.7 Complete combustion of carbon to carbon dioxide

Complete combustion of carbon occurs when it is burnt with sufficient supply of oxygen. The combustion equation is:

$$C + O_2 = CO_2 \qquad\qquad [16.1]$$

This means that one molecule of carbon combines with one molecule of oxygen to form one molecule of carbon dioxide. With reference to the relative molecular masses given in Table 16.2, equation [16.1] becomes:

$$12 \text{ kg C} + 32 \text{ kg O}_2 = 44 \text{ kg CO}_2$$
or $\quad 1 \text{ kg C} + 2\frac{2}{3} \text{ kg O}_2 = 3\frac{2}{3} \text{ kg CO}_2$

Thus, 1 kg of carbon requires $2\frac{2}{3}$ kg of oxygen for complete combustion and as a result $3\frac{2}{3}$ kg of carbon dioxide is produced.

The heat energy released by 1 kg of carbon in burning to carbon dioxide is 33.8 MJ.

16.8 Incomplete combustion of carbon to carbon monoxide

When carbon is burnt with insufficient oxygen, carbon monoxide is formed and the combustion is said to be **partial** or **incomplete**. This is because less oxygen is required to form carbon monoxide. If carbon monoxide is burnt, it will burn to carbon dioxide (see Section 16.9). In this case, the partial combustion equation is:

$$2C + O_2 = 2CO \qquad\qquad [16.2]$$

This equation states that two molecules of carbon combine with one molecule of oxygen to form two molecules of carbon monoxide.

Note that equation [16.2] cannot be written as $C + O = CO$, because the smallest particle of oxygen that can exist on its own is a molecule, consisting of two atoms and written O_2.

Substituting the relative molecular masses, we get:

$$2C + O_2 = 2CO$$
$$(2 \times 12) + 32 = (2 \times 28)$$
i.e. $\quad 24 \text{ kg C} + 32 \text{ kg O}_2 = 56 \text{ kg CO}$
or $\quad 1 \text{ kg C} + 1\frac{1}{3} \text{ kg O}_2 = 2\frac{1}{3} \text{ kg CO}$

Thus, 1 kg of carbon taking $1\frac{1}{3}$ kg of oxygen produces $2\frac{1}{3}$ kg of carbon monoxide, and this will release approximately 10.3 MJ of heat energy.

It will be observed that the heat liberated when carbon is burnt to **carbon monoxide** is much less than when it is burnt to completion. Such combustion is therefore wasteful of energy.

16.9 Combustion of carbon monoxide to carbon dioxide

The process is represented by the equation

$$2CO + O_2 = 2CO_2 \hspace{4cm} [16.3]$$

that is, two molecules of carbon monoxide combine with one molecule of oxygen to form two molecules of carbon dioxide.

Putting in the relative molecular masses, we get:

$$
\begin{aligned}
2CO + O_2 &= 2CO_2 \\
(2 \times 28) + 32 &= (2 \times 44) \\
\text{i.e.} \quad 56 \text{ kg CO} + 32 \text{ kg O}_2 &= 88 \text{ kg CO}_2 \\
\text{or} \quad 1 \text{ kg CO} + \tfrac{4}{7} \text{ kg O}_2 &= 1\tfrac{4}{7} \text{ kg CO}_2
\end{aligned}
$$

Thus, 1 kg of carbon monoxide requires $\tfrac{4}{7}$ kg of oxygen to produce $1\tfrac{4}{7}$ kg of carbon dioxide, and this will release approximately 10.1 MJ of heat energy.

16.10 Complete combustion of hydrogen to water vapour

This process is represented by the following combustion equation:

$$2H_2 + O_2 = 2H_2O \hspace{4cm} [16.4]$$

that is, two molecules of hydrogen combine with one molecule of oxygen to form two molecules of water vapour or steam.

Substituting the relative molecular masses, we get:

$$
\begin{aligned}
2H_2 + O_2 &= 2H_2O \\
(2 \times 2) + 32 &= (2 \times 18) \\
\text{i.e.} \quad 4 \text{ kg H}_2 + 32 \text{ kg O}_2 &= 36 \text{ kg H}_2O \\
\text{or} \quad 1 \text{ kg H}_2 + 8 \text{ kg O}_2 &= 9 \text{ kg H}_2O
\end{aligned}
$$

Thus, 1 kg of hydrogen requires 8 kg of oxygen for complete combustion and as a result 9 kg of water vapour is produced. The heat energy released is approximately 144 MJ.

16.11 Complete combustion of sulphur to sulphur dioxide

This process is represented by the following combustion equation:

$$S + O_2 = SO_2 \hspace{4cm} [16.5]$$

One molecule of sulphur combines with one molecule of oxygen to form one molecule of sulphur dioxide.

With reference to the relative molecular masses (Table 16.2), we get:

$$32 \text{ kg S} + 32 \text{ kg O}_2 = 64 \text{ kg SO}_2$$
$$\text{or} \quad 1 \text{ kg S} + 1 \text{ kg O}_2 = 2 \text{ kg SO}_2$$

Thus, 1 kg of sulphur requires 1 kg of oxygen for complete combustion and as a result 2 kg of sulphur dioxide is produced. The heat energy released is approximately 9.2 MJ.

16.12 Theoretical mass of air required for combustion

It was mentioned in Section 16.5 that air contains 23 per cent oxygen by mass, with the remainder being mainly nitrogen. As the oxygen for a combustion process is supplied from the atmosphere, it is necessary to know the theoretical quantity of air required for combustion. Thus, from the above mass analysis of air, we get:

Theoretical mass of air required for combustion

$$= \text{Mass of oxygen required} \times \frac{100}{23}$$

Hence, from Section 16.7, theoretical mass of air required for complete combustion of 1 kg of carbon

$$= 2\tfrac{2}{3} \text{ kg} \times \frac{100}{23} = \underline{11.6 \text{ kg of air}}$$

Also, from Section 16.10, theoretical mass of air required for complete combustion of 1 kg of hydrogen

$$= 8 \text{ kg} \times \frac{100}{23} = \underline{34.8 \text{ kg of air}}$$

Again, from Section 16.11, theoretical mass of air required for complete combustion of 1 kg of sulphur

$$= 1 \text{ kg} \times \frac{100}{23} = \underline{4.35 \text{ kg of air}}$$

In practice, complete combustion would not be likely to occur if the theoretical quantity of air were supplied. This is because it is virtually impossible to achieve the distribution of oxygen necessary to produce complete combustion. For example, in an internal combustion engine the mixing process inside the cylinder is not sufficiently good to produce combustion of all the carbon present in the fuel to carbon dioxide (CO_2) in the very short time available. Instead, a mixture of carbon dioxide and carbon monoxide (CO) is produced. It is always necessary, therefore, to supply excess air if complete combustion of the fuel is to take place and even then, if the process is very rapid, as in a high-speed internal combustion engine, complete combustion will not necessarily occur.

The mass of air required for complete combustion per unit mass of fuel used is known as the *air–fuel ratio*.

A typical air–fuel ratio for the complete combustion of petrol in an engine running at normal operating temperature is 15 to 1.

16.13   Liquid fuels

These are derived from one or other of the following sources:

1. Petroleum or crude oil.
2. By-products from coal gas manufacture.
3. Vegetable matter.

Fuels used in spark-ignition engines are of the volatile type, e.g. petrol, kerosene, benzole and alcohol. Those used in compression-ignition engines are of the non-volatile type, e.g. diesel oil and gas oil.

Volatility is a measure of the ease with which a fuel vaporizes at normal atmospheric temperatures.

Fuels that have their chemical structures based on molecules of linked hydrogen and carbon atoms are called *hydrocarbons*.

Alcohol fuels are compounds of carbon, hydrogen and oxygen.

16.14   Petroleum or crude oil

Petroleum or crude oil is a thick, dark-coloured liquid which is found in underground deposits, and contains a large number of different compounds of hydrogen and carbon. The separation of petroleum into the various 'fractions' is achieved by *distillation*, i.e. by heating the petroleum and condensing the vapour which evaporates at various temperatures and pressures.

Crude petroleum is separated into the following fractions in turn: petrol, paraffin, kerosene, diesel oil, gas oil, fuel oils used in marine type engines and in the furnaces of oil-fired boilers, paraffin wax and bitumen or asphalt.

Petrol

This is the principal hydrocarbon fuel used in motor vehicle engines. Its distillation temperature is between 30 °C and 200 °C, and it has a composition of about 85 per cent carbon and 15 per cent hydrogen by mass. Petrol is obtained from crude oil by a process known as *cracking distillation*. This is a process whereby the large 'heavy' hydrocarbon molecules are decomposed into simpler molecules by subjecting the crude oil to high temperature and pressure.

To improve 'startability', i.e. to aid starting in cold conditions, most commercial petrols contain a good proportion, usually from 30 to 40 per cent, of the lighter fractions which volatize easily at normal atmospheric temperatures. Special substances, known as 'fuel dopes' or 'anti-detonators', are also added to reduce the tendency for detonation or 'pinking' and thus allow for the use of high compression ratios (see Section 15.12). In some instances, alcohol and benzole are used on account of their good anti-knock qualities. Other additives are used to prevent the fouling of sparking plugs and to prevent gummy deposits forming in the fuel pipes, and solvent oils to maintain cleanliness in the induction system are also added. The relative density of petrol is about 0.74.

Kerosene

This is less volatile than petrol, the temperature range being from 150 °C to 300 °C for distillation. It has a relative density of about 0.81 and is generally used for tractor engines and for heating and lighting purposes. Engines using this type of fuel are often started and warmed up on petrol.

Fuel oils

These are the non-volatile fuels and are the heavier distillates of crude petroleum. Those which distil at temperatures in the range 200 °C to 350 °C are the light grade fuel and gas oils (relative density about 0.85) which are suitable for use in motor vehicle compression-ignition engines. Those which distil at temperatures in the range 340 °C to 430 °C are the heavy grade fuel oils (relative density 0.87−0.90) used for marine engines and for the furnaces of oil-fired boilers.

The chemical composition (by mass) of a diesel fuel oil suitable for a motor vehicle compression-ignition engine is about 87 per cent carbon, 11 per cent hydrogen, 1 per cent oxygen and 1 per cent sulphur. The sulphur content should be a minimum as this produces harmful deposits in the engine cylinder.

The volatile hydrocarbon fuels obtained from crude petroleum may be classified into two series, as shown below.

Series	Fuel	Chemical symbol
Paraffins	Pentane	C_5H_{12}
General chemical	Hexane	C_6H_{14}
formula: C_nH_{2n+2}	Heptane	C_7H_{16}
	Octane	C_8H_{18}
	Nonane	C_9H_{20}
	Decane	$C_{10}H_{22}$
	Undecane	$C_{11}H_{24}$
	Duodecane	$C_{12}H_{26}$

Series	Fuel	Chemical symbol
Naphthenes General chemical formula: C_nH_{2n}	Cyclohexane Hexahydrotoluene Hexahydroxylene	C_6H_{12} C_7H_{14} C_8H_{16}

16.15 By-products from coal gas manufacture

Benzole is a hydrocarbon fuel like petrol but is produced from tar, a by-product from coal gas manufacture. It has a distillation range of 80 °C to 120 °C, and is a mixture of the aromatic series represented by the general chemical formula C_nH_{2n-6}. These include *benzene* (C_6H_6), *toluene* (C_7H_8) and *xylene* (C_8H_{10}). An important feature of such fuels is that they are much less liable to detonation than petrol and can therefore be used in engines with high compression ratios.

Benzole has a relative density of about 0.88 and is usually blended with petrol, up to about 30 per cent, to improve the qualities of the fuel.

16.16 Vegetable matter

Alcohol is a highly volatile fuel formed by fermentation of vegetable matter (e.g. grain, potatoes, sugar-beet, etc.). It has the advantage that it can be employed under the higher compression ratio conditions (up to about 16 to 1) without exhibiting any tendencies to detonate or knock. Alcohol has a relative density of about 0.80.

Two valuable fuel fractions belonging to the alcohol series are *methyl alcohol* (CH_4O) and *ethyl alcohol* (C_2H_6O), boiling point temperatures being respectively 78 °C and 64 °C.

Alcohol fuels are blended with petrol to produce an anti-knock mixture suitable for use in high-performance engines.

16.17 Properties of liquid fuels

Flash point

The *flash point* of a fuel is defined as the lowest temperature at which inflammable vapour is given off by the fuel to ignite when a flame is applied to it.

Petrol has a fairly low flash point and should always be treated with the maximum amount of care. The risk of fire with fuel oils is, however, remote as these have a high flash point and do not usually give off inflammable vapours at normal atmospheric temperatures.

The flash point of a fuel can be determined experimentally by special apparatus, e.g. Pensky-Martin, Grays, etc.

Ignition temperature

The *ignition temperature* of a fuel is defined as the lowest temperature at which the fuel will self-ignite, i.e. without the help of a flame or spark.

The ignition temperature should be high for petrol engines and lower for diesel engines.

Calorific value

The *calorific value* of a fuel is defined as the amount of heat energy released when unit mass of the fuel is burnt completely in sufficient air.

Fuels containing hydrogen have two calorific values, the higher or gross calorific value (HCV) and the lower or net calorific value (LCV).

The *higher calorific value* is the energy output from the complete combustion of unit mass of the fuel when the products of combustion are cooled to the original temperature of the fuel.

When the fuel is burnt in an engine cylinder, the steam formed by the hydrogen and oxygen during the combustion process cannot give up its latent heat because the temperature is too high for the condensation of the steam to take place in the cylinder. The steam therefore passes out through the exhaust. Hence, the available calorific value of the fuel in this case is the *lower calorific value*. The lower calorific value of the fuel is therefore obtained by subtracting the amount of latent heat of vaporization of the steam from the higher calorific value.

The experimental determination of the calorific value of a liquid fuel is carried out in a specially designed calorimeter, known as the *bomb calorimeter*. The 'bomb' is a strong stainless steel vessel in which a small quantity of the fuel under test is ignited in an atmosphere of pure oxygen under high pressure, ensuring perfect combustion. The heat energy liberated is measured and hence the calorific value of the fuel determined.

Average figures for the higher calorific value of some liquid fuels are given in Table 16.3.

Octane number

The term *octane number* is applied to petrols and is a measure of their tendency to resist detonation or pinking. High-octane fuels resist detonation very powerfully and are needed for use with modern high compression ratio engines, whereas low-octane fuels detonate easily at low compression ratios.

In the determination of the octane number of a fuel, a test mixture consisting of iso-octane (C_8H_{18}) and normal heptane (C_7H_{16}) is used. The former is a very effective anti-knock fuel and is given an octane rating of 100, while the latter makes an engine detonate readily and is given the value of 0. The octane number of a fuel is measured by that

260

Table 16.3 Higher calorific values of liquid fuels

Fuel	Higher calorific value (MJ/kg)
Ethyl alcohol	24
Methyl alcohol	29
Benzole	40
Diesel oil	45
Kerosene	46
Petrol	47

percentage of iso-octane in an iso-octane/heptane mixture which detonates under the same conditions as the fuel to be rated.

Cetane number

An important property of a diesel fuel for use in high-speed compression-ignition engines is its self-ignition quality. This is governed by the *cetane number*; the higher the cetane number (60 to 70), the more suitable is the fuel for compression-ignition work.

The cetane number of a fuel is obtained by comparing the ignition qualities of a mixture of hexadecane ($C_{16}H_{34}$) and alpha-methyl-naphthalene ($C_{10}H_7CH_3$) with those of the fuel under test. The former (commonly called cetane) ignites easily while the latter has very low ignition properties. The percentage of cetane in a reference mixture of these two compounds, which gives the same ignition characteristics as the fuel under consideration, determines the cetane number of that fuel.

Exercise 16.1 – Review questions

1 Complete the following statements:
   (a) An element is ......
   (b) At atom is ......
   (c) A molecule is ......
2 Name three combustible elements.
3 Distinguish between a 'compound' and a 'mixture'.
4 Which of the following statements is incorrect?
   (a) The properties of a mixture are in general derived from the properties of its component parts.
   (b) Compounds are formed from elements by the union of atoms in fixed proportions only.
   (c) When compounds are made, the constituent elements can always be separated by physical means.
5 The 'relative atomic mass' of an element is the ......

6 The 'relative molecular mass' of a substance is the ......
7 The relative molecular mass of sulphur dioxide (SO_2) is
   (a) 28   (b) 32   (c) 44   (d) 64   (e) 72
8 Give the chemical symbol for the following:
   (a) Water ......
   (b) Carbon monoxide ......
   (c) Carbon dioxide ......
9 The chemical symbol for ethyl alcohol (relative molecular mass 46) is
   (a) CH_4 (b) CH_4O (c) C_6H_6 (d) C_2H_6O
10 The product of the complete combustion of
   (a) carbon is ......
   (b) hydrogen is ......
   (c) sulphur is ......
11 The chemical equation for the complete combustion of
   (a) carbon is ......
   (b) hydrogen is ......
   (c) sulphur is ......
12 The product of the combustion of carbon when the supply of air is not sufficient for complete combustion is
   ...... This is represented by the chemical equation
   ......
13 Name three fuels used in internal combustion engines.
14 State what is meant by the 'calorific value' of a fuel.
15 What do you understand by the 'higher calorific value' of a fuel, and how does this differ from the 'lower calorific value'?
16 Describe an experiment to determine the calorific value of a liquid fuel.
17 The average higher calorific value, in MJ/kg, of diesel oil is
   (a) 30   (b) 40   (c) 45   (d) 46   (e) 47
18 What do you understand by the 'ignition temperature' of a fuel?
19 State what is meant by the 'volatility' of a fuel. Give **one** reason why a high-volatile fuel is desired for spark-ignition engines.
                                                    (NWRAC/ULCI)
20 What do you understand by the 'flash point' of a fuel?
21 Describe, with the aid of a sketch, the apparatus used in a laboratory experiment to determine the flash point of a fuel.
                                                    (NWRAC/ULCI)
22 What are the properties of petrol that make it particularly suitable for use as a fuel in a motor car engine?
                                                    (EMEU)
23 (a) State the two main chemical elements in a petrol.
   (b) State the approximate calorific value of petrol and give the average proportion of air to petrol by mass for normal running.
   (c) State the three main gases contained in the exhaust assuming complete combustion has taken place.
                                                    (NWRAC/ULCI)

24 The approximate chemical composition of petrol by mass is carbon
...... per cent and hydrogen ...... per cent.

25 Give the chemical composition (by mass) of a fuel suitable for use
in a motor vehicle compression-ignition engine.

26 Answer true (T) or false (F) to each of the following statements.
  (*a*) The principal chemical elements contained in an alcohol fuel
     are carbon, hydrogen and oxygen.
  (*b*) The flash point of petrol is higher than that of diesel oil.
  (*c*) A good liquid fuel should burn completely and leave no
     deposits in the combustion chamber.
  (*d*) Diesel is the term used for the light fuel oils produced from
     coal.
  (*e*) For use in spark-ignition engines a fuel should have good
     vaporizing qualities.

27 Explain briefly what is meant by
  (*a*) the octane rating of petrol
  (*b*) the cetane rating of diesel fuel.

(EMEU)

28 The use of high-octane fuel is usually associated with high efficiency
engines. Explain the reason for this.
  What is the effect of using 101 octane fuel in an engine which is
designed to run on a 94 octane fuel?

(CGLI)

Chapter 17

Engine cycles

17.1 The constant volume or Otto cycle

The constant volume or Otto cycle is the theoretical basis of the spark-ignition or petrol engine cycle. This theoretical cycle is represented on the pressure–volume diagram given in Fig. 17.1. The working substance is an ideal gas. Starting at 1, the gas is compressed to the point 2 as the piston moves from bottom dead centre (b.d.c.) to top dead centre (t.d.c.). At 2, the gas is heated at constant volume, when its pressure increases to the value given by 3. From 3, the gas expands to 4. At 4, heat is rejected until its pressure returns to the original value given by 1.

The actual pressure–volume diagram traced out by an engine in practice using an air–petrol charge instead of air is shown in Fig. 17.2.

Curve 0–1 represents the *induction* stroke. The piston draws into the cylinder a vaporized mixture of petrol and air from the carburettor. The inlet valve is arranged to open about 10° before t.d.c. and to close about 50° after b.d.c. in an attempt to get as much air–fuel mixture into the cylinder as possible. The pressure in the cylinder will be slightly less than that of the atmosphere.

Curve 1–2 represents the *compression* stroke. The mixture is compressed by the piston into the combustion space of the cylinder, and the pressure rises to an amount dependent upon the compression ratio, the speed of the engine and the throttle opening. A typical value is about 900 kPa (900 kN/m²).

Just before the end of the compression stroke, the mixture is ignited

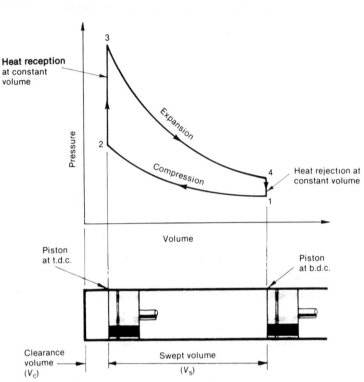

Figure 17.1 Constant volume or Otto cycle (theoretical)

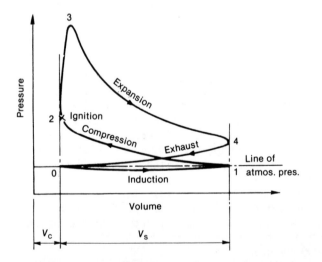

Figure 17.2 Constant volume or Otto cycle (practical)

by means of a sparking plug. This is necessary because the temperature of the mixture is not as high as its ignition temperature. Heat is then released from the fuel and the pressure in the cylinder rises rapidly to about 3500 kPa. This is denoted by point 3. Notice that between the points 2−3 the heat release occurs while the piston is almost at rest at t.d.c. position (i.e. heat addition at constant volume).

Curve 3−4 represents the *expansion* or *power* stroke. The high-pressure gases expand and drive forward the piston and thus turn the crankshaft. At point 4 the pressure in the cylinder falls to about 250 kPa.

Curve 4−0 represents the *exhaust* stroke. This is the fourth stroke and completes the cycle of operations. The piston discharges the products of combustion through the exhaust valve, and, in order to expel as much of the spent gases as possible, the exhaust valve is arranged to open about 55° before b.d.c. and to close about 15° after t.d.c. The pressure in the cylinder will be slightly above that of the atmosphere.

On a modern high-speed petrol engine the inlet valve opens about 30° before t.d.c. while the exhaust valve closes some 35° after t.d.c., giving 65° of valve overlap. The inlet valve closes about 75° after b.d.c. and the exhaust valve opens about 70° before b.d.c.

17.2 The constant pressure or Diesel cycle

The *constant pressure or Diesel cycle* is suitable for slow-speed compression-ignition engines, and it differs from the constant volume or Otto cycle in that the heat intake is at **constant pressure** instead of at constant volume.

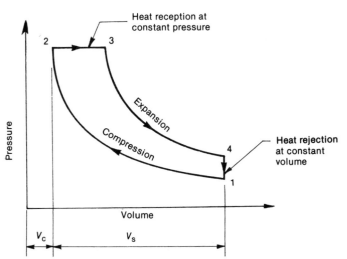

Figure 17.3 Constant pressure or Diesel cycle (theoretical)

The constant pressure or Diesel cycle is shown in its ideal or theoretical form in Fig. 17.3. This is arranged as follows:

1−2 Compression. The pressure increases as the piston moves from b.d.c. to t.d.c.

2−3 Constant pressure heating. The heat supply stops at point 3; this is called the point of cut-off.

3−4 Expansion. The pressure decreases to the value given by 4.

4−1 Constant volume cooling. At 4, heat is rejected until the pressure returns to the original value given by 1.

The diesel engine uses heavy oil as a fuel and ignition is always brought about by compression alone. The air is compressed into the clearance volume to such a high pressure that its temperature is sufficient to ignite the oil fuel when it is injected into the cylinder combustion space at the end of the compression stroke. With an effective compression ratio of 14 to 1 and an initial temperature and pressure of, say, 60 °C and 100 kPa respectively at the commencement of the compression stroke, the final temperature and pressure of the air at the end of compression at full load and full speed conditions would be about 680 °C and 4000 kPa respectively. The temperature of 680 °C would be more than sufficient to ignite the fuel oils used which have self-ignition temperatures ranging from 350 °C to 450 °C at normal atmospheric pressure. Even with a compression ratio of 12 to 1 the compression temperature in the cylinder rises to about 530 °C.

17.3 The dual combustion cycle

Most modern compression-ignition engines, including the high-speed oil engines used for heavy road vehicles, operate on a cycle known as the *dual combustion or mixed cycle* in which the intake of heat is partly at constant volume and partly at constant pressure. Due to the high speed of the engine, it is necessary to start injection of the fuel oil into the combustion chamber before the air temperature is sufficient to ignite it and to ensure that the correct quantity of fuel is mixed with the air before the piston reaches t.d.c. position.

The dual combustion cycle is given in its ideal or theoretical form in Fig. 17.4. To avoid confusion with engines operating on the Diesel cycle, oil engines working on the dual combustion cycle are generally referred to as compression-ignition engines.

The cycle is arranged as follows:

1−2 Compression. The pressure increases as the piston moves from b.d.c. to t.d.c.

2−3 Constant volume heating. The pressure is further increased to the value given by 3 while the piston is still at t.d.c. position.

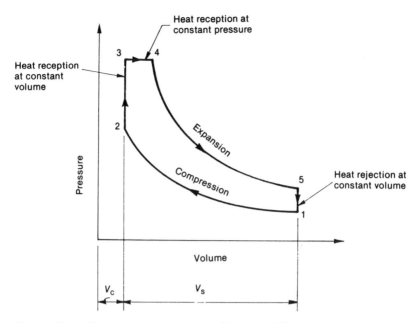

Figure 17.4 Dual combustion cycle (theoretical)

3–4 Constant pressure heating.
4–5 Expansion. The pressure decreases to the value given by 5.
5–1 Constant volume cooling. At 5, heat is rejected until the pressure returns to the original value given by 1.

The actual pressure–volume diagram traced out by a four-stroke cycle high-speed compression-ignition engine is given in Fig. 17.5. The lower loop shows the induction and exhaust processes.

Typical values of the maximum temperature and pressure produced in a compression-ignition engine having a compression ratio of 15 to 1 are 1300 °C and 6200 kPa respectively.

Due to the high combustion pressures in a compression-ignition engine, large forces are exerted on the engine parts which necessitate a heavier and more expensive construction than for a spark-ignition engine. Consequently, the power-to-weight ratio is lower than for a spark-ignition engine. On the other hand, the higher compression ratio gives a greater thermal efficiency and, therefore, a compression-ignition engine is more economical than a spark-ignition engine of comparable size and power output. Also, since the fuel has a higher self-ignition temperature (about 400 °C) and is of the non-volatile type, the danger of fire is considerably reduced. The higher flash point is in the region of 60 °C.

Note: All pressures quoted in this chapter are absolute pressures.

268

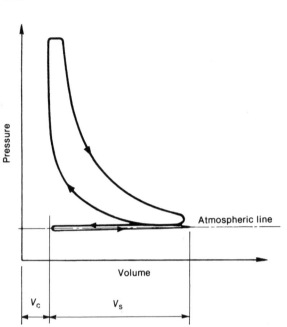

Figure 17.5   Dual combustion cycle (practical)

Exercise 17.1 − Review questions

1   The combustion cycle upon which a spark-ignition engine operates is the ......
2   The combustion cycle upon whcih a modern high-speed compression-ignition engine operates is the ......
3   One reason why a compression-ignition engine has a higher compression ratio than most spark-ignition engines is ......
4   The compression-ignition engine is more heavily built than a spark-ignition engine of comparable power output because ......
5   Which of the following statements are true?
   (*a*) In the compression stroke of a spark-ignition engine a mixture of petrol and air is compressed.
   (*b*) In the compression stroke of a compression-ignition engine air alone is compressed.
   (*c*) The maximum compression temperature in a compression-ignition engine is well below the self-ignition temperature of the fuel.
   (*d*) The theoretical Diesel cycle differs from the constant volume cycle by having no change in pressure during compression.
   (*e*) In the theoretical Diesel cycle the burnt gases are cooled at constant volume.

(f) One advantage of a compression-ignition engine compared with a spark-ignition engine is that it uses fuel having a higher flash point, so reducing risk of fire.

6 (a) Sketch **two** theoretical pressure—volume diagrams, one for a spark-ignition engine and the other for a modern compression-ignition engine.

(b) Label **each** diagram and indicate on each line of **each** diagram what is happening in the cycle.

(c) State **one** reason why the pressure—volume diagrams which occur in practice vary from the theoretical diagrams.

(CGLI)(Modified)

7 (a) Make a simple line sketch of the probable pressure—volume diagram that might be obtained from a modern high-speed compression-ignition engine when under load.

(b) What is the name given to this cycle of operations, and why is it so called?

(EMEU)

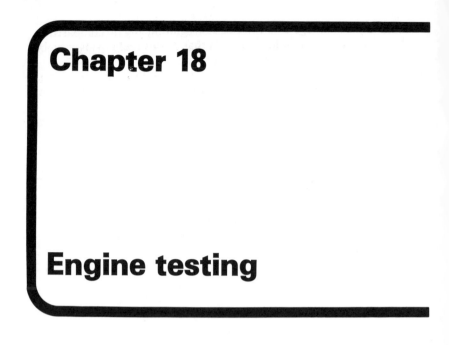

Chapter 18

Engine testing

18.1 Introduction

In order to determine the performance characteristics of a motor vehicle engine it is necessary to conduct a series of tests on that engine. In factories, these tests are usually carried out with the engine running on a test bed. The characteristics so determined are tabulated and, where possible, suitable performance curves are plotted. These curves are of utmost value to the engineer, especially when the engine is being developed.

Some of the general performance characteristics of an engine and their method of determination will now be discussed in the following sections of this chapter.

18.2 Brake power and engine torque

It is appropriate at this stage to first describe what is meant by the term 'torque' and then to show the calculation of the power developed when a torque is transmitted.

The moment of a force about a given point is the product of the force and the perpendicular distance from the line of action of the force to that point. The perpendicular distance is the leverage of the force (see Section 9.2).

When the moment has a tendency to twist or rotate a body, such as turning a shaft in its bearings, it is usually called a *torque* or *turning moment*.

Consider a shaft of radius *r* metres (Fig. 18.1) being acted upon by a tangential force of *F* newtons to a point A on its circumference.

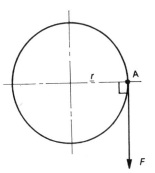

Figure 18.1

Then:

Torque applied to shaft = Force × Radius
$$= F \times r \text{ N m}$$

If the point A makes one complete revolution under the action of *F*, then:

Work done = Force × Distance moved
$$= \text{Force} \times \text{Circumference}$$
$$= F \times 2\pi r \quad [\text{Units: N m} = \text{J}]$$

If point A makes *N* revolutions per minute, in one second it makes *N*/60 revolutions.

$\therefore$ Work done per second $= F \times 2\pi r \times \dfrac{N}{60}$ [Units: J/s]

Since 1 watt (W) = 1 joule/second (J/s), then:

Power developed $= \dfrac{2\pi NFr}{60}$ W

Engine brake power developed

The *brake power* (b.p.) of an engine is the useful power available at the crankshaft of the engine. It is measured by running the engine against some form of absorption brake, hence its name.

    For high-speed motor vehicle engines, the type of brake widely used is the *Heenan and Froude hydraulic dynamometer*. A diagrammatic layout of a hydraulic dynamometer is illustrated in Fig. 18.2. It consists essentially of a rotor running in a casing through which water flows steadily via the inlet and outlet pipes. The rotor is coupled to the

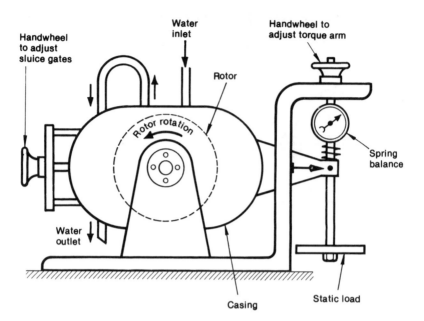

Figure 18.2 Hydraulic dynamometer

engine output shaft, and the casing is freely mounted on bearings fitted to the trunnion brackets. At the periphery of the rotor there is a series of semi-elliptical pockets or cups and at the inside of the casing there is an identical set of pockets, so that, when the rotor is driven by the engine, the water is flung out of its pockets by centrifugal action and transferred to the pockets in the casing. This results in a tendency to turn the casing with the rotor. The casing is prevented from rotating by the resistance of a spring and a static (or dead) load applied to the torque arm which projects from the casing.

A handwheel is provided on top of the balance frame to adjust the torque arm to a horizontal position; this is facilitated by a small pointer, as shown. The amount of load and, hence, the torque absorbed by the dynamometer can be varied by controlling the flow of water. This is usually done by operating another handwheel which slides thin metal plates between the rotor and the casing pockets, thus, blanking-off a number of effective pockets.

As the length of the torque arm, together with the static load and spring balance reading, is known, the torque on the casing can be determined. This is balanced by the torque transmitted by the engine.

Hence, if S = spring balance reading (N)

$\quad\quad W_1$ = static load (N)

$\quad\quad W$ = effective load on torque arm (N)

$\quad\quad R$ = length of torque arm (m)

then,

Torque (T) transmitted by engine
= Effective load × Length of torque arm

i.e. $\quad T = WR$ N m $\qquad$ [18.1]

where $\quad W = S + W_1$ $\qquad$ [18.2]

If the engine is running at N rev/min, then:

Brake power (b.p.) $= \dfrac{2\pi NWR}{60}$ W $\qquad$ [18.3]

From equation [18.1], equation [18.3] becomes:

$$\text{b.p.} = \frac{2\pi NT}{60} \text{ W} \qquad [18.4]$$

It should be noted that since R is a fixed length for a given dynamometer, the terms $(2\pi R)/60$ in expression [18.3] may be written:

$$\frac{2\pi R}{60} = \frac{1}{K}$$

The value of the constant K is usually stamped on the nameplate attached to the dynamometer. Thus, the b.p. formula for the dynamometer may be reduced to the simple form

$$\text{b.p.} = \frac{WN}{K} \text{ W} \qquad [18.5]$$

18.3 Brake power and torque curves

Figure 18.3 shows typical b.p. and torque curves plotted against a base of engine speed. The falling off of the torque curve at increased engine speeds is due to the decrease in the 'volumetric efficiency' of the engine. This efficiency represents the degree of completeness with which the cylinder is filled with a fresh charge, and varies with different engines and also with the speed.

The b.p. of the engine increases with the speed, and will continue to increase until it reaches its maximum value at the 'peak' point of the curve. Thereafter, it decreases very rapidly as the engine approaches its maximum speed. This is due mainly to the fall in the 'brake mean effective pressure' (see Sections 18.10 and 18.15).

The maximum torque transmitted by the engine will be at that speed where the tangent (shown dotted) drawn from the origin touches the b.p. curve, i.e. at point A. This is also the point of maximum brake mean effective pressure.

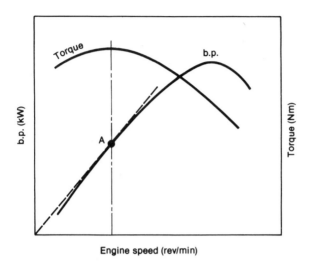

Engine speed (rev/min)

Figure 18.3 Typical brake power and torque curves

Example 18.1

An engine working on the four-stroke cycle was coupled to a dynamometer having a torque arm length of 0.56 m. When the engine was running at 3000 rev/min the effective load on the dynamometer was found to be 160 N. Calculate the b.p. developed by the engine.

Solution

Effective load $= W = 160$ N
Engine speed $= N = 3000$ rev/min
Torque arm length $= R = 0.56$ m

Using equation [18.3], we get:

Engine b.p. developed $= \dfrac{2\pi NWR}{60}$ W

$$= \dfrac{2 \times 22 \times 3000 \times 160 \times 0.56}{7 \times 60}\ \text{W}$$

$$= 28\ 160\ \text{W} = 28.16\ \text{kW}$$

Answer: Engine b.p. developed $= 28.16$ kW

Example 18.2

A six-cylinder, four-stroke petrol engine was coupled to a hydraulic dynamometer for testing. The engine developed maximum power at a speed of 4800 rev/min and the combined static load and spring balance reading was found to be 285 N. If the constant K for the dynamometer is 16, determine:

(a) the b.p. developed by the engine
(b) the torque transmitted.

Solution
(a) Effective brake load $= W = 285$ N
Engine speed $= N = 4800$ rev/min
Dynamometer constant $= K = 16$
Using equation [18.5], we get:

$$\text{Engine b.p. developed} = \frac{WN}{K}\,W$$

$$= \frac{285 \times 4800}{16} = 85\,500 \text{ W}$$

$$= 85.5 \text{ kW}$$

(b) Let T be the torque transmitted by the engine, in N m. Then:

$$\text{Engine b.p. developed} = \frac{2\pi NT}{60}\,W$$

i.e. $$85\,500 = \frac{2\pi \times 4800 \times T}{60}$$

so that $$T = \frac{85\,500 \times 60}{2\pi \times 4800} = 170 \text{ N m}$$

Answer: (a) Engine b.p. developed $= 85.5$ kW
(b) Torque transmitted $= 170$ N m

Example 18.3
An engine, tested against a dynomemeter having a formula b.p. $= WN/20$ W, gave the following results:

Speed, N (rev/min)	1000	1400	2000	2500	3000	3800	4200	4750
Load, W (N)	163.4	172	167	163.4	158	147.5	138	119

Plot the engine characteristic curve and from it deduce the approximate speed at which the engine develops its maximum power and the approximate speed at which it develops its maximum torque.

Solution

Using the formula b.p. = $WN/20$ W, we get:

$$\text{b.p. at 1000 rev/min} = \frac{163.4 \times 1000}{20} = 8170 \text{ W}$$

$$= 8.17 \text{ kW}$$

The b.p. developed by the engine at the other given speeds is calculated in a similar manner and the results are tabulated as follows:

Speed, N (rev/min)	1000	1400	2000	2500	3000	3800	4200	4750
Break power (kW)	8.17	12	16.7	20.43	23.7	28	29	28.3

These values are plotted in Fig. 18.4.

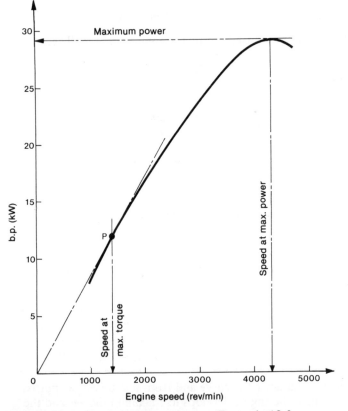

Figure 18.4 Engine power curve – Example 18.3

The maximum power of the engine is the peak point of the b.p. curve. From the graph, the speed at which this occurs is approximately 4300 rev/min.

The speed at which the engine develops its maximum torque is that point at which the tangent drawn from the origin of the graph touches the b.p. curve, i.e. at the point P. The speed at this point is approximately 1400 rev/min.

18.4   The indicator diagram

An *indicator diagram* is a pressure–volume (or pressure–stroke) graph of the conditions inside the cylinder of an engine during a complete cycle of operations. An indicator diagram can be obtained while the engine is running by using an instrument known as the *engine indicator*.

An indicator diagram can give valuable information about the process of combustion, ignition timing and valve operation. A typical indicator diagram for a four-stroke cycle petrol engine is given in Fig. 17.2. The diagram may be seen to consist of two loops. The upper and larger loop is known as the 'positive' loop, since its area represents the work done by the engine during each cycle. The lower and smaller loop is the 'negative' loop, since its area represents the loss of work from the engine during the inlet and exhaust operations. The negative loop is very often referred to as the *pumping loop*.

18.5   Mean effective pressure

The *mean effective pressure* (m.e.p.) is the average net pressure which, acting on the piston over the full length of its stroke, does the same amount of work as is actually obtained during a complete engine cycle.

The m.e.p. is given by the mean height of the indicator diagram, and the method of determination is fully explained in the Level 3 Science Book.

It should be noted that since the m.e.p. is obtained direct from an indicator diagram, it is generally known as the *indicated mean effective pressure* (i.m.e.p.)

18.6   Indicated power

The *indicated power* (i.p.) of an engine is the power actually developed in its cylinders. The i.p. is always greater than the b.p. of an engine, because there will always be some power losses between the cylinder and the output shaft, due, mainly, to friction between the moving parts

278

of the engine and the pumping power needed to clean and recharge the cylinder. The frictional losses also include the power needed to drive the essential engine auxiliaries, such as the water pump, the fuel feed pump, the dynamo and fan, etc.

The difference between the indicated power (i.p.) and the brake power (b.p.) of an engine is termed the *friction power* (f.p.). Thus:

f.p. = i.p. − b.p.   [18.6]

18.7 Calculation of indicated power

From a knowledge of the i.m.e.p., the power developed in the cylinders of an engine (i.e. the i.p.) can be calculated as follows:

Let P_m = i.m.e.p. (Pa = N/m²)
    A = cross-sectional area of piston (m²)
    L = length of stroke (m)
    n = number of working strokes per minute

Then, with reference to Fig. 18.5,

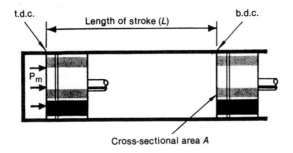

Figure 18.5

Force on piston
        = i.m.e.p. × Cross-sectional area of piston
        = $P_m × A$ [Units: N/m² × m² = N]

Work done per working stroke
        = Force on piston × Length of stroke
        = $P_m × A × L$ [Units: N × m = N m = J]

Work done per minute
        = Work done per working stroke
          × Number of working strokes per minute
        = $P_m × A × L × n$ [Units: J/min]

Work done per second

$$= \frac{P_m \times A \times L \times n}{60} \quad \text{[Units: J/s]}$$

This is usually written as $\dfrac{P_m LAn}{60}$

Since 1 watt (W) = 1 joule/second (J/s), then:

$$\text{i.p.} = \frac{P_m LAn}{60} \text{ W} \qquad [18.7]$$

It should here be pointed out that in a four-stroke cycle engine there is only one working stroke in two revolutions of the crankshaft, while in a two-stroke cycle engine there is one working stroke in each revolution.

Hence, if N = engine speed in rev/min, then:

(1) For a four-stroke cycle engine,

$$n = \frac{N}{2} \times \text{Number of cylinders} \qquad [18.8]$$

(2) For a two-stroke cycle engine,

$$n = N \times \text{Number of cylinders} \qquad [18.9]$$

Note: In expression [18.7], the quantity $(L \times A)$ is equal to the swept volume of the cylinder.

18.8 Mechanical efficiency

The ratio of the useful power available at the output shaft to the power developed in the cylinders of an engine is known as the *mechanical efficiency* of the engine. Thus:

$$\text{Mechanical efficiency} = \frac{\text{Brake power}}{\text{Indicated power}} \qquad [18.10]$$

It is common practice to express the mechanical efficiency as a percentage by multiplying the above ratio by 100.

The mechanical efficiency of an engine is dependent upon engine speed, cylinder jacket and inlet air temperature and also upon the degree of carburettor throttling. In general, the mechanical efficiency decreases at the higher engine speeds and increases with increase in jacket water temperature. In modern petrol engines, the maximum values of mechanical efficiency range from 85 to 90 per cent, and in some cases values higher than 90 per cent have also been obtained.

18.9 Curves of i.p., b.p., f.p. and mechanical efficiency

Typical curves of i.p., b.p., f.p. and mechanical efficiency plotted on a base of engine speed are shown in Fig. 18.6.

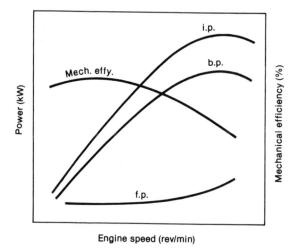

Figure 18.6 Typical power and mechanical efficiency curves

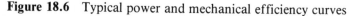

Example 18.4

During a test carried out on a four-cylinder, four-stroke petrol engine of cylinder bore 76 mm and stroke 100 mm, the following readings were recorded:

Speed = 2800 rev/min; i.m.e.p. = 860 kPa; effective brake load = 198 N at a radius of 0.5 m.

Determine (a) the i.p., (b) the b.p., (c) the f.p. and (d) the mechanical efficiency of the engine.

Solution

(a) i.m.e.p., $P_m = 860$ kPa $= 860\ 000$ N/m^2

Length of stroke, $L = 0.1$ m

Area of cylinder bore, $A = \dfrac{\pi}{4} \times 0.076^2 = 0.004\ 54$ m^2

Working strokes/min, $\quad n = \dfrac{\text{rev/min}}{2} \times \text{Number of cylinders}$

$$= \dfrac{2800}{2} \times 4 = 5600$$

Now,

$\quad$ i.p. $= \dfrac{P_m L A n}{60}$ W $\qquad$ from equation [18.7]

$\qquad = \dfrac{1}{60} \times 860\ 000 \times 0.1 \times 0.004\ 54 \times 5600$ W

$\qquad = 36\ 440$ W $= 36.44$ kW

(b) Effective brake load, $\quad W = 198$ N
$\quad$ Effective brake radius, $\quad R = 0.5$ m
$\quad$ Engine speed, $\qquad\quad N = 2800$ rev/min

$\quad$ b.p. $= \dfrac{2\pi N W R}{60}$ W $\qquad$ from equation [18.3]

$\qquad = \dfrac{1}{60} \times 2\pi \times 2800 \times 198 \times 0.5$ W

$\qquad = 29\ 040$ W $= 29.04$ kW

(c) From equation [18.6],
$\quad$ f.p. $=$ i.p. $-$ b.p.
$\qquad = 36.44 - 29.04 = 7.4$ kW

(d) From equation [18.10],

$\quad$ Mechanical efficiency (%) $= \dfrac{\text{b.p.}}{\text{i.p.}} \times 100$

$\qquad = \dfrac{29.04\ \text{kW}}{36.44\ \text{kW}} \times 100 = 79.7\%$

Answer: (a) i.p. $= 36.44$ kW $\qquad$ (b) b.p. $= 29.04$ kW
$\qquad$ (c) f.p. $= 7.4$ kW $\qquad$ (d) mechanical efficiency $= 79.7\%$

18.10 Brake mean effective pressure

When the mean effective pressure is based on the brake power of an engine it is known as the *brake mean effective pressure* (b.m.e.p.), and is obtained by multiplying the i.m.e.p. by the mechanical efficiency of the engine. Hence:

b.m.e.p. = i.m.e.p. × Mechanical efficiency [18.11]

The b.m.e.p. is proportional to the engine torque (or load). If a suitable scale is used, the b.m.e.p.–speed curve becomes the torque–speed curve shown in Fig. 18.3. (See also Fig. 18.8.)

Whereas the torque transmitted depends on the size of the engine, the b.m.e.p. is used by engine designers as a method of comparison of the performances of internal combustion engines of different sizes.

The factors influencing the value of the b.m.e.p. are:
1. Mixture strength (air–fuel ratio)
2. Compression ratio
3. Cylinder bore diameter
4. Engine speed.

The b.m.e.p. is also dependent on engine design, valve timing, ignition timing, air inlet pressure and temperature, exhaust back pressure, as well as sparking plug location and cylinder temperatures.

If the b.m.e.p. of an engine is known, then the power developed at the crankshaft of the engine can be determined by using an expression of the same form as that used in the case of i.p.

Hence, if P_{mb} = b.m.e.p. in N/m^2 (or Pa)

then b.p. $= \dfrac{P_{mb}LAn}{60}$ W [18.12]

Example 18.5
A certain six-cylinder engine is known to have a total swept volume of $0.0015 \ m^3$. If it develops a brake power of 24.2 kW at 2200 rev/min, calculate the b.m.e.p. of the engine under these conditions.

Solution
From equation [18.12],

b.p. developed $= \dfrac{P_{mb}LAn}{60}$ W

The product LA in the above expression gives the swept volume of one cylinder. Hence:

$$LA = \frac{0.0015}{6} = 0.000\ 25 \ m^3$$

For a six-cylinder engine working on the four-stroke cycle,

Working strokes/min, $n = \dfrac{2200}{2} \times 6 = 6600$

Hence, equation [18.12] becomes:

$$24.2 \times 10^3 = \frac{P_{mb} \times 0.000\ 25 \times 6600}{60}$$

so that
$$P_{mb} = \frac{24.2 \times 10^3 \times 60}{0.000\ 25 \times 6600} = 880 \times 10^3 \text{ N/m}^2$$

$$= 880 \text{ kN/m}^2 \text{ or } 880 \text{ kPa}$$

Answer: b.m.e.p. = 880 kPa

Example 18.6

A four-cylinder, four-stroke engine develops 33.6 kW b.p. at
3300 rev/min. If the b.m.e.p. is 1100 kPa and the stroke-bore ratio is
1:1, determine the diameter of the cylinder bore.

(CGLI)

Solution

Let d be the cylinder bore diameter in metres. Since the stroke–bore
ratio is 1:1, then the length of stroke, L, is equal to d metre.

Area of cylinder bore, $A = \dfrac{\pi}{4} \times d^2$

Brake m.e.p., P_{mb} $= 1100 \text{ kPa} = 1100 \times 10^3 \text{ N/m}^2$

Working strokes/min, $n = \dfrac{\text{rev/min}}{2} \times \text{No. of cylinders}$

$$= \frac{3300}{2} \times 4 = 6600$$

Now,

$$\text{b.p. developed} = \frac{P_{mb}LAn}{60} \text{ W}$$

i.e. $33.6 \times 10^3 = 1100 \times 10^3 \times d \times \dfrac{\pi}{4} \times d^2 \times \dfrac{6600}{60}$

so that
$$d^3 = \frac{33.6 \times 4 \times 60}{\pi \times 1100 \times 6600} = 0.000\ 354 \text{ m}^3$$

$\therefore$ $d = 0.0707 \text{ m} = 70.7 \text{ mm}$

Answer: Cylinder bore diameter = 70.7 mm

18.11 The Morse test

The *Morse test* is a method of determining, without the use of an engine indicator, the indicated power of a high-speed, multi-cylinder, internal combustion engine.

In this method, the engine under test is coupled to a dynamometer and run at a certain speed. The b.p. of the engine is first measured with all the cylinders working. One of the cylinders is then 'cut out'. This can be achieved, in the case of a petrol engine, by short-circuiting the sparking plug of that cylinder and, in the case of a compression-ignition engine, by interrupting the fuel supply to the cylinder. As a result of cutting out the cylinder, the engine speed will drop. The load on the dynamometer is therefore reduced until the original speed is restored. By so doing, the friction and pumping losses are kept as nearly constant as possible. The b.p. of the engine is again measured from the new brake load, but the result will obviously be lower than the first one. The difference between the two values of b.p. gives the i.p. of the idle cylinder. This procedure is adopted for each cylinder in turn; the sum of the results giving the total i.p. of the engine.

Let us consider the case of a four-cylinder engine.

If $\qquad A$ = b.p. of the engine with all cylinder working

B_1, B_2, B_3 and B_4 = b.p. of the engine with each of the cylinders cut out in turn

then,

$$\text{Total i.p.} = (A - B_1) + (A - B_2) + (A - B_3) + (A - B_4)$$
$$= (A \times 4) - (B_1 + B_2 + B_3 + B_4) \qquad [18.13]$$

It should be noted that the total i.p. so determined is just a close approximation, since the friction and pumping losses while a cylinder is cut out are not the same as when it is working. The test must also be carried out quickly in order to reduce the effect of cooling of the cut-out cylinder.

Note: Since in a Morse test both the b.p. and the i.p. of an engine are determined, an approximate estimate of the friction and pumping losses as well as the mechanical efficiency of the engine can also be obtained by using expressions [18.6] and [18.10] respectively.

Example 18.7

A Morse test on a six-cylinder petrol engine gave the following results when the speed was maintained at 2000 rev/min.

Cylinder 'cut out'	None	No. 1	No. 2	No. 3	No. 4	No. 5	No. 6
Brake power (kW)	40.65	32.44	31.32	32.44	32.8	32.1	31.7

From the above results, calculate (*a*) the indicated power, (*b*) the friction and the pumping losses, and (*c*) the mechanical efficiency of the engine.

Solution

(*a*) For a six-cylinder engine, equation [18.13] becomes:

Indicated power
= (40.65 × 6) − (32.44 + 31.32 + 32.44 + 32.8 + 32.1 + 31.7)
= 243.9 − 192.8 = 51.1 kW

(*b*) From equation [18.6],

Friction and pumping losses = i.p. − b.p.
= 51.1 − 40.65 = 10.45 kW

(*c*) Mechanical efficiency (%) $= \dfrac{\text{b.p.}}{\text{i.p.}} \times 100$

$$= \frac{40.65}{51.1} \times 100 = 79.55\%$$

Answer: (*a*) Indicated power   = 51.1 kW
    (*b*) Friction and pumping losses = 10.45 kW
    (*c*) Mechanical efficiency   = 79.55%

18.12 Fuel consumption

A knowledge of the amount of fuel consumed by a motor vehicle engine in a given time is essential when assessing the qualities of that engine. Motorists assess fuel consumption in terms of kilometres per litre, but engine designers compare the fuel consumption of different engines by the amount of fuel used in a period of one hour for each kilowatt of power developed. The latter is referred to as the *specific fuel consumption*, and depends on the calorific value of the fuel used. (In Section 16.17 the term 'calorific value' is defined and explained.)

The specific fuel consumption may be stated for either the i.p. or the b.p. of an engine. Thus:

Indicated specific $= \dfrac{\text{Fuel consumed/h}}{\text{Indicated power in kW}}$ [18.14]
fuel consumption

This gives the amount of fuel required, in kilograms or in litres, to develop an indicated power of 1 kilowatt for a period of 1 hour at the load considered.
(The units are kg/kW h, or litre/kW h.)

$$\text{Brake specific fuel consumption} = \frac{\text{Fuel consumed/h}}{\text{Brake power in kW}} \qquad [18.15]$$

This gives the amount of fuel required, in kilograms or in litres, to develop a brake power of 1 kilowatt for a period of 1 hour at the load considered.

(The units are kg/kW h, or litre/kW h.)

On the test bed, the fuel consumption of an engine is measured by allowing the fuel to run through a special measuring device. This can take the form of a tank of fuel of known quantity, and the time for the engine to consume this measured quantity of fuel is noted by means of a stop-watch.

Another form of accurate measurement is to allow the fuel to flow through a special *flow-meter* which is calibrated to give the fuel consumption, in kg/h or litre/h, by direct reading.

18.13 Thermal efficiency

A motor vehicle engine cannot convert all the heat energy in the fuel into useful work. Even with the most efficient engine only about one-third of the heat energy in the fuel is converted into mechanical work done, the remaining two-third being lost in the exhaust gases, the cooling water, and in radiation to the surroundings.

The thermal efficiency of an engine is the ratio

$$\frac{\text{Work done per second}}{\text{Heat energy supplied from the fuel per second}}$$

There are two cases to be considered. These are the *indicated thermal efficiency*, based on the i.p. of the engine, and the *brake thermal efficiency*, based on the b.p. of the engine. The former is preferred because it does not include the inefficiency of the engine due to frictional losses. However, since it is not always possible to take indicator diagrams for measuring the i.p., the brake thermal efficiency is also acceptable.

$$\text{Indicated thermal efficiency} = \frac{\text{i.p. (W)}}{\text{kg of fuel used/s} \times \text{C.V.}} \qquad [18.16]$$

Similarly,

$$\text{Brake thermal efficiency} = \frac{\text{b.p. (W)}}{\text{kg of fuel used/s} \times \text{C.V.}} \qquad [18.17]$$

Alternatively,

$$\text{Indicated thermal efficiency} = \frac{\text{i.p.(W)} \times 3600}{\text{kg of fuel used/h} \times \text{C.V.}} \qquad [18.18]$$

and,

$$\text{Brake thermal efficiency} = \frac{\text{b.p. (W)} \times 3600}{\text{kg of fuel used/h} \times \text{C.V.}} \qquad [18.19]$$

where C.V. is the calorific value of the fuel in joules per kilogram (J/kg).
Also,

Brake thermal efficiency
= Indicated thermal efficiency × Mechanical efficiency   [18.20]

The thermal efficiency of an engine is dependent upon a number of different influencing factors; these include the following:

1. Mixture strength (air−fuel ratio)
2. Compression ratio
3. Engine speed
4. Throttle opening
5. Valve timing
6. Ignition timing
7. Nature of fuel employed
8. Dimensions of engine
9. Combustion chamber design
10. Inlet charge temperature
11. Cylinder temperature.

18.14   Curves of fuel consumption and thermal efficiency

Typical curves showing the variation of fuel consumption per kilowatt hour and thermal efficiency with load (at constant speed) for a petrol engine are given in Fig. 18.7.

18.15   Other performance curves

Other performance curves obtained from the results of tests carried out on a four-cylinder, four-stroke cycle petrol engine at full load and variable speed are given in Fig. 18.8. On a base representing the engine speed in rev/min are shown plotted curves of b.p., b.m.e.p., and fuel consumption per kilowatt hour (brake basis).

It will be observed that the minimum brake specific fuel consumption (0.3 litre/kW h) occurs at a speed of 2600 rev/min. This condition corresponds to the maximum thermal efficiency and is the most economical speed for the engine when running under the conditions used in the test. As the speed is increased beyond this value, the brake specific fuel consumption increases and the thermal efficiency of the engine is consequently reduced. The b.p. curve shows that the brake

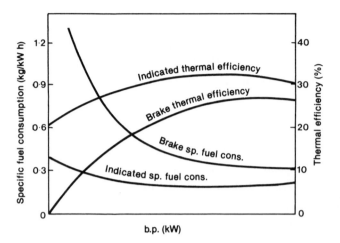

Figure 18.7 Variation of specific fuel consumption and thermal efficiency with load

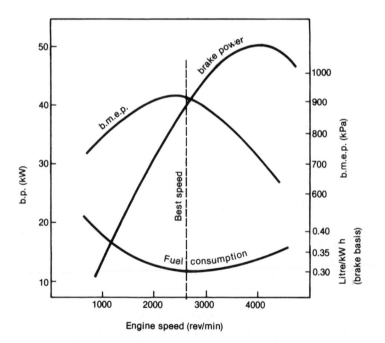

Figure 18.8 Full load b.p., b.m.e.p. and fuel consumption characteristics of a four-cylinder, four-stroke cycle petrol engine

power increases with speed until the peak figure (51 kW) is reached at 4000 rev/min. Hence, the maximum power output does not occur at the condition for maximum thermal efficiency. The b.m.e.p. curve falls off somewhat steeply after the peak figure (920 kPa) is reached at a speed slightly below the most economical speed.

Example 18.8
Calculate the amount of heat energy contained in 10 litre of petrol of relative density 0.72 and calorific value 45 MJ/kg. (1 litre of water has a mass of 1 kg.)

Solution
Mass of 10 litre of water = 10 kg

∴   Mass of 10 litre of petrol
= Mass of 10 litre of water × Relative density of petrol
= 10 × 0.72 = 7.2 kg

Amount of heat energy contained in 10 litre of petrol
= Mass of petrol × Calorific value

$$= 7.2 \text{ [kg]} \times 45 \left[\frac{MJ}{kg}\right] = 324 \text{ MJ}$$

Answer: Heat energy contained in 10 litre of petrol = 324 MJ

Example 18.9
A diesel engine developing an i.p. of 37.4 kW consumes fuel of calorific value 45 400 kJ/kg at the rate of 9 kg/h. If 8.5 kW are absorbed by friction and pumping losses within the engine, determine:

(a) the brake power
(b) the brake specific fuel consumption
(c) the mechanical efficiency
(d) the indicated thermal efficiency
(e) the brake thermal efficiency of the engine.

Solution
(a) From equation [18.5],

b.p. = i.p. − f.p.
= 37.5 − 8.5 = 29 kW

(b) From equation [18.15],
Brake specific fuel consumption

$$= \frac{\text{kg of fuel used/h}}{\text{b.p. (kW)}}$$

$$= \frac{9 \text{ kg/h}}{29 \text{ kW}} = 0.31 \text{ kg/kW h}$$

(c) Mechanical efficiency (%) $= \dfrac{\text{b.p.}}{\text{i.p.}} \times 100$

$$= \frac{29 \text{ kW}}{37.5 \text{ kW}} \times 100 = 77.3\%$$

(d) From equation [18.18],
Indicated thermal efficiency (%)

$$= \frac{\text{i.p. (W)} \times 3600}{\text{kg of fuel used/h} \times \text{C.V.}} \times 100$$

$$= \frac{37.5 \times 10^3 \times 3600}{9 \times 45\,400 \times 10^3} \times 100 = 33\%$$

(e) Brake thermal efficiency
= Indicated thermal efficiency × Mechanical efficiency
= 0.33 × 0.773 = 0.255 or 25.5%

Answer: (a) Brake power   = 29 kW
           (b) Brake specific fuel consumption = 0.31 kg/kW h
           (c) Mechanical efficiency   = 77.3%
           (d) Indicated thermal efficiency   = 33%
           (e) Brake thermal efficiency   = 25.5%

Example 18.10

An engine on test consumes fuel of relative density of 0.8 at the rate of 9 litre/h. If the brake thermal efficiency is 28 per cent and the calorific value of the fuel used is 45 MJ/kg, determine the b.p. developed by the engine.
(1 litre of water has a mass of 1 kg.)

Solution

Fuel consumption = 9 litre/h
$$= 9 \times 1 \times 0.8 = 7.2 \text{ kg/h}$$

From equation [18.19],

Brake thermal efficiency (%) $= \dfrac{\text{b.p. (W)} \times 3600}{\text{kg of fuel used/h} \times \text{C.V.}} \times 100$

i.e. $28 = \dfrac{\text{b.p.} \times 3600 \times 100}{7.2 \times 45 \times 10^6}$

$$\therefore \qquad \text{b.p.} = \frac{28 \times 7.2 \times 45 \times 10^6}{3600 \times 100} \text{ W}$$

$$= 25.2 \times 10^3 \text{ W} = 25.2 \text{ kW}$$

Answer: Brake power developed = 25.2 kW

Example 18.11

A petrol engine when coupled to an absorption dynamometer applies a torque of 115 N m at a speed of 2500 rev/min to a floating brake lever. The brake specific fuel consumption is 0.36 kg/kW h and the calorific value of the fuel is 45 MJ/kg. Calculate:

(*a*) the brake power
(*b*) the brake thermal efficiency
(*c*) the heat dispersed by the brake per minute.

(CGLI)(Modifided)

Solution

(*a*) From equation [18.4],

$$\text{b.p. developed} = \frac{2\pi NT}{60 \times 10^3} \text{ kW}$$

$$= \frac{2\pi \times 2500 \times 115}{60 \times 10^3} = 30.1 \text{ kW}$$

(*b*) From equation [18.19],
Brake thermal efficiency (%)

$$= \frac{\text{b.p. (W)} \times 3600}{\text{kg of fuel used/h} \times \text{C.V.}} \times 100$$

But from equation [18.15],

$$\frac{\text{kg of fuel used/h}}{\text{b.p. (kW)}} = \text{Specific fuel consumption (kg/kW h)}$$

Hence, equation [18.19] becomes:

Brake thermal efficiency (%)

$$= \frac{3600 \times 10^3 \times 100}{\text{Specific fuel consumption (kg/kW h)} \times \text{C.V.}}$$

$$= \frac{3600 \times 10^3 \times 100}{0.36 \times 45 \times 10^6} = 22.22\%$$

292

(c) Heat energy equivalent to 30.1 kW = 30.1 kJ/s
Hence,

Heat dispersed by the brake/min
= 30.1 × 60 = 1806 kJ/min

Answer: (a) Brake power developed   = 30.1 kW
        (b) Brake thermal efficiency = 22.22%
        (c) Heat dispersed by brake   = 1806 kJ/min

Exercise 18.1 – Review questions

1 Define the terms 'brake power' and 'indicated power' as applied to a motor vehicle engine.
2 Explain the reason for the difference between the brake power and the indicated power of an internal combustion engine.

(CGLI)

3 The mechanical efficiency of an engine is given by

$$\frac{\ldots\ldots}{\ldots\ldots}.$$

4 Three factors which affect the mechanical efficiency of a spark-ignition engine are:
(1) ......   (2) ......   (3) ......
5 State what is meant by 'engine torque'.
6 The units of engine torque are ......
7 A device which measures engine torque is ......
8 The equation which gives the relationship between engine torque and brake power is ......
9 Sketch typical torque and brake power curves on a base of engine speed. Explain briefly why they are of the shape shown.
10 Distinguish between 'indicated mean effective pressure' and 'brake mean effective pressure'.
11 Three factors which affect the value of the brake mean effective pressure of a spark-ignition engine are:
(1) ......   (2) ......   (3) ......
12 Define the term 'specific fuel consumption'.
13 Complete the following equations:
(a) i.p. − b.p. = ...
(b) b.m.e.p. = i.m.e.p. × ......

14 The thermal efficiency of an engine is the ratio $\frac{\ldots\ldots}{\ldots\ldots}$

15 Three factors which affect the thermal efficiency of a spark-

ignition engine are:

(1) ......   (2) ......   (3) ......

16 Describe a laboratory test on a four-cylinder, spark-ignition engine to determine the torque delivered by the crankshaft and the brake power at various speeds.

(NWRAC/ULCI)

17 (*a*) Describe an experiment to find the approximate indicated power of a four-cylinder internal combustion engine, using the Morse test.

(*b*) Show a typical formula used to find (*i*) brake power, (*ii*) indicated power, and (*iii*) mechanical efficiency.

(*c*) Indicate on a base of engine speed the types of graph which may be plotted as a result of this experiment.

(NWRAC/ULCI)

18 Describe how an engine is tested under laboratory conditions for power and fuel consumption. State the equipment and calculations required to obtain the final conclusions. Show a typical fuel consumption and power curve.

(NWRAC/ULCI)

19 State how the brake thermal efficiency of the engine can be determined from the results obtained in the experiment of Question 18 above.

Exercise 18.2 − Problems

1 An engine is tested against a dynamometer at 3300 rev/min and exerts a force of 200 N at the end of a torque arm of length 0.35 m. Calculate:

(*a*) the torque transmitted by the engine

(*b*) the brake power developed by the engine at this speed.

2 Calculate the torque of an engine which develops 22 kW at a speed of 21 rev/s.

(EMEU)

3 Using the values given in the table below, plot the graph for engine torque against speed.

Engine torque (N m)	450	492	500	490	453	410	360
Speed (rev/min)	1200	1500	1800	2100	2400	2700	3000

(*a*) From the graph, obtain the maximum torque and the speed at which it occurs.

(*b*) Calculate the power at that speed.

4 (a) Plot torque and brake power curves for both spark and compression-ignition engines from the following data:

Petrol engine

Speed (rev/min)	600	1200	1800	2400	3000	3600	4200	4800
Torque (N m)	90	110	104	90	74	59	44	26
Brake power (kW)	14	22	29	35.5	41	45	46	38

Compression-ignition engine

Speed (rev/min)	600	1200	1800	2400	3000	3600
Torque (N m)	95	98	97	95	90	83
Brake power (kW)	10	22	32	41	47	46

(b) In what way may these graphs be used in putting forward an argument in favour of the compression-ignition engine?

(WMAC/UEI)(Modified)

5 A six-cylinder, four-stroke petrol engine, having a cylinder bore diameter of 82 mm and a stroke of 80 mm, develops maximum power at a speed of 4800 rev/min. The i.m.e.p. at this speed was found to be 1100 kPa, the engine being coupled to a hydraulic dynamometer having a value of $K = 16$. The load on the dynamometer was 290 N. Calculate the indicated power, brake power and mechanical efficiency of the engine.

6 A single-cylinder engine has a bore of 70 mm and a stroke of 76 mm. The average pressure during each working stroke is 620 kPa. Calculate:
(a) the average force on the piston
(b) the work done on the piston during one working stroke
(c) the power developed in the cylinder if the piston makes 2000 working strokes per minute
(d) the power available at the flywheel if the engine has a mechanical efficiency of 85 per cent.

(CGLI)

7 The average pressure acting on each piston crown of a four-cylinder, four-stroke engine on test was 850 kPa, the piston diameter being 60 mm, and piston stroke 75 mm.
(a) Calculate the power developed by the engine, the crankshaft speed being 4200 rev/min

(*b*) If the mechanical efficiency of the engine is 80 per cent, calculate the torque developed at the output shaft of the engine.

8 A single-cylinder, two stroke diesel engine developes 7 kW at 2800 rev/min. Calculate the work done on the piston, in joules, in one stroke.

If the piston is 100 mm diameter and the stroke is 150 mm, calculate the average pressure on the piston, in kPa.

(WMAC/UEI)(Modified)

9 The following results were obtained from an engine tested with a dynamometer having a b.p. formula $WN/20\ 000$ kilowatts.

Speed, N (rev/min)	1000	1500	2000	2500	3000	3500	4000	4500
Load, W (N)	104	108	110	110	105		96	86.5	77.2

On a base of rev/min, plot the engine load and b.p. curves. Make comments on these curves and indicate the speed at which maximum torque occurs.

(NWRAC/ULCI)(Modified)

10 A four-cylinder, four-stroke engine produces an indicated power of 61 kW when rotating at 50 rev/s. The compression ratio is 8.5 to 1 when using a clearance volume of 66.4 cm^3. Calculate:
(*a*) the swept volume of the cylinder
(*b*) the indicated mean effective pressure at 50 rev/s.

(WMAC/UEI)

11 A single-cylinder, four-stroke engine of bore 120 mm and stroke 150 mm overcomes a resistance of 140 N at a radius of 0.5 m when running at 600 rev/min. Calculate the brake power developed by the engine and the brake mean effective pressure.

12 Calculate the diameter of the cylinder bore of a six-cylinder, four-stroke engine which develops a brake power of 46 kW at 3500 rev/min. The brake mean effective pressure is 700 kPa and the engine bore and stroke have the same dimension.

(CGLI)

13 A six-cylinder engine is to develop an output power of 30 kW at 2500 rev/min, at which speed the b.m.e.p. is expected to be 840 kPa. If the ratio of stroke to bore is to be 1.4, determine the bore and stroke of the engine.

(CGLI)(Modified)

14 A vee-eight, four-stroke compression-ignition engine has a bore of 119 mm and a stroke of 89 mm, and the clearance volume is 58 cm^3. The engine develops its maximum torque of 450 N m at 1900 rev/min and its maximum brake power of 250 kW at 3800 rev/min. Calculate:

(a) the compression ratio

(b) the brake power at maximum torque

(c) the b.m.e.p. at maximum power

(d) the i.m.e.p. and friction power at maximum power if the mechanical efficiency is 90 per cent.

(CGLI)

15 During a Morse test on a four-cylinder engine the following results were recorded.

Cylinder cut out	None	No. 1	No. 2	No. 3	No. 4
Brake power developed (kW)	33.6	23.1	23.2	23.0	23.1

For normal running at test speed the engine used 0.23 kg/min of petrol of calorific value 44 000 kJ/kg. Calculate:

(a) the indicated power

(b) the mechanical efficiency

(c) the indicated thermal efficiency.

(CGLI)

16 Using a dynamometer having a torque arm length of 0.6 m, the following brake loads were obtained during a Morse test on a four-cylinder engine at a test speed of 2250 rev/min.

Cylinder firing	All 4	2, 3, 4	1, 3, 4	1, 2, 4	1, 2, 3
Brake force (N)	135	90	89.5	91.5	91

From the above data calculate:

(a) the brake power

(b) the indicated power

(c) the friction power

(d) the mechanical efficiency of the engine.

(WMAC/UEI)

17 Calculate the brake thermal efficiency of an engine which uses fuel at the rate of 0.003 kg/s of 40 000 kJ/kg calorific value to produce 36 kW.

(EMEU)

18 A petrol engine develops an indicated power of 43.5 kW while consuming 8.6 kg of fuel per hour. Given that the calorific value of the fuel is 42 200 kJ/kg, and that friction and pumping losses account for 9.25 kW, calculate:

(a) the brake power

(b) the brake specific fuel consumption

(c) the mechanical efficiency

(*d*) the indicated thermal efficiency

(*e*) the brake thermal efficiency.

(WMAC/UEI)

19 Calculate the brake power of an engine which uses 15 kg of fuel per hour, the fuel having a calorific value of 44 MJ/kg. It is known that only 25 per cent of the energy in the fuel will be converted into brake power.

(CGLI)

20 A petrol engine develops an indicated power of 30 kW and uses fuel having a calorific value of 43 MJ/kg. If the indicated thermal efficiency is 32 per cent, determine the number of litres of fuel consumed by the engine per hour.

(1 litre of the fuel used has a mass of 0.74 kg.)

21 During a test on a compression-ignition engine of 25.5 kW (brake), 7.5 kg of oil were used in one hour. If the mechanical efficiency was 80 per cent, determine the brake thermal efficiency and the indicated thermal efficiency.

The calorific value of the fuel was 45 MJ/kg.

(CGLI)(Modified)

22 A six-cylinder, four-stroke engine developing 100 kW at 42 rev/s has a bore and stroke of 100 mm. The thermal efficiency is 30 per cent and the calorific value of the fuel 40 000 kJ/kg. Calculate:

(*a*) the brake mean effective pressure

(*b*) the specific fuel consumption.

(EMEU)

23 The following are the mean values of observations made during a series of tests on a four-cylinder petrol engine coupled to a dynamometer. The speed of the engine was kept constant throughout the tests at 2500 rev/min. Readings were obtained with all cylinders working and then each cylinder was cut out in turn. The calorific value of the fuel used was 43 MJ/kg.

Cylinder cut out	None	No. 1	No. 2	No. 3	No. 4
Fuel consumption (kg/h)	5.45	5.5	5.61	5.58	5.48
Brake power (kW)	13.05	9.25	9.32	8.95	9.0

Calculate:

(*a*) the indicated power

(*b*) the friction power

(*c*) the brake thermal efficiency

(*d*) the mechanical efficiency of the engine.

(CGLI)(Modified)

24 A four-cylinder, two-stroke cycle petrol engine has a cylinder bore diameter of 76 mm and a piston stroke of 90 mm. When running at 2400 rev/min, the engine develops a brake mean effective pressure of 725 kPa and uses 9.2 kg of fuel per hour of calorific value 44 MJ/kg. Calculate:

(a) the brake power
(b) the specific fuel consumption, in kg/kW h
(c) the brake thermal efficiency.

25 In a test on a small petrol engine the fuel used had a calorific value of 44 MJ/kg, and the power was absorbed by a brake through which water circulated. When the output of the engine was 41 kW, petrol was used at the rate of 12 kg/h. Calculate the brake thermal efficiency of the engine.

Also calculate the rate of flow of water required by the brake, in kg/min, assuming that all the power is converted into heat, for the rise in water temperature to be 45 K.

(Take the specific heat capacity of water as 4.2 kJ/kg K.)

(WMAC/UEI)(Modified)

26 A four-cylinder, four-stroke engine developing 78.5 kW at 50 rev/s has a fuel consumption of 0.25 kg/kW h and a bore and stroke of 100 mm. Calculate:

(a) the brake mean effective pressure
(b) the thermal efficiency assuming the calorific value of the fuel is 45 000 kJ/kg.

(EMEU)

27 The following results were obtained during a test using a spark-ignition engine under varying load, to determine the fuel consumption at various speeds.

Speed (rev/min)	1000	1500	2000	2500	3000	3500	4000	4500
Brake power (kW)	11	15.4	19.4	23	26.3	28.8	29	27.5
Fuel consumption (kg/kW h)	0.45	0.375	0.346	0.34	0.347	0.36	0.39	0.46

Using a base of speed, plot curves for brake power and fuel consumption and determine:

(a) the maximum brake power developed and the speed at which it is produced
(b) the speed at which minimum specific fuel consumption occurs.

28 The following results were obtained during tests on a four-cylinder petrol engine using fuel having a calorific value of 45 MJ/kg.

Brake power (kW)	10	15	20	25	30
Fuel consumption (kg/kW h)	0.371	0.347	0.337	0.337	0.353

From the above results, calculate the brake thermal efficiency in each case and plot curves on a base of brake power of (*a*) fuel consumption and (*b*) brake thermal efficiency. From these curves, estimate the most economical power of the engine.

(CGLI)(Modified)

Answers

Answers to review questions

Chapter 2
7 60 kg m/s   **11** 0.5 m/s^2 **13** 490.5 N   **15** (*c*)   **16** (*b*)   **17** (*a*)   **18** (*g*)
19 (*e*)   **20** (*c*)   **21** (*b*)   **22** (*e*)   **23** (*b*)   **24** (*d*)

Chapter 4
9 (*b*)   **10** (*b*)   **11** (*a*)   **12** (*d*)   **13** (*b*)   **14** (*d*)   **15** (*d*)   **16** (*c*)
17 (*b*)   **18** (*b*)

Chapter 5
11 (*c*)   **12** (*b*)

Chapter 6
17 (*a*) 475;   (*b*) 500;   (*c*) 215;   (*d*) 162 000

Chapter 7
9 (*d*)   **10** (*a*) T;   (*b*) F;   (*c*) T;   (*d*) T;   (*e*) F;   (*f*) F

Chapter 12
4 273   **5** −73 °C; 333 K   **13** (*d*)   **14** (*c*)   **15** (*c*)   **16** (*a*)   **17** (*b*)
18 (*c*)   **19** (*d*)   **20** (*d*)

Chapter 13
16 (*b*)   **17** (*c*)   **18** (*c*)

Chapter 16
7 (*d*)   **9** (*d*)   **17** (*c*)
26 (*a*) T;   (*b*) F;   (*c*) T;   (*d*) F;   (*e*) T

Chapter 17
5 (*a*);   (*b*);   (*e*);   (*f*)

Answers to problems

Chapter 1

1 (*a*) 0.5 rad;   (*b*) 28.64°
2 125 rev/min;   13.1 rad/s;   65.5 rad
3 (*a*) 15.7 rad/s;   (*b*) 5.5 m/s   **4** 2.5 rad/s²
5 24 rad/s; 96 rad   **6** 70 rev   **7** 3 m/s   **8** 50 rad/s   **9** 63.36 km/h
10 (*a*) 4 rad/s²;   (*b*) 154 rev;   (*c*) 0.72 m/s²
11 (*a*) 0.469 m/s²;   (*b*) 20 rad/s;   (*c*) 1.25 rad/s²
12 (*a*) 630 rev/min;   (*b*) 8.8 rad/s²
13 (*a*) 200 rad/s;   (*b*) 2864 rev;   (*c*) 2 rad/s²

Chapter 2

1 400 N   **2** 1000 m/s²   **3** 1250 kg   **4** 3.75 kN; 4 s
5 (*a*) 6 kN;   (*b*) 12 m/s (43.2 km/h);   (*c*) 96 m
6 75 m   **7** 7.5 m/s   **8** (*a*) 7.5 s;   (*b*) 93.75 m;   (*c*) 2000 N
9 3.5 m/s² in the direction of the 120 N force   **10** 950 N
11 (*a*) 175 000 kg m/s;   (*b*) 8.75 kN, 12.25 kN
12 9600 kg m/s   **13** 800 N   **14** 4000 kg
15 (*a*) 1.2 m/s²;   (*b*) 135 m;   (*c*) 18 m/s (64.8 km/h)
16 (*a*) 8 kN;   (*b*) 9.2 kN;   (*c*) 6.8 kN   **17** 1750 N

Chapter 3

1 52.5 kJ   **2** 24 m   **3** 3 kN   **4** (*a*) 600 J;   (*b*) 75 W
5 (*a*) 375 N;   (*b*) 12 s   **6** 1.75 kW   **7** 1000 N   **8** 2.45 kW   **9** 50 kg
10 3 s   **11** (*a*) 1.05 MJ/min;   (*b*) 17.5 kW   **12** (*a*) 1.2 MJ;   (*b*) 6kW
13 490.5 W; 11.77 kJ   **14** 4 m   **15** (*a*) 1230 J;   (*b*) 750 J
16 330 kJ; 150 m   **17** 1.6 J   **18** 150 kJ   **19** 72 km/h
20 (*a*) 10 kJ, 0;   (*b*) 4 kJ, 6 kJ;   (*c*) 0, 10 kJ
21 (*a*) 1521 J;   (*b*) 3.1 m   **22** 408.6 J   **23** 55.8 km/h

Chapter 4

1 (*a*) 294.3 N;   (*b*) 0.238   **2** 8.24 kN   **3** 35.68 kg
4 (*a*) 240 N; (*b*) 3.6 kJ   **5** (*a*) 10 N m;   (*b*) 2.2 kW   **6** 0.03
7 (*a*) 1.508 kW;   (*b*) 90.48 kJ/min   **8** 264 mm   **9** 35.64 kW
10 77 kW   **11** 2 kN   **12** (*a*) 3.41 kN;   (*b*) 45.8 mm   **13** 4.48 kN
14 (*a*) 141.4 N m;   (*b*) 14.81 kW
15 (*a*) 28.8 N m;   (*b*) 65 153 J/min;   (*c*) 65 153 J/min
16 (*a*) 105 N m;   (*b*) 10.56 kW;   (*c*) 633.6 kJ/min
17 80 Nm   **18** (*a*) 600 N;   (*b*) 237.6 kJ
19 (*a*) 86.4 N m;   (*b*) 3.168 kW;   (*c*) 190.1 kJ/min

Chapter 6

1 40 MPa   **2** 50 MPa   **3** 160 mm²   **4** 125 MPa   **5** 58.43 MPa
6 220 kN   **7** 21 mm   **8** 45.45 MPa   **9** 35.65 MPa   **10** 0.000 02
11 1.5 m   **12** (*a*) 82.5 kN;   (*b*) 20.625 kN;   (*c*) 33 MPa

13 (*a*) 114.6 MPa; (*b*) 0.000 55; (*c*) 208 GPa **14** 0.45 mm
15 80 kN **16** (*a*) 143.2 MPa; (*b*) 0.000 716; (*c*) 2.864 mm
17 25 mm; 200 GPa **18** 200 GPa
19 (*a*) 200 GPa; (*b*) 465 MPa; (*c*) 32.5%; (*d*) 35%
20 260 MPa; 475 MPa; 34%; 47.2% **21** 5
22 7.98 mm (say 8 mm); 0.5 mm **23** 53 MPa **24** 25.53 kN
25 19.48 MPa **26** (*a*) 70.7 MPa; (*b*) 26 MPa
27 (*a*) 35.2 MPa; (*b*) 33.2 MPa

Chapter 8
1 27.4 kN; 14° 39′ **2** 3090 N; 54° 28′ South of West
3 1790 N; 1470 N **4** 866 N; 1732 N
5 Tension in BC = 14.2 kN; Tension in AC = 18.1 kN
6 52 g, 90° relative to 30 g mass and 150° relative to 60 g mass
7 120°; 105°; 135° **8** (*a*) 4.635 kN; (*b*) 14.265 kN
9 152 kN; 113 kN **10** 6000 N; 7500 N
11 (*a*) 10°; (*b*) 5100 N; (*c*) 900 N
12 (*a*) 380 N; (*b*) 720 N; (*c*) 63°
13 25.4 kN at $117\frac{1}{2}°$ clockwise from the vertical
14 31.5 g at 78° anticlockwise from the vertical position
15 31 N at 75° anticlockwise from the vertical
16 52 N at 18° clockwise to force *W*
17 *P* = 11.4 N; *Q* = 9 N

Chapter 9
1 15 N **2** 75 N **3** Left 16 kN; Right 12 kN
4 R_A = 400 N; R_B = 500 N
5 (*a*) R_A = 40 kN, R_B = 50 kN; (*b*) R_A = R_B = 70 kN; 2.4 m
6 R_A = 11.67 kN; R_B = 48.33 kN **7** (*a*) 5.5 kN; (*b*) 8.5 kN
8 1.75 m from A **9** 8.25 kN; 13 kN
10 (*a*) R_A = 15 kN, R_B = 25 kN; (*b*) 1.4 m from left-hand end

Chapter 10
1 (*a*) 50; (*b*) 20; (*c*) 40% **2** (*a*) 75%; (*b*) 500 N; (*c*) 4.5 kJ
3 6.4 kN **4** 130 N; 30.77%; Limiting efficiency 33.33%
5 (*a*) *P* = 0.05*W* + 20; (*b*) 170 N, 73.53%; (*c*) 83.33%
6 *P* = 0.1*W* + 5 **7** *P* = 0.07*W* + 10
8 (*a*) 3; (*b*) 750 N; (*c*) 2; (*d*) 66.67%
9 (*a*) 43.75%; (*b*) 1.68 kJ **10** (*a*) 600 N; (*b*) 450 J
11 18; 6.3; 35% **12** 130 mm
13 (*a*) 25%; (*b*) 440 J; (*c*) 1320 J **14** 7.7 kN
15 (*a*) 264; (*b*) (*i*) 40 N, (*ii*) 37.5, (*iii*) 14.2%
16 (*a*) 3, 2.7, 90%; (*b*) 135 N **17** 1080 N **18** 60
19 (*a*) 200 rev/min anticlockwise; (*b*) 150 rev/min clockwise
20 28 **21** (*a*) 0.25; (*b*) 1200 rev/min

Chapter 11

1 (*a*) 2.4;   (*b*) 3;   (*c*) 80%
2 3.2 to 1; 2.25 to 1; 1.75 to 1; 1 to 1
3 (*a*) 23 to 1;   (*b*) 150 rev/min   **4** 6.5 to 1   **5** 14.08 km/h
6 280 N m   **7** (*a*) 5 to 1;   (*b*) 312.5 N m   **8** 475 .2 N m
9 1480 rev/min   **10** (*a*) 5.85 to 1;   (*b*) 90%
11 (*a*) 150 rev/min;   (*b*) 425 N m   **12** (*a*) 410 rev/min;   (*b*) 1195 N m
13 (*a*) (*i*) 4.5 to 1, (*ii*) 4.5, 6.75, 9;   (*b*) 4.5 to 1
14 20 to 1   **15** 10 to 1

Chapter 12

1 58.5 kJ   **2** (*a*) 1680 kJ;   (*b*) 90°   **3** 441 kJ/min
4 400 J/kg K   **5** 11.22 kJ/s   **6** 77.55 K   **7** 9.6 min
8 10.72 litre/min   **9** 127.6 J/kg K   **10** 109.5 kg
11 (*a*) 52.16 °C;   (*b*) 7174 kJ   **12** 462.5 J/kg K
13 18.03 kg   **14** 887 J/kg K   **15** 967 °C

Chapter 13

1 (*a*) 4880 kJ;   (*b*) 36 min, 25 min   **2** 26 kJ/kg; 7.8 kJ
3 1027 kJ   **4** 12 140 kJ   **5** 6744 kJ   **6** 6093 kJ
7 36.05 °C   **8** (*a*) 2120 kJ;   (*b*) 2.4 kg   **9** 0.045 kg
10 38.66 °C   **11** − 18 °C; 26%

Chapter 14

1 16.67×10^{-6}/K   **2** 0.1404 mm   **3** 200.36 mm
4 438.8 °C   **5** 12×10^{-6}/K   **6** 50.252 mm   **7** 2.5 m
8 4.4 mm   **9** 265.7 °C   **10** 0.086 mm   **11** 0.1 mm
12 0.000 02/K   **13** 0.0675 mm   **14** (*a*) 70 °C;   (*b*) 0.025 mm
15 120 mm^2 **16** 17×10^{-6}/K   **17** 95.8 °C
18 6.75 mm^3 **19** 4512 mm^3

Chapter 15

1 60 kPa abs   **2** 440 K   **3** 300 kPa abs   **4** 0.2913 litre
5 0.0896 m^3; 8.07 bar   **6** (*a*) 2.44 bar;   (*b*) 2.26 bar
7 750 kPa abs; 150 kPa abs   **8** (*a*) 4200 cm^3;   (*b*) 3962 cm^3
9 (*a*) 367 °C;   (*b*) 15 °C, 1.26 MPa abs   **10** 327 °C
11 (*a*) 1100 cm^3;   (*b*) 6.6 litre   **12** 14.97 to 1   **13** 69 300 mm^3
14 (*a*) 498 cm^3;   (*b*) 90.74 mm   **15** 704 cm^3; 6.25 to 1
16 (*a*) 78.16 mm;   (*b*) 0.65 mm   **17** (*a*) 15.68 to 1;   (*b*) 512.7 °C
18 12 to 1   **19** 3927 kPa abs   **20** 509 °C; 1291 °C   **21** 17.4 to 1

Chapter 18

1 (*a*) 70 N m;   (*b*) 24.2 kW   **2** 166.7 N m
3 (*a*) 500 N m, 1800 rev/min;   (*b*) 94.25 kW
5 111.6 kW; 87 kW; 78%

6 (*a*) 2387 N;   (*b*) 181.4 J;   (*c*) 6.047 kW;   (*d*) 5.14 kW
7 (*a*) 25.25 kW;   (*b*) 46 N m   **8** 150 J; 127.4 kPa
9 2300 rev/min   **10** (*a*) 498 cm³;   (*b*) 1225 kPa
11 4.4 kW; 519 kPa   **12** 78 mm   **13** 63.8 mm; 89.3 mm
14 (*a*) 19.07 to 1;   (*b*) 89.55 kW;   (*c*) 996.8 kPa
(*d*) 1108 kPa, 27.8 kW   **15** (*a*) 42 kW;   (*b*) 80%;   (*c*) 24.9%
16 (*a*) 19.09 kW;   (*b*) 25.17 kW;   (*c*) 6.08 kW;   (*d*) 75.84%
17 30%   **18** (*a*) 34.25 kW;   (*b*) 0.251 kg/kW h;   (*c*) 78.74%
(*d*) 43.15%;   (*e*) 33.98%   **19** 45.83 kW   **20** 10.61 litre/h
21 27.2%; 34%   **22** (*a*) 1010 kPa;   (*b*) 0.3 kg/kW h
23 (*a*) 15.68 kW;   (*bv*) 2.63 kW;   (*c*) 20%;   (*d*) 83.2%
24 (*a*) 23.7 kW;   (*b*) 0.338 kg/kW h;   (*c*) 24.2%
25 28%; 13 kg/min   **26** (*a*) 999.4 kPa;   (*b*) 32%
27 (*a*) 29.3 kW at 3800 rev/min;   (*b*) 2400 rev/min   **28** 23 kW

Index

Absolute pressure, 228
Absolute temperature, 187
Absolute zero of temperature, 186
Acceleration, 1
  angular, 7
  due to gravity, 20
Action of springs, 99, 100
Additives to lubricating oils, 67–9
Air–fuel ratio, 256
Alcohol, 256, 258
Allowable working stress, 87
Angular acceleration, 7
Angular motion, 1, 4
Angular velocity, 5
Anti-detonators, 257
Anti-foam preventers, 68
Anti-freeze solution, 201
Anti-oxidants, 68
Anti-wear additives, 69
Atmospheric pressure, 209, 227
Atom, 250
Average velocity, 2

Balancing, road wheel, 114
Bar, 227
Barometer, 227
Beam reactions, 127
  experimental determination of, 136
Beams, 127
Bearing friction, 45
Benzole, 258
Bimetallic strip, 215
Boiling point of liquid, 206
  effect of pressure on, 209

Bomb calorimeter, 259
Bourdon pressure gauge, 230
Bow's notation, 109
Boyle's law, 231
Brake hydraulic, 271
  mean effective pressure, 281
  power, 271, 273
  specific fuel consumption, 285–6
  thermal efficiency, 286
Brakes
  disc, 50
  shoe, 53
Braking torque, 54, 55
Brittle material, 84

Calorific value of a fuel, 259
Celsius temperature scale, 186
Cetane number, 260
Change of state, 199
Charles' law, 234
Clearance volume, 240
Clutch
  power transmitted by, 47, 48
  torque transmitted by, 47, 48
Coefficient of
  cubic expansion, 220
  friction, 41
  linear expansion, 215
  superficial expansion, 220
Coil springs, 101
Combination of Boyle's and Charles'
  laws, 236
Combustion, 249, 251
  equations, 252

incomplete, 253
mass of air required for, 255
of carbon, 253
of carbon monoxide, 254
of hydrogen, 254
of sulphur, 254
Compounds, 250
Compression, 71
Compression ratio, 240
Compressive force, 71
Compressive strain, 75
Compressive stress, 71
Concentrated load, 127
Concurrent forces, 107
Condensation, 207
Conservation of energy, 32
Constant pressure cycle, 265
Constant spring rate, 102
Constant volume cycle, 263
Cooling curve, 205
Coplanar forces, 107
Corrosion and rust inhibitors, 68
Cracking distillation, 256
Crude oil, 256
Cubic expansion, coefficient of, 220
Cycles, engine, 263–9

Deformation, 74
Degree celsius, 186
Depression, 231
Detergents, 68
Detonation, 241
Diagram, force (vector), 108–17, 120
indicator, 277
space, 107–17, 120
Diesel cycle, 265
Direct strain, 74
Direct stress, 71
Disc brakes, 50
Dispersants, 68
Distillation of petrol, 256
Double shear, 89
Dual combustion cycle, 266
Ductility, 83

Effective pressure
brake mean, 281
indicated mean, 277
mean, 277
Efficiency, brake thermal, 286, 287
gearbox, 169
indicated thermal, 286
limiting, 144
mechanical, 279
curves of, 280
of a machine, 141, 144

steering box, 180, 181
thermal, 286
curves of, 287
Effort, 140
ideal, 142
Elastic limit, 76, 82
Elasticity, 76
modulus of, 77
Electrolyte, 201
freezing point of, 202
Elementary theory of the shoe brake, 53
Elements, 249
Elongation, percentage, 83
Energy, 29
conservation of, 32
heat, 188
possessed by a fuel, 259
kinetic, 30
potential, 29
Engine capacity, 240
Engine cycles, 263–9
Engine testing, 270–99
Engine torque, 270
curve of, 273
Equation, gas, 236
Equations
combustion, 252
of angular motion, 8
of linear motion, 1
Equilibrant, 107
Equilibrium, 106
Expansion of solids and liquids, 214–25
Extension, 75
Extreme pressure additives, 69

Factor of safety, 87
Flash point of a fuel, 258
Force
compressive, 71
of friction, 40
of gravity, 20
representation of, 106
resolution of, 117
tensile, 71
unit of, 16
Force and acceleration, 14, 16
Force diagram, 108–17, 120
Force ratio, 140, 169
Forces
concurrent, 107
coplanar, 107
equilibrant of, 107
parallelogram of, 107
polygon of, 115
resultant of, 107
triangle of, 108

Fortin barometer, 228
Freezing, 202
Freezing points, 200
Friction
  advantages and disadvantages of, 42
  bearing, 45
  coefficient of, 41
  force of, 40
  laws of, 40
  power, 278
  sliding (or dynamic), 40, 41
  static, 40, 41
Frictional torque, 48, 51
Fuel additives, 257
Fuel consumption, 285
  curves of, 287, 288
  specific, 285
Fuel oils, 257
Fuels, 249
  calorific value of, 259
  combustion of, 251
  liquid, 256
    properties of, 258
Fusion, latent heat of, 200
  specific, 202

Gas
  absolute pressure of, 228
  general equation, 236
  laws, 236−48
  pressure exerted by, 226
Gauge length, 81
Gauge pressure, 228
Gauges
  pressure, 229
  vacuum, 231
Gear ratio, 160, 170, 176, 179
  overall, 173
Gear systems, 159
Gear trains
  compound, 161
  single, 161
Gearbox efficiency, 169
Gearbox ratios, 170
Gravity
  acceleration due to, 20
  force of, 20

Heat energy, 188
  possessed by a fuel, 259
  transfer in mixtures, 191
  unit of, 188
Higher calorific value, 259
Hooke's law, 76
Hydraulic dynamometer, 271
Hydrocarbons, 256

Hydrogen, combustion of, 254
Hypoid oils, 69

Ideal effort, 142
Ideal machine, 142
Idler gearwheel, 160
Ignition temperature of a fuel, 259
Index, viscosity, 66
Indicated mean effective pressure, 277
Indicated power, 277
  calculation of, 278
  curves of, 280
Indicated specific fuel consumption, 285
Indicated thermal efficiency, 286
Indicator diagram, 277
Indicator, engine, 277
Inertia, 15

Joule, 26
Journal friction, 45

Kelvin, 186
Kelvin temperature scale, 186
Kerosene, 256, 257
Kilogram, 15

Laminated plate or leaf springs, 98−100
Latent heat, 199, 200
Law
  Boyle's, 231
  Charles', 234
  Hooke's, 76
  of machine, 143
  pressure, 239
Laws
  combination of Boyle's and Charles',
    236
  of friction, 40
  of motion, Newton's, 14, 15, 20
Leading and trailing shoe brakes, 53
Levers, 156
Limit
  elastic, 76, 82
  of proportionality, 76, 81
Limiting efficiency, 144
Linear and angular motion, 1−13
  relatonship between, 8
Linear expansion, 214
  coefficient of, 215
Liquid, boiling point of, 206
  effect of pressure on, 209
Liquid cooling system, 201
Liquid fuels, 256
  properties of, 258
Load−extension graph, 77, 82, 85
Load, concentrated (or point), 127
  maximum, 83

Loop, pumping, 277
Lower calorific value, 259
Lubricating oils, properties of, 61–70
Lubrication, forms of, 62

Machine
  definition of, 140
  efficiency of, 141, 144
  ideal, 142
  law of, 143
Manometer, 229
Mass, 15
Maximum load, 83
Mean effective pressure, 277
  brake, 281
  indicated, 277
Mechanical advantage, 140
Mechanical efficiency, 279
  curves of, 280
Melting point, 200
  determination of from cooling curve,
    204
Mercury barometer, simple, 227, 228
Mixed cycle, 266
Mixtures, 250
Modulus
  of elasticity, 77
  of rigidity, 91
Molecular mass, relative, 251
Molecule, 251
Moment of a force, 127, 270
Moments, principle of, 129
Momentum, 15
  rate of change of, 16
Morse test, 284
Movement ratio, 141, 169
Multi-grade oil, 66

Necking, 83
Newton, 16
Newton's laws of motion, 14, 15, 20
Normal stresses, 71

Octane number, 259
Oil
  crude, 256
  freezing point of, 202
  hypoid, 69
  multi-grade, 66
  viscosity tests, 63
Oiliness, 63
Otto cycle, 263
Overall gear ratio, 173
Oxidation inhibitors, 68

Parallelogram of forces, 107
Pascal, 227

Permanent set, 82
Petrol
  freezing point of, 202
  production of, 256
Petrol engine cycle, 263
Petroleum, 256
Point load, 127
Polygon of forces, 115
Power, 35
  brake, 271
  friction, 278
  indicated, 277, 278
  curves of, 280
Power absorbed by disc brake, 53
Power absorbed by journal friction, 46
Power transmitted by clutch, 47, 48
Pressure
  absolute, 228
  atmospheric, 209, 227
  brake mean effective, 281
  gauge, 228
  indicated mean effective, 277
  law, 239
  mean effective, 277
  unit of, 227
Pressure effect on boiling point, 209
Pressure gauges, 229
Pressure of gas, 226
Pressure–volume diagram, 263–8
Pressurized cooling system, 210
Principle
  of conservation of energy, 32
  of moments, 129
Progressive spring, 103
Properties of liquid fuels, 258
Properties of lubricating oils, 61–70
Proprtionality, limit of, 76, 81
Pulley systems, 148
Pumping loop, 277

Quantity of heat, 188

Radian, 4
Rate of spring, 102
Ratio
  air–fuel, 256
  compression, 240
  force, 140
  gear, 160, 170, 176, 179
  movement, 141
  overall, 173
  rear-axle, 171
  speed, 176
  steering box, 179
  torque, 175
  velocity, 141
Rear-axle ratio, 171

Rear-axle torque, 179
Rectangular components, 117
Reduction in area, percentage, 83
Redwood viscometer, 64
Relationship between linear and angular
    motion, 8
Relative atomic mass, 250
Relative molecular mass, 251
Representation of a force, 106
Resolution of a force, 117
Resultant, 107
Rigidity, modulus of, 91

SAE viscosity rating, 65
Safe working stress, 87
Safety, factor of, 87
Saybolt viscometer, 63
Scales, temperature, 186
Screw jack, 154
Sensible heat, 199
Shear
    double, 89
    modulus, 91
    single, 88
    strain, 90
    stress, 88
Shoe brake, elementary theory of, 53
Simple barometer, 227, 228
Simple machines, 140–85
Simply supported beams, 127–39
    definition of, 131
Single shear, 88
Sliding (or dynamic) friction, 40, 41
Space diagram, 107–17, 120
Specific fuel consumption, 285
Specific heat capacity, 189
Specific latent heat
    of fusion, 202
    of vaporization, 207
Spring
    coil, 101
    leaf (or laminated), 98–100
    rate, 102
    stiffness, 78, 102
    suspension, 98–105
    torsion bar, 101
State, change of, 199
Static friction, 40, 41
Steering box calculations, 179
Stiffness of spring, 78, 102
STP, 238
Strain
    compressive, 75
    direct, 74
    shear, 90
    tensile, 74

Strength, tensile, 83
Stress, 71
    allowable, 87
    compressive, 71
    direct, 71
    intensity of, 71
    shear, 88
    –strain graph, 84
    tensile, 71
    working, 87
    yield, 82
Sulphur, combustion of, 254
Superficial expansion, 220
    coefficient of, 220
Suspension springs, 98–105
Swept volume, 240

Temperature, 186
    absolute, 187
    absolute zero of, 186
    scales, 186
    unit of, 186
Tensile strain, 74
Tensile strength, 83
Tensile stress, 71
Tensile testing of materials, 81
Tension, 71
Thermal efficiency, 286
    brake, 286, 287
    curves of, 287
    indicated, 286
Thermodynamic temperature scale, 186
Torque, 270
    braking, 54, 55
    engine, 270
        curve of, 273
    frictional, 48, 51
    ratio, 175
    rear-axle, 179
    steering box, 180
    transmitted by clutch, 47, 48
Torsion, 91
    bars, 101
Torsional stress, 91
Transfer of heat energy in mixtures, 191
Transmission efficiency, 178
Triangle of forces, 108

U-tube manometer, 229

Vacuum gauges, 231
Value, calorific, 259
Vaporization, latent heat of, 200
Vector diagrams, 108–17, 120
Velocity
    angular, 5

angular–linear relationship, 9
average, 2
ratio, 141, 169
-time graph, 1, 2
Viscometer, 63
Viscosity, 63
  index, 66
    improvers, 67
  tests for oils, 63
Volatility, 256
Volume
  clearance, 240
  swept, 240

Watt, 35
Weight, 20
Weston differential block, 152
Work, 26
  unit of, 26
Work done in lifting objects, 27
Working stress, 87

Yield point, 82
Yield stress, 82
Young's modulus of elasticity, 77

Zero, absolute, of temperature, 186